THE

# BRITISH ESSAYISTS;

WITH

## PREFACES

BIOGRAPHICAL, HISTORICAL,

AND CRITICAL.

BY THE

### REV. LIONEL THOMAS BERGUER,

LATE OF ST. MARY HALL, OXON: FELLOW EXTRAORDINARY OF THE
ROYAL MEDICAL SOCIETY OF EDINBURGH.

---

IN FORTY-FIVE VOLUMES.

## VOL. XXXIX.

---

## LONDON:

PRINTED FOR T. AND J. ALLMAN, PRINCES STREET,
HANOVER SQUARE:

W. Baynes and Son, Paternoster Row ; A. B. Dulau and Co. Soho Square ;
W. Clarke, New Bond Street ; R. Jennings, Poultry ; J. Hearne, Strand ;
R. Triphook, Old Bond Street ; Westley and Parrish, Strand ; W. Wright,
Fleet Street ; C. Smith, Strand : H. Mozley, Derby : W. Grapel, and
Robinson and Sons, Liverpool : Bell and Bradfute, J. Anderson, jun. and
H. S. Baynes and Co. Edinburgh: M. Keene, and J. Cumming, Dublin.

1823.

# CONTENTS TO VOL. XXXIX.

No.

# OBSERVER.

## No. 52—108.

———Multorum providus urbes
Et mores hominum inspexit——— HORAT.

## By RICHARD CUMBERLAND, Esq.

# THE
# OBSERVER.

## NUMBER LII.

Singula lætus
Exquiritque, auditque, virûm monumenta priorum.

VIRGIL.

OF all our dealers in second-hand wares, few bring
their goods to so bad a market, as those humble
wits who retail other people's worn-out jokes. A
man's good sayings are so personally his own, and
depend so much upon manner and circumstances,
that they make a poor figure in other people's mouths,
and suffer even more by printing than they do by
repeating: it is also a very difficult thing to pen a
witticism; for by the time we have adjusted all the
descriptive arrangements of this man said, and t'other
man replied, we have miserably blunted the edge of
the repartee. These difficulties however have been
happily overcome by Mr. Joseph Miller and other
facetious compilers, whose works are in general circulation, and may be heard of in most clubs and
companies where gentlemen meet, who love to say a
good thing without the trouble of inventing it. We
are also in a fair train of knowing every thing that a
late celebrated author said, as well as wrote, without
an exception even of his most secret ejaculations.
We may judge how valuable these diaries will be to
posterity, when we reflect how much we should now

be edified, had any of the ancients given us as minute a *collectanea* of their illustrious contemporaries.

We have, it is true, a few of Cicero's table-jokes; but how delightful would it be to know what he said, when nobody heard him! How piously he reproached himself when he laid in bed too late in a morning, or eat too heartily at Hortensius's or Cæsar's table. We are told, indeed, that Cato the Censor loved his jest, but we should have been doubly glad to have partaken of it: what a pity it is that nobody thought it worth their while to record some pleasanter specimen than Macrobius has given us of his retort upon Q. Albidius, a glutton and a spendthrift, when his house was on fire—' What he could not eat, he has burnt,' said Cato; where the point of the jest lies in the allusion to a particular kind of sacrifice, and the good humour of it with himself. It was better said by P. Syrus the actor, when he saw one Mucius, a malevolent fellow, in a very melancholy mood—' Either some ill fortune has befallen Mucius, or some good has happened to one of his acquaintance.'

A man's fame shall be recorded to posterity by the trifling merit of a jest, when the great things he has done would else have been buried in oblivion: Who would now have known that L. Mallius was once the best painter in Rome, if it was not for his repartee to Servilius Geminus? ' You paint better than you model,' says Geminus, pointing to Mallius's children, who were crooked and ill favoured. —' Like enough,' replied the artist; ' I paint in the daylight, but I model, as you call it, in the dark.'

Cicero, it is well known, was a great joker, and some of his good sayings have reached us; it does not appear as if his wit had been of the malicious sort, and yet Pompey, whose temper could not stand a jest, was so galled by him, that he is reported to have said with great bitterness—' Oh! that Cicero would go over to my enemies, for then he would be afraid of me.'—If Cicero forgave this sarcasm, I should call him not only a better-tempered, but a braver man than Pompey.

But of all the ancient wits, Augustus seems to have had the most point, and he was as remarkable for taking a jest, as for giving it. A country fellow came to Rome, who was so like the emperor, that all the city ran after him; Augustus heard of it, and ordering the man into his presence—' Harkye, friend!' says he, ' when was your mother in Rome?' —' Never, an please you!' replied the countryman, ' but my father has been here many a time and oft.' The anecdote of the old soldier is still more to his credit: he solicited the emperor to defend him in a suit: Augustus sent his own advocate into court: the soldier was dissatisfied, and said to the emperor —' I did not fight for you by proxy at Actium.'— Augustus felt the reproof, and condescended to his request in person. When Pacuvius Taurus greedily solicited a largess from the emperor, and to urge him to the greater liberality added, that all the world would have it, that he had made him a very bountiful donation—' But you know better,' said Augustus, ' than to believe the world,'—and dismissed the sycophant without his errand. I shall mention one more case, where by a very courtly evasion, he parried the solicitation of his captain of the guard, who had been cashiered, and was petitioning the emperor to allow him his pay: telling him that he did not ask that indulgence for the sake of the money which might accrue to him, but that he might have it to say he had resigned his commission, and not been cashiered—' If that be all your reason, says the emperor, ' tell the world that you have received it, and I will not deny that I have paid it.'

Vatinius, who was noted to a proverb as a common slanderer, and particularly obnoxious for his scurrility against Cicero, was pelted by the populace in the amphitheatre, whilst he was giving them the Gladiators : he complained to the Ædiles of the insult, and got an edict forbidding the people to cast any thing into the area but apples. An arch fellow brought a furious large fir-apple to the famous lawyer Cascellius, and demanded his opinion upon the edict.—' I am of opinion,' says Cascellius, ' that your fir-apple is literally and legally an apple, with this proviso however, that you intend to throw it at Vatinius's head.'

As there is some danger in making too free with *old jokes,* I shall hold my hand for the present ; but if these should succeed in being acceptable to my readers, I shall not be afraid of meeting Mr. Joseph Miller and his modern witticisms with my ancients. In that case I shall not despair of being able to lay before the public a veritable Roman newspaper, compounded of events in the days of Julius Cæsar : by what happy chance I traced this valuable relic, and with what pains I possessed myself of it, may be matter of future explanation : I have the satisfaction however to premise to the reader, that it is written with great freedom, and as well sprinkled with private anecdotes as any of the present day, whose agreeable familiarity is so charming to every body but the parties concerned ; it has also a good dash of the dramatic, and as some fastidious people have been inclined to treat our intelligencers and reviewers with a degree of neglect bordering upon contempt, I shall have pleasure in shewing that they have classical authority for all their quirks and conceits, and that they are all written in the true quaint spirit of criticism : it is to be lamented that the Roman theatre furnishes no ladies to match the heroines of our stage; but I can produce some encomiums upon Laberius, Roscius, and the famous Publius Syrus, which would not be unapplicable to some of our present capital actors: I am sorry to be obliged to confess, that they were not in the habit of speaking epilogues in those days: but I have a substitute in a prologue written and spoken by Decimus Laberius, which I am tempted to throw out as a lure to my newspaper; but I must first explain upon what occasion it was composed.

This Laberius was a Roman knight of good family, and a man withal of high spirit and pretensions, but unfortunately he had a talent for the drama: he read his own plays better than any man then living could act them, for neither Garrick nor Henderson was yet born. P. Clodius, the fine gentleman and rake of the age, had the indecorum to press Laberius to come forward on the public stage, and take the principal character in one of his own plays: Laberius was indignant, and Clodius proceeded to menaces: —' Do your worst,' says the Roman knight, ' you can but send me to Dyracchium and back again'— proudly intimating that he would suffer the like banishment with Cicero, rather than consent to his demand: for acting was not then the amusement of people of fashion, and private theatres were not thought of. Julius Cæsar was no less captivated with Laberius's talents than Clodius had been, and being a man not apt to be discouraged by common difficulties, took up the same solicitation, and assailed our Roman knight, who was now sixty years of age, and felt his powers in their decline: conscious of this decline no less than of his own dignity, he resisted the degrading request: he interceded, he implored of Cæsar to excuse him: it was to no purpose, Cæsar had made it his point, and his point he would carry: the word of Cæsar was law, and

Laberius, driven out of all his defences, was obliged to submit and comply. Cæsar makes a grand spectacle for all Rome; bills are given out for a play of Laberius, and the principal part is announced to be performed by the author himself; the theatre is thronged with spectators; all Rome is present, and Decimus Laberius presents himself on the stage, and addresses the audience in the following prologue:

### PROLOGUE BY DECIMUS LABERIUS.

O strong Necessity! of whose swift course
So many feel, so few escape the force,
Whither, ah! whither, in thy prone career,
Hast thou decreed this dying frame lo bear?
Me in my better days nor foe, nor friend,
Nor threat, nor bribe, nor vanity, cou'd bend;
Now lur'd by flattery in my weaker age,
I sink my knighthood and ascend the stage,
Yet muse not therefore—How shall man gainsay
Him, whom the Deities themselves obey?
Sixty long years I've liv'd without disgrace
A Roman knight: let dignity give place!
I'm Cæsar's actor now, and compass more
In one short hour, than all my life before.

O Fortune! fickle source of good and ill,
If here to place me 'twas thy sovereign will,
Why, when I'd youth and faculties to please
So great a master and such guests as these,
Why not compel me then, malicious power!
To the hard task of this degrading hour?
Where now, in what profound abyss of shame,
Dost thou conspire with Fate to sink my name?
Whence are my hopes? What voice can age supply
To charm the ear; what grace to please the eye?
Where is the action, energy, and art,
The look, that guides its passion to the heart?
Age creeps like ivy o'er my wither'd trunk,
Its bloom all blasted, and its vigour shrunk:
A tomb, where nothing but a name remains
To tell the world whose ashes it contains.

The original is so superiorly beautiful, that to prevent a pathos I shall insert it after the translation.

Necessitas, cujus cursûs transversi impetum
Voluerunt multi effugere, pauci potuerunt,
Quò me detrusit pœnè extremis sensibus?
Quem nulla ambitio, nulla unquam largitio,
Nullus timor, vis nulla, nulla auctoritas
Movere potuit in juventâ de statu;
Ecce in senectâ ut facilè labefecit loco,
Viri excellentis, mente clemente edita,
Submissa, placidè blandiloquens oratio!
Etenim ipsi Dii negare cui nil potuèrunt,
Hominem me denegare quis possit pati?
Ego bis tricenis annis actis sine notâ,
Eques Romanus, lare tandem egressus meo,
Domum revertar mimus: Nimirum hoc die
Uno plùs vixi, mihi quàm vivendum fuit.
Fortuna, immoderata in bono æquè atque in malo,
Si tibi erat libitum literarum laudibus
Floris cacumen nostræ famæ frangere,
Cur cùm vigebam membris præviridantibus,
Satisfacere populo et tali cùm poteram viro,
Non flexibilem me concurvâsti ut carperes?
Nunc me quò dejicis? quid ad scenam affero?
Decorem formæ, an dignitatem corporis,
Animi virtutem, an vocis jucundæ sonum?
Ut hedera serpens vires arboreas necat,
Ità me vetustas amplexa annorum enecat;
Sepulchri similis nil, nisi nomen, retineo.

The play which this pathetic prologue was attached to was a comedy, in which Laberius took the character of a slave, and in the course of the plot (as usual) was beaten by his master: in this condition, having marked his habit with counterfeited stripes, he runs upon the stage, and cries out amain—*Porrò, Quirites! libertatem perdimus*—'In good faith, countrymen, there is an end of freedom.' The indignant spectators sent up a shout; it was, in the language or our present playhouse bills, 'a burst of applause; a most violent burst of applause from a most crowded and brilliant house, overflowing in all parts.' Laberius, not yet content with this atonement to the manes of his knighthood, subjoins the following pointed allusion: *Necesse est multos timeat,*

*quem multi timent—*' The man whom many fear,
must needs fear many.' All eyes were now turned
upon Cæsar, and the degraded Laberius enjoyed a
full revenge.

We may naturally suppose this conduct lost him
the favour of Cæsar, who immediately took up
Publius Syrus, a Syrian slave who had been ma-
numitted for his ingenious talents, and was acting
in the country theatres with much applause: Cæsar
fetched him out of his obscurity, as we bring up an
actress from Bath or York, and pitted him against
Laberius. It was the triumph of youth and vigour
over age and decay, and Cæsar, with malicious
civility, said to Laberius, *Favente tibi me victus es,
Laberi, a Syro*—' You are surpassed by Syrus in
spite of my support.' As Laberius was going out
of the theatre, he was met by Syrus, who was inconsiderate enough to let an expression escape him,
which was very disrespectful to his veteran competitor: Laberius felt the unbecoming insult, and
turning to Syrus, gave him this extemporary answer—

> To stand the first is not the lot of all;
> 'Tis now your turn to mount and mine to fall:
> 'Tis slippery ground; beware you keep your feet;
> For public favour is a public cheat.

> Non possunt primi esse omnes omni in tempore;
> Summum ad gradum cùm claritatis veneris,
> Consistes ægrè; et quum descendas, decides:
> Cecidi ego: Cadet qui sequitur. Laus est publica.

I need not remind the learned reader in what
credit the sayings of this Publius Syrus have been
justly held by all the *literati* from Seneca to Scali-
ger, who turned them into Greek; and it is for the
honour of the fraternity of the stage, that both he
and Sophron, whose moral sentences were found
under Plato's pillow when he died, were actors by
profession.

I shall now only add, that my newspaper contains a very interesting description of two young actors, Hylas and Pylades, who became great favourites with Augustus, when he was emperor, and made their first appearance at the time this journal was written. If the reader shall find any allusion to two very promising young performers, now living, whose initials correspond with the above, I can promise him that our contemporaries will not suffer by the comparison. I may venture to say, in the words of Dr. Young—

> The Roman wou'd not blush at the mistake.

---

# NUMBER LIII.

THERE is no period of ancient history would afford a more useful study to a young prince, than an accurate delineation of the whole life of Tiberius: this ought to be done with great care and ability, for it is a character extremely difficult to develope, and one that by a continued chain of incidents furnishes a lesson in every link of its connexion, highly interesting to all pupils, but most to those who are on the road to empire. To trace the conduct of Tiberius from his first appearance in history to his death, is as if we should begin with the last acts of Augustus, and read his story backwards to its commencement in the civil wars; each narration would then begin with honour, and conclude with infamy. If Augustus had never attained to empire, he would have had a most disgraceful page in history; on the other hand, had Tiberius died with Germanicus, he would have merited a very glorious one: it should

seem therefore that he was by nature a better man
than his predecessor. The cautious timid character
of Augustus kept him under constant awe of those
he governed, and he was diligent to secure to himself the opinions of mankind; but there are rents
and fissures enough in the veil, which adulation has
thrown over him, through which to spy out the impurities and meannesses of his natural disposition.
Tiberius seems on his part also to have had a jealous
holding and respect towards Germanicus, which had
an influence over the early part of his reign; but it
was a self-restraint founded in emulation, not in fear.
It is hinted that Augustus had in mind to restore the
commonwealth, and give back her liberties to Rome;
and these may very possibly have been his meditations; but they never arose in his mind till he found
his life in the last stage of decay, when, having no
heir of his own body, he would willingly have had
the empire cease with him, and left posterity to draw
the conclusion, that no successor could be found fit
to take it after him; this I can readily believe he
would have done in his last moments if he could, and
even before his last moments if he dared; but the
shock which such a revolution might possibly have
occasioned, alarmed his fears, and he was too tena-
cious of power to quit it upon any other motives than
those of absolute conviction that he could hold it no
longer. This is so much in character, that I think
it very probable he might have tried it upon Tiberius
in his long death-bed conversation with him at
Nola—*Revocatum ex itinere Tiberium diu secreto ser-
mone detinuit, neque post ulli majori negotio animum
accommodavit.* (*Suetonius.*) This passage is very
curious, and some important conjectures may fairly
be grounded upon it. Suetonius says that the conference was *long*, and also that it was *private*; and
he adds that Augustus, after his conversation with

his successor, never turned his thoughts to any important business, or, in other words, any matter of state whatever. The *secrecy* of this conference very much favours my conjecture, that he made an attempt to dissuade Tiberius from holding on the empire, and the *length* of time it took up corroborates the probability of that conjecture; and I farther incline to think it likely that it might make serious impressions on Tiberius's mind, as to the measure proposed; for I can never believe that the repugnance with which Tiberius took the charge of the government upon him, was wholly feigned, though historians agree in giving it that turn; his long and voluntary exile in the island of Rhodes, where he seemed for a time to have renounced all desire of succeeding to the empire, might be a reason with Augustus for making this experiment upon a man of his cold and sequestered habits. At all events I think it highly natural to suppose, that Augustus would not have closeted him in this manner, if it were only for the purpose of giving him lessons and instructions in the arts of government; for in that case his vanity, which made him act a part for applause even in his expiring moments, would have opened the doors to his family and attendants, that they might have been present to record his sayings; and we should have had as many fine maxims in his dying speech, as Socrates uttered in his prison, or Seneca in his bath: add to this, that he certainly bore no goodwill to Tiberius, who was not a successor to his mind, nor could he wish to elevate the Claudian family to the throne. It is not likely however that he altogether succeeded with Tiberius, or brought him to make any absolute promise of abdication; for in that case he would not have failed to have taken credit with the people about him, for having been the means of restoring the liberties of his country, and he would have made as great a parade of patriotism, as would have become a Cato or a Solon; but the author above quoted says he took no farther account of public business, and therefore we may conclude the conference, if it took that turn, did not come to any satisfactory conclusion on the point.

Tiberius on his accession found the empire in a critical situation, for besides the movements which Clemens on one part, and Scribonius Libo on another, were making, the Pannonian and German armies were in absolute revolt. This was no time for making any change in the constitution of the imperial power, had he been so disposed; as he was a man of deep measures, he held himself on the reserve with the senate, and suffered them to solicit his acceptance of the sovereign power upon their knees. He wished to have assessors in the government; he would take his share, and whatever department in the state they should recommend to his charge, he would readily undertake. Had he persisted in refusing the empire, or had he attempted to throw the constitution back to its first principles of freedom, the mutinous legions would have forced the sovereignty upon Germanicus; but by this suggestion of a partition he artfully sounded the temper of the senate, where there were some leading men of very doubtful characters, whom Augustus had marked out in his last illness; from two of these, Asinius Gallus and L. Aruntius, Tiberius's proposal drew an answer, in which they demanded of him to declare what particular department of the state he would choose to have committed to him. This was opening enough for one of his penetration, and he drew his conclusions upon the spot, evading for the time the snare that was laid for him.

The servile and excessive adulation of the senate soon convinced him, that the Roman spirit had suffered a total change under the reign of Augustus, and that the state might indeed be thrown into convulsions by any attempt at a change in favour of freedom, but that slavery and submission under a despotic master was their determined choice, and if the alternative was to lie between himself and any other, there was little room for hesitation. Who more fit than the adopted heir of Augustus, and a descendant of the Claudian house, which ranked so high in the Patrician nobility, and so superior in pretensions of ancestry and merit to the Julian and Octavian gentry, from whom his predecessors were ignobly descended?

When the German and the Pannonian mutinies were appeased, there seems to have been a period of repose, when he might have new modelled the constitution had he been so disposed; but this I take to be appearance only, for those mutinies had been quelled by Germanicus and Drusus, and both these princes were in the adoption; and the latter of a very turbulent and ambitious spirit.

For the space of two complete years, Tiberius never stirred out of the doors of his palace, devoting this whole time to the affairs of government. In this period he certainly did many excellent things; and though his manners were not calculated for popularity, yet his reputation through the empire was universal; he regulated all domestic matters with consummate prudence, and on some occasions with a liberal and courteous spirit: in the distant provinces, where wars and disturbances were more frequent, public measures were more indebted for their success to the good policy of his instructions, than to the courage and activity of his generals, though Germanicus was of the number.

The death of that most amiable and excellent prince, which was imputed to the machinations of

Cneius Piso, involved Tiberius in some degree in the same suspicion; but as Tacitus, in his account of the event, gives admission to an idle story of sorceries and incantations, practised by Piso for compassing the death of Germanicus, and states no circumstance that can give any reasonable ground for belief that he actually poisoned him, I am not inclined to give credit to the transaction, even in respect to Piso's being guilty of the murder, much less with regard to Tiberius. Tacitus indeed hints at secret orders supposed by some to have been given by the emperor to Piso; but this, which at best is mere matter of report, does not go to the affair of the poisoning, but only to some private intimations, in which the empress was chief mover, for mortifying the pride of Agrippina. It is not to be supposed, when Piso openly returned to Rome, and stood a public trial, that these orders, had any such existed, could have been so totally suppressed, that neither the guilty person should avail himself of them, nor any one member of so great and numerous a family produce them in vindication of him when yet living, or of his memory after death; and this in no period of time, not even when the Claudian family were superseded in the empire, and anecdotes were industriously collected to blacken the character of Tiberius.

The death of Drusus followed that of Germanicus, and the same groundless suspicions were levelled at the emperor; but these are rejected by Tacitus with contempt, and the words he uses, which are very strong, are a proper answer to both imputations—
*Neque quisquam scriptor tam infensus extitit, ut Tiberio objectaret, cùm omnia conquirerent, intenderentque.*

It would have been most happy for the memory of Tiberius had his life been terminated at this fatal period; henceforward he seems to have been surrendered to desperation and disgust; he retired to the Campania, and devolved the government upon his minister Sejanus; there were times in which some marks of his former spirit appeared, but they were short and transient emanations; the basest of mankind had possession of his soul, and whether he was drugged by Sejanus and his agents, or that his brain was affected by a revulsion of that scrophulous humour which broke out with such violence in his face and body, it seems highly natural to conjecture, that he was never in his sound mind during his secession in the island of Capreæ. A number of circumstances might be adduced in support of this conjecture; it is sufficient to instance his extraordinary letter to the senate; can words be found more expressive of a distracted and desperate state of mind than the following? *Quid scribam vobis, Patres Conscripti, aut promodo scribam, aut quid omninò non scribam hoc tempore, Dii me deæque pejùs perdant, quàm perire quotidie sentio, si scio.*

I beg leave now to repeat what I advanced in the outset of this paper, and which alone led me to the subject of it, that a detail comprising all the great and interesting events within the life of Tiberius, with reasonings and remarks judiciously interspersed as these occurrences arise in the course of the narration, would compound such a body of useful precepts and instructions, as would apply to every species of example, which a prince should be taught either to imitate or avoid; and these lessons would carry the greater force and recommendation with them, and have an advantage over all fabulous morals, by being incorporated with a real history of the most interesting sort.

# NUMBER LIV.

HOWEVER disposed we may be to execrate the bloody act of the regicides, yet we must admit the errors and misconduct of Charles's unhappy reign to be such as cannot be palliated; in our pity for his fate we must not forget the history of his failings, nor, whilst we are sympathizing in the pathos of the tragedy, overlook its moral.

Four successive parliaments, improvidently dissolved, were sufficient warnings for the fifth to fall upon expedients for securing to themselves a more permanent duration, by laying some restraints upon a prerogative so wantonly exerted.

Let us call to mind the inauspicious commencement of this monarch's reign; before the ceremony of his coronation had taken place, he espoused a sister of France, and set a Catholic princess on the throne of a Protestant kingdom, scarce cool from the ferment of religious jealousies, recently emancipated from the yoke of Rome, and of course intolerant through terror, if not by principle: the most obnoxious man in the kingdom was Montague, author of the proscribed tract, entitled *Appello Cæsarem*, and him Charles enrolled in his list of royal chaplains. By throwing himself incontinently into the hands of Buckingham, he shewed his people they were to expect a reign of favouritism, and the choice of the minister marked the character of the monarch: he levied musters for the Palatinate of twelve thousand men, exacted contributions for coat and conduct money, declared martial law in the kingdom, and furnished his brother of France with a squadron of ships for the unpopular reduction of Rochelle, and the mariners refused the service : these measures stirred the parliament then sitting to move for a redress of grievances, before they provided for his debts, and their remonstrances provoked him upon the instant to dissolve them.

Every one of these proceedings took place before his coronation, and form the melancholy prelude to his misguided government.

A second parliament was called together, and to intimidate them from resuming their redress of grievances, and divert their attempts from the person of his favourite, he haughtily informs them, that he cannot suffer an inquiry even on the meanest of his servants. What was to be expected from such a menacing declaration? They, disdaining *illam osculari, quâ sunt oppressi, manum*, proceed to impeach Buckingham; the king commits the managers of that process to the Tower, and resorting to his prerogative, dissolves his second parliament, as suddenly, and more angrily, than his first.

A third parliament meets, and in the interim new grievances of a more awakening sort had supplied them with an ample field for complaint and remonstrance ; in the intermission of their sittings, he had exacted a loan, which they interpreted a tax without parliament, and of course a flagrant violation of the constitution : this he enforced with so high a hand, that several gentlemen of name in their counties had been committed to close imprisonment for refusing payment; ship-money also at this time began to be questioned as an intolerable grievance, and being one of the resources for enabling the crown to govern without a parliament, it was considered by many as a violation of their rights, an inequitable and oppressive tax, which ought to be resisted, and accordingly it was resisted: this parliament therefore, after a short and inefficient sitting, shared the sudden fate of its predecessors.

The same precipitancy, greater blindness, a more confirmed habit of obstinacy, and a heightened degree of aggravation marked this period of intermission from parliaments for now the leading members of the late house were sent to close imprisonment in the Tower, and informations were lodged against them in the Star-Chamber.

The troubles in Scotland made it necessary for the king once more to have resort to a parliament; they met for the fourth time on the thirteenth of April 1640, and the fifth day of the following month sent them back to their constituents to tell those grievances in the ears of the people, which their sovereign disdained to listen to.—— Ill-counselled sovereign! but will that word apologize for conduct so intemperate? It cannot: a mind, so flexible towards evil counsel, can possess no requisites for government: what hope now remained for moderate measures, when the people's representatives should again assemble? In this fatal moment the fuel was prepared and the match lighted, to give life to the flames of civil war; already Scotland had set those sparks into a blaze; the king, unable to extinguish the conflagration by his own power and resources, for the fifth and last time convenes his parliament: but it was now too late for any confidence or mutual harmony to subsist between the crown and commons; on the third of November following their last dissolution, the new elected members take possession of their seats, and the house soon resounds with resolutions for the impeachment of the minister Strafford, and the primate Laud: the humble monarch confirms the fatal bill of attainder, and sends Strafford to the scaffold; he ratifies the act for securing parliament against future dissolution, and subscribes to his own death-warrant with the same pen.

The proceedings of this famous parliament are of a mixt nature; in many we discern the true spirit of patriotism, and not a few seem dictated by revenge and violence: the Courts of High Commission and Star-Chamber are abolished, and posterity applauds their deliverers; the city-crosses are pulled down, the bishops sent to the Tower, and their whole order menaced with expulsion from parliament, and here we discover the first dawnings of fanatic frenzy: an incurable breach is made in the constitution; its branches are dissevered, and the axe of rebellion is laid to the root of the tree: the royal standard is set up; the father of his people becomes the general of a party, and the land is floated with the blood of its late peaceable inhabitants: great characters start forth in the concussion, great virtues and great vices: equal courage and superior conduct at length prevail for the leaders of the people; a fanatic champion carries all before him; the sovereign surrenders himself weakly, capitulates feebly, negotiates deceitfully, and dies heroically.

And this is the reign, this is the exit of a king! Let kings ponder it, for it is a lesson, humbling perhaps to their pride of station, but pointedly addressed to their instruction.

If there is a trust in life, which calls upon the conscience of a man who undertakes it more strongly than any other, it is that of the education of an heir-apparent to a crown: the training such a pupil is a task indeed; how to open his mind to a proper knowledge of mankind, without letting in that knowledge which inclines to evil; how to hold off flattery, and yet admit familiarity; how to give the lights of information, and shut out the false colours of seduction, demands a judgment for distinguishing and an

authority for controlling, which few governors in that
delicate situation ever possess, or can long retain :
to educate a prince, born to reign over an enlightened people, upon the narrow scale of secret and
sequestered tuition, would be an abuse of common
sense ; to let him loose upon the world is no less
hazardous in the other extreme, and each would probably devote him to an inglorious destiny : that he
should know the leading characters in the country
he is to govern, be familiar with its history, its constitution, manners, laws, and liberties, and correctly
comprehend the duties and distinctions of his own
hereditary office, are points that no one will dispute :
that he should travel through this kingdom I can
hardly doubt, but whether those excursions should
reach into other states, politically connected with,
or opposed to, his own, is more than I will presume
to lay down as a general rule, being aware that it
must depend upon personal circumstances : splendour he may be indulged in, but excess in that, as
in every thing else, must be avoided, for the mis-
chiefs cannot be numbered which it will entail upon
him ; excess in expense will subject him to obligations of a degrading sort; excess in courtesy will lay
him open to the forward and assuming, raise mountains of expectation about him, and all of them un-
dermined by disappointment, ready charged for explosion, when the hand of presumption shall set fire
to the train : excess in pleasure will lower him in
character, destroy health, respect, and that becoming dignity of mind, that conscious rectitude, which
is to direct and support him, when he becomes the
dispenser of justice to his subjects, the protector and
defender of their religion, the model of their imitation, and the sovereign arbiter of life and death
in the execution of every legal condemnation.  To
court popularity is both derogatory and dangerous,

nor should he who is destined to rule over the whole, condescend to put himself in the league of a party. To be a protector of learning, and a patron of the arts, is worthy of a prince, but let him beware how he sinks himself into a pedant or a virtuoso. It is a mean talent which excels in trifles; the fine arts are more likely to flourish under a prince, whose ignorance of them is qualified by general and impartial good-will towards their professors, than by one, who is himself a dabbler; for such will always have their favourites, and favouritism never fails to irritate the minds of men of genius concerned in the same studies, and turns the spirit of emulation into the gall of acrimony.

Above all things let it be his inviolable maxim to distinguish strongly and pointedly in his attentions between men of virtuous morals and men of vicious: there is nothing so glorious, and at the same time nothing so easy; if his countenance is turned to men of principle and character, if he bestows his smile upon the worthy only, he need be at little pains to frown upon the profligate, all such vermin will crawl out of his path, and shrink away from his presence. Glittering talents will be no passport for dissolute morals, and ambition will then be retained in no other cause, but that of virtue; men will not choose crooked passages and by-alleys to prefer-ment, when the broad highway of honesty is laid open and straight before them. A prince, though he gives a good example in his own person, what does he profit the world, if he draws it back again by the bad example of those whom he employs and fa-vours? Better might it be for a nation, to see a li-bertine on its throne, surrounded by virtuous coun-sellors, than to contemplate a virtuous sovereign, delegating his authority to unprincipled and licen-tious servants.

The king who declares his resolution of coun-
tenancing the virtues only amongst his subjects,
speaks the language of an honest man : if he makes
good his declaration, he performs the functions of
one, and earns the blessings of a righteous king ; a
life of glory in this world, and an immortality of
happiness in the world to come.

## NUMBER LV.

### Non erat his locus.

THERE is a certain delicacy in some men's nature,
which though not absolutely to be termed a moral attribute, is nevertheless so grateful to society at large,
and so recommendatory of those who possess it, that
even the best and worthiest characters cannot be
truly pleasing without it. I know not how to describe
it better than by saying it consists in a happy discernment of ' times and seasons.'

Though this engaging talent cannot positively be
called a virtue, yet it seems to be the result of many
virtuous and refined endowments of the mind, which
produces it; for when we see any man so tenderly
considerate of our feelings, as to put aside his own
for our accommodation and repose, and to consult
opportunities with a respectful attention to our ease
and leisure, it is natural to us to think favourably of
such a disposition, and although much of his discernment may be the effect of a good judgment and
proper knowledge of the world, yet there must be a
great proportion of sensibility, candour, diffidence,
and natural modesty, in the composition of a faculty

so conciliating and so graceful. A man may have many good qualities, and yet, if he is unacquainted with the world, he will rarely be found to understand those apt and happy moments, of which I am now speaking; for it is a knowledge not to be gained without a nice and accurate observation of mankind, and even when that observation has given it, men, who are wanting in the natural good qualities above described, may indeed avail themselves of such occasions to serve a purpose of their own ; but, without a good heart, no man will apply his experience to general practice.

But as it is not upon theories that I wish to employ these papers, I shall now devote the remainder of my attention to such rules and observations as occur to me upon the subject of *the times and seasons*.

Men, who in the fashionable phrase *live out of the world,* have a certain awkwardness about them, which is for ever putting them out of their place in society, whenever they are occasionally drawn into it. If it is their studies which have sequestered them from the world, they contract an air of pedantry, which can hardly be endured in any mixed company without exposing the object of it to ridicule; for the very essence of this contracted habit consists in an utter ignorance *of times and seasons*. Most of that class of men who are occupied in the education of youth, and not a few of the young men themselves, who are educated by them, are of this description: we meet with many of Jack Lizard's cast in the Spectator, who will learnedly maintain *there is no heat in fire.* There is a disputatious precision in these people, which lets nothing pass in free conversation, that is not mathematically true; they will confute a jest by syllogism, canvas a merry tale by cross-examination and dates, work every common calculation by X, *the unknown quantity,* and in the festive sallies of ima-

gination convict the witty speaker of false grammar,
and nonsuit all the merriment of the table.

The man of form and ceremony, who has shaped
his manners to the model of what is commonly called
*The Old Court,* is another grand defaulter against
*times and seasons:* his entrances and exits are to be
performed with a stated regularity; he measures his
devoirs with an exactitude that bespeaks him a correct interpreter of *The Red Book;* pays his compli-
ments with a minuteness, that leaves no one of your
family unnamed, inquires after the health of your
child who is dead, and desires to be kindly remembered to your wife, from whom you are divorced.
Nature formed him in straight lines, habit has stiffened
him into an unrelenting rigidity, and no familiarity
can bend him out of the upright. The uneducated
squire of rustic manners forms a contrast to this
character, but he is altogether as great an intruder
upon *times and seasons,* and his total want of form
operates to the annoyance of society as effectually as
the other's excess. There cannot be in human nature a more terrible thing than vulgar familiarity;
a low-bred fellow, who affects to put himself at his
ease amongst his superiors, and be pleasant company
to them, is a nuisance to society; there is nothing
so ill understood by the world in general as familiarity; if it was not for the terror which men have
of the very troublesome consequences of condescen-
sion to their inferiors, there would not be a hundredth part of that pride and holding-back amongst
the higher ranks, of which the low are so apt to
complain. How few men do we meet with, who,
when the heart is open and the channel free, know
how to keep their course within the buoys and
marks, that true good-manners have set up for all
men to steer by! Jokes out of season, unpleasant
truths touched upon incautiously, *plump questions* (as

they are called) put without any preface or refinement, manual caresses compounded of hugs and
slaps and squeezes, more resembling the gambols of
a bear than the actions of a gentleman, are sure to
follow upon the overflowing ebullitions of a vulgar
familiarity broke loose from all restraints. It is a
painful necessity men of sensibility are under, when
they find themselves compelled to draw back from
the eager advances of an honest heart, only because
the shock of its good-humour is too violent to be endured; it is very wounding to a social nature to
check festivity in any degree, but there is nothing
sinks the spirits so effectually as boisterous mirth,
nobody so apt to overact his character as a jolly
fellow, and stunned with the vociferation of his own
tongue to forget that every other man is silent and
suffering: in short, it is a very difficult thing to be
properly happy and well pleased with the company
we are in, and none but men of good education, great
discernment, and nice feelings know how to be familiar. These rural gentry are great dealers in long
stories of their own uninteresting achievements;
they require of you to attend to the narrative of their
paltry squabbles and bickerings with their neighbours; they are extremely eloquent upon the laws
against poachers, upon turnpike roads and new en-
closures, and all these topics they will thrust in by
the neck and shoulders to the exclusion of all others.

Plain speaking, if we consider it simply as a mark
of truth and honesty, is doubtless a very meritorious
quality, but experience teaches that it is too frequently under bad management, and obtruded on
society out of *time and season* in such a manner as to
be highly inconvenient and offensive. People are
not always in a fit humour to be told of their faults,
and these plain-speaking friends sometimes perform
their office so clumsily, that we are inclined to sus-

pect they are more interested to bring us to present
shame than future reformation: it is a common
observation with them, when things turn out amiss,
to put us in mind how they dissuaded us from such
and such an undertaking, that they foresaw what
would happen, and that the event is neither more
nor less than they expected and predicted. These
retorts, cast in our teeth in the very moment of
vexation, are what few tempers, when galled with
disappointment, can patiently put up with; they may
possibly be the result of zeal and sincerity, but they
are so void of contrivance, and there is so little delicacy in the timing of them, that it is a very rare
case indeed, when they happen to be well understood
and kindly taken. The same want of sensibility
towards human infirmities, that will not spare us in
the moments of vexation, will make no allowances
for the mind's debility in the hours of grief and
sorrow: if a friend of this sort surprises us in the
weakness of the soul, when death perhaps has robbed us of some beloved object, it is not to contribute
a tear, but to read us a lecture, that he comes; when
the heart is agonized, the temper is irritable, and as
a moralizer of this sort is almost sure to find his ad-
monitions take the contrary effect from what he intended, he is apt to mistake an occasional impatience in us for a natural one, and leaves us with the
impression that we are men who are ill prepared
against the common vicissitudes of life, and endowed with a very small share of fortitude and resignation; this early misconception of our character, in
the course of time leads him to another, for he no
sooner finds us recovered to a proper temper of
mind, than he calls to mind our former impatience,
and, comparing it with our present tranquillity, concludes upon appearances, that we are men of light
and trivial natures, subject indeed to fits and starts

of passion, but incapable of retention, and as he has then a fine subject for displaying his powers of plain-speaking, he reminds us of our former inattention to his good advice, and takes credit for having told us over and over again that we ought not to give way to violent sorrow, and that we could not change the course of things by our complaining of them. Thus, for want of calculating *times and seasons,* he begins to think despisingly of us, and we, in spite of all his sincerity, grow tired of him, and dread his company.

Before I quit this subject, I must also have a word with the valetudinarians, and I wish from my heart I could cure them of their *complaints,*—that species I mean which comes under my notice as an Observer, without intruding upon the more important province of the physician. Now, as this island of ours is most happily supplied with a large and learned body of professors under every medical description and character, whether operative or deliberative, and all these stand ready at the call, and devoted to the service of the sick or maimed, whether it be on foot, on horseback, or on wheels, to resort to them in their distresses, it cannot be for want of help that the valetudinarian states his case to all companies so promiscuously. Let the whole family of death be arrayed on one side, and the whole army of physic, regulars and irregulars, be drawn out on the other, and I will venture to say, that for every possible disease in the ranks of the besieger, there shall be a champion in the garrison ready to turn out and give him battle. Let all who are upon the sick-list in the community be laid out between the camps, and let the respective combatants fight it out over the bodies, but let the forces of life and health have no share in the fray: why should their peace be disturbed, or their society contaminated by the infectious communication? It is as much out of *time and place* for a man to be giving the diary of his disease in company, who are met for social purposes, as it is for a doctor to be talking politics or scandal in a sick man's chamber; yet so it is, that each party are for ever out of character; the chatterer disgusts his patient by an inattention to his complaints, and the valetudinarian disgusts his company by the enumeration of them, and both are equally out of season.

Every man's observation may furnish him with instances not here enumerated, but if what I have said shall seem to merit more consideration than I have been able to give it in the compass of this paper, my readers may improve upon the hint, and society cannot fail to profit by their reflections.

## NUMBER LVI.

———῀Ω τρισάθλιοι
"Ἅπαντες οἱ φυσῶντες ἐφ᾽ ἑαυτοῖς μέγα,
Αὐτοὶ γὰρ οὐκ ἴσασιν ἀνθρώπου φύσιν.

MENANDER. Gubernatoribus.

Oh wretched mortals! by false pride betray'd,
Ye know not of what nature man is made.

THOUGH I think our nation can never be accused of want of charity, yet I have observed with much concern a poor unhappy set of men amongst us, whose case is not commiserated as it ought to be; and as I would gladly contribute any thing in my power towards their relief, the best proof I can give them of my good will is by endeavouring to convince them of a certain truth, which all the world except themselves has discovered long ago, viz. 'That a proud man is

the most contemptible being in nature.' Now if
these proud men to whom I address myself, and for
whose miserable situation I have such compassion,
shall once find a friend to convince them, that they
are truly 'the most contemptible beings in nature,'
it can never be supposed they will persist to entertain a companion in their bosoms who affords them
so little pleasure, and yet involves them in so much
disgrace. I must consider them therefore as mistaken rather than obstinate, and treat them accordingly; for how can I suppose there would be such an
absurdity in the world as a proud man, if the poor
creature was not behind-hand with the rest of mankind in a discovery that concerns himself so mate-
rially? I admit indeed that pride is a very foolish
thing, but I contend that wise men are sometimes surprised into very foolish things, and, if a little friendly
hint can rescue them, it would be an ill-natured action to withhold the information: ' If you are proud,
you are a fool,' says an old Greek author called
Sotades—Ἂν ἀλαζὼν ᾖς, τοῦτ' ἀνοίας ἐστὶ φρύαγμα
—but I hope a little plain English, without the help
of Sotades, will serve to open the eyes of a plain
Englishman, and prevent him from strutting about
the world merely to make sport for his neighbours;
for I declare in truth, that so far from being annoyed
and made splenetic, as some folks are, when I fall
into company with a proud fellow-creature, I feel no
other impulse than of pity, with now and then a
small propensity to titter, for it would be downright
rudeness to laugh in a man's face on such an occasion; and it hurts me to see an honest gentleman,
who may have many more natural good qualities
than he himself is aware of, run about from house to
house only to make sport for the scoffers, and to take
a world of pains, and put on an air of gravity and importance, for no better purpose than to provoke ridicule

and contempt—' Why is earth and ashes proud?'
says the Son of Sirach; 'Pride was not made for men.'

As I am determined to put these poor men upon
their guard in all points, I shall remind them of another error they are in, which sadly aggravates their
misfortunes, and which arises from a circumstance of
a mere local nature, viz. ' That England is the worst
country a proud man can exhibit himself in.'—I do
really wish they would well consider the land they
live in; if they do not know, they ought to be told,
that we are a free people; that freedom tends to
make us independent of one another, fearless in our
persons, warm in our resentments, bold of tongue,
and vindictive against insult; England is the place
upon earth, where a proud stomach finds the least to
feed upon; indeed it is the only stomach that can here
complain of its entertainment: if the proud man
thinks it will be sufficient to pay his fine of affability
to his neighbours once in seven years upon a parlia-
mentary canvas, he is cruelly mistaken; the common people in this country have such a share of intuition, understand their own strength so well, and
scrutinize into the weaknesses of their superiors so
acutely, that they are neither to be deceived nor in-
timidated; and on that account (as the proud man's
character is compounded of the impostor and
bully) they are the very worst people he can deal
with. A man may strut in Spain, vapour in France,
or kick and cuff the vulgar as he likes in Russia; he
may sit erect in his palanquin in India without dropping his eyes upon the earth he moves over; but if
he carries his head in the air here, and expects the
crowd to make way for him, he will soon run foul of
somebody that will make him repent of his stateli-
ness. Pride then, it seems, not only exposes a man
to contempt, but puts him in danger; it is also a
very expensive frolic, if he keeps it up as it should

be kept, for what signifies his being proud, if there is not somebody always present to exercise his pride upon? He must therefore of necessity have a set of humble cousins and toad-eaters about him, and as such cattle cannot be had for nothing in this country, he must pay them according to the value of their services; common trash may be had at a common price, but clever fellows know their own consequence, and will stand out upon terms. If Nebuchadnezzar had not had ' all people, nations, and languages,' at his command, he might have called till he was hoarse before any one would have come to worship his ' image in the plain of Dura;' let the proud man take notice withal, that Nebuchadnezzar's *image* was made of *gold*, and if he expects to be worshipped by all people after this fashion, and casts himself in the same mould, he must also cast himself in the same metal. Now, if I am right in my assertion, that sycophants bear a higher price in England than elsewhere (and, if scarcity makes things dear, I trust they do), let the proud man consider if it be worth his while to pay dear for bad company, when he may have good-fellowship at an easy rate. Here then is another instance of his bad policy, and sure it is a sorrowful thing to be poor and proud.

That I may thoroughly do my duty to an order of men, to whose service I dedicate this short essay, I must not omit to mention, that it behoves a proud man, in all places, and on all occasions, to preserve an air of gloominess and melancholy, and never to suffer so vulgar an expression as mirth or laughter to disarrange the decorum of his features: other men will be apt to make merry with his humour, but he must never be made merry by theirs: in this respect he is truly to be pitied, for if once he grows sociable he is undone. On the contrary, he must for ever remain in the very predicament of the proud man described

in the fragment of Euripides's Ixion—Φίλοις ἄμικτος
καὶ πάσῃ πόλει—*Urbi atque amicis pariter insociabilis.*
He must have no friend, for that would be to admit
an equal; he must take no advice, for that would be
to acknowledge a superior.  Such society as he can
find in his own thoughts, and such wisdom as he was
sent into the world with, such he must go on with:
as wit is not absolutely annexed to pedigree in this
country, and arts and sciences sometimes condescend to throw their beams upon the low-born and
humble, it is not possible for the proud man to descend amongst them for information and society; if
truth does not hang within his reach, he will never
dive into a well to fetch it up: his errors, like some
arguments, move *in a circle:* for his pride begets ignorance, and his ignorance begets pride; and thus
in the end he has more reasons for being *melancholy*
than Master Stephen had, not only because it is
*gentleman-like,* but because he can't help it, and don't
know how to be merry.

I might enumerate many more properties of this
contemptible character, but these are enough, and a
proud man is so dull a fellow at best, that I shall
gladly take my leave of him; I confess, also, that I
am not able to treat the subject in any other than a
vague and desultory manner, for I know not how to
define it myself, and at the same time am not reconciled to any other definition of pride, which I have
met in Mr. Locke's essay or elsewhere.  It is called
a passion, and yet it has not the essentials of a passion; for I can bring to mind nothing under that
description, which has not reference either to God,
to our fellow-creatures, or to ourselves.  The sensual passions for instance, of whatever sort, have
their end in selfish gratification; the generous attributes, such as valour, friendship, public spirit, munificence, and contempt of danger, have respect to

our fellow-creatures; they look for their account in an honourable fame, in the enjoyment of present praise, and in the anticipation of that which posterity shall bestow; whilst the less ostentatious and purer virtues of self-denial, resignation, humility, piety, forbearance, and many others, are addressed to God alone, they offer no gratification to self, they seek for no applause from man. But in which of these three general classes shall we discover the passion of pride? I have indeed sometimes seen it under the cloak of religion, but nothing can be more opposite to the practice of it: it is in vain to inquire for it amongst the generous and social attributes, for its place is no where to be found in society; and I am equally at a loss to think how that can be called a selfish gratification, which brings nothing home to a man's heart but mortification, contempt, abhorrence, secret discontent, and public ridicule. It is composed of contraries, and founded in absurdity; for, at the same time that it cannot subsist without the world's respect, it is so constituted as never to obtain it. Anger is proverbially termed a short madness, but pride methinks is a perpetual one; if I had been inclined to use a softer word, I would have called it folly; I do confess I have often seen it in that more venial character, and therefore, not to decide upon the point too hastily, I shall leave the proud man to make his choice between folly and madness, and take out his commission from which party he sees fit.

Good heaven! how pleasant, how complacent to itself and others, is a humble disposition! To a soul so tempered how delightfully life passes in brotherly love and simplicity of manners! Every eye bestows the cheering look of approbation upon the humble man; every brow frowns contempt upon the proud. Let me therefore advise every gentleman, when he finds himself inclined to take up the cha-

racter of pride, to consider well whether he can be
quite proud enough for all purposes of life : whether
his pride reaches to that pitch as to meet universal
contempt with indifference; whether it will bear him
out against mortification, when he finds himself excluded from society, and understands that he is ridiculed by every body in it ; whether it is convenient
to him always to walk with a stiff back and a stern
countenance; and, lastly, whether he is perfectly
sure, that he has that strength and self-support in
his own human nature, as may defy the power and
set at nought the favour of God, *who resisteth the
proud, but giveth grace to the humble.*

There is yet another little easy process, which I
would recommend to him as a kind of probationary
rehearsal before he performs in public : I am persuaded it will not be amiss if he first runs over a few
of his airs and graces by himself in his own closet :
let him examine himself from head to foot in his
glass, and if he finds himself no handsomer, no
stronger, no taller than the rest of his fellow-creatures, he may venture, without risk, to conclude that
he like them is a man, and nothing more. Having
settled this point, and taken place in the human
creation, he may next proceed to consider what that
place ought to be : for this purpose he may consult
his pedigree and his rent-roll, and if, upon a careful
perusal of these documents, he shall find (as most
likely he will) that he is not decidedly the noblest
and the richest man in the world, perhaps he will see
no good cause, why he should strut over the face of
it as if it was his own : I would then have him go
back to his glass, and set his features in order for
the very proudest and most arrogant look he can put
on ; let him knit his brow, stretch his nostrils, and
bite his lips with all the dignity he can summon;
and after this, when he has reversed the experiment,

by softening them into a mild complacent look, with as much benignity as he can find in his heart to bestow upon them, let him ask himself honestly and fairly, which character best becomes him, and whether he does not look more like a man with some humanity than without it; I would, in the next place, have him call his understanding to a short audit, and upon casting up the sum total of his wit, learning, talents, and accomplishments, compute the balance between others and himself, and if it shall turn out that his stock of all these is not the prodigious thing it ought to be, and even greater than all other mens, he will do well to husband it with a little frugal humility. The last thing he must do (and if he does nothing else I should hope it would be sufficient), is to take down his Bible from the shelf, and look out for the parable of the Pharisee and Publican; it is a short story and soon read, but the moral is so much to his purpose, that he may depend upon it, if that does not correct his pride, his pride is incorrigible, and all the Observers in the world will be but waste paper in his service.

## NUMBER LVII.

Μακάριος, ὅστις οὐσίαν καὶ νοῦν ἔχει·
Χρῆται γὰρ οὗτος, εἰς ἃ δεῖ, ταύτῃ καλῶς·
Οὕτω μαθεῖν δεῖ, πάντα καὶ πλοῦτον φέρειν·
Ἀσχημοσύνης γὰρ γίνετ' ἐνίοις αἴτιος.

MENANDER. Circulatore.

Abundance is a blessing to the wise;
The use of riches in discretion lies:
Learn this, ye men of wealth—a heavy purse
In a fool's pocket is a heavy curse.

THERE are so many striking advantages in the possession of wealth, that the inheritance of a great

estate devolving upon a man in the vigour of mind
and body, appears to the eye of speculation as a lot
of singular felicity.

There are some countries where no subject can
properly be said to be independent; but in a constitution so happily tempered as ours, that blessing
seems peculiarly annexed to affluence. The English
landed gentleman, who can set his foot upon his
own soil, and say to all the world—*This is my free-
hold; the law defends my right: Touch it who dare!*—
is surely as independent as any man within the rules
of society can be, so long as he encumbers himself
by no exceedings of expense beyond the compass of
his income: if a great estate therefore gives a man
independence, it gives him that which all, who do
not possess it, seem to sigh for.

When I consider the numberless indulgences,
which are the concomitants of a great fortune, and
the facility it affords to the gratification of every
generous passion, I am mortified to find how few,
who are possessed of these advantages, avail themselves of their situation to any worthy purposes:
that happy temper, which can preserve a medium between dissipation and avarice, is not often to be found,
and where I meet one man, who can laudably acquit
himself under the test of prosperity, I could instance numbers, who deport themselves with honour
under the visitation of adversity. Man must be in a
certain degree the artificer of his own happiness;
the tools and materials may be put into his hands
by the bounty of Providence, but the workmanship
must be his own.

I lately took a journey into a distant county, upon
a visit to a gentleman of fortune whom I shall call
Attalus. I had never seen him since his accession
to a very considerable estate; and as I have met
with few acquaintance in life of more pleasant qua-

lities, or a more social temper than Attalus, before
this great property unexpectedly devolved upon him,
I flattered myself that fortune had in this instance
bestowed her favours upon one who deserved them;
and that I should find in Attalus's society the pleasing gratification of seeing all those maxims, which I
had hitherto revolved in my mind as matter of speculation only, now brought forth into actual practice; for amongst all my observations upon human
affairs, few have given me greater and more frequent
disappointment, than the almost general abuse of
riches. Those rules of liberal economy, which would
make wealth a blessing to its owner and to all he
were connected with, seem so obvious to me, who
have no other interest in the subject than what meditation affords, that I am apt to wonder how men
can make such false estimates of the true enjoyments
of life, and wander out of the way of happiness, to
which the heart and understanding seem to point
the road too plainly to admit of a mistake.

With these sanguine expectations I pursued my
journey towards the magnificent seat of Attalus, and
in my approach it was with pleasure I remarked the
beauty of the country about it; I recollected how
much he used to be devoted to rural exercises, and
I found him situated in the very spot most favourable to his beloved amusements; the soil was clean,
the hills easy, and the downs were chequered with
thick copses, that seemed the finest nurseries in nature for a sportsman's game. When I entered upon
his ornamented demesne, nothing could be more enchanting than the scenery; the ground was finely
shaped into hill and vale; the horizon every where
bold and romantic, and the hand of art had evidently improved the workmanship of nature with consummate taste; upon the broken declivity stately
groves of beech were happily disposed; the lawn

was of the finest verdure gently sloping from the
house; a rapid river of the purest transparency ran
through it, and fell over a rocky channel into a noble
lake within view of the eastern mansion; behind this upon
the northern and eastern flanks I could discern the
tops of very stately trees, that sheltered a spacious
enclosure of pleasure-ground and gardens, with all
the delicious accompaniments of hot-houses and
conservatories.

It was a scene to seize the imagination with rapture: a poet's language would have run spontane-
ously into metre at the sight of it: ' What a subject,' said I within myself, ' is here present for those
ingenious bards, who have the happy talent of describing nature in her fairest forms!  Oh! that I
could plant the delightful author of *The Task* in this
very spot! perhaps whilst his eye—*in a fine frenzy
rolling*—glanced over this enchanting prospect, he
might burst forth into the following, or something
like the following rhapsody—'

> Blest above men, if he perceives and feels
> The blessings he is heir to. He! to whom
> His provident forefathers have bequeathed
> In this fair district of their native isle
> A free inheritance, compact and clear.
> How sweet the vivifying dawn to him,
> Who with a fond paternal eye can trace
> Beloved scenes, where rivers, groves, and lawns
> Rise at the touch of the Orphean hand,
> And Nature, like a docile child, repays
> Her kind disposer's care! Master and friend
> Of all that blooms or breathes within the verge
> Of this wide-stretcht horizon, he surveys
> His upland pastures white with fleecy flocks,
> Rich meadows dappled o'er with grazing herds,
> And valleys waving thick with golden grain.
>     Where can the world display a fairer scene?
> And what has Nature for the sons of men
> Better provided than this happy isle?
> Mark! how she's girded by her watery zone,

Whilst all the neighb'ring continent is trench'd
And furrow'd with the ghastly seams of war:
Barriers and forts and arm'd battalions stand
On the fierce confines of each rival state,
Jealous to guard, or eager to invade ;
Between their hostile camps a field of blood,
Behind them desolation void and drear,
Where at the summons of the surly drum
The rising and the setting sun reflects
Nought but the gleam of arms, now here, now there
Flashing amain, as the bright phalanx moves :
Wasteful and wide the blank in Nature's map,
And far, far distant where the scene begins
Of human habitation, thinly group'd
Over the meagre earth ; for there no youth
No sturdy peasant, who with limbs and strength
Might fill the gaps of battle, dares approach ;
Old age instead, with weak and trembling hand,
Feebly solicits the indignant soil
For a precarious meal, poor at the best.

Oh, Albion ! oh, blest isle, on whose white cliffs
Peace builds her halcyon nest, thou, who embrac'd
By the uxorious ocean sit'st secure,
Smiling and gay and crown'd with every wreath,
That Art can fashion or rich Commerce waft
To deck thee like a bride ; compare these scenes
With pity not with scorn, and let thy heart,
Not wanton with prosperity, but warm
With grateful adoration, send up praise
To the great Giver—thence thy blessings come.

　The soft luxurious nations will complain
Of thy rude wintry clime, and chide the winds
That ruffle their fine forms ; trembling they view
The boisterous barrier that defends thy coast,
Nor dare to pass it till their pilot bird,
The winter-sleeping swallow, points the way ;
But envy not their suns, and sigh not thou
For the clear azure of their cloudless skies ;
The same strong blast, that beds the knotted oak
Firm in his clay-bound cradle, nerves the arm
Of the stout hind, who fells him to the ground.
These are the manly offspring of our isle ;
Theirs are the pure delights of rural life,
Freedom their birth-right and their dwelling peace
The vine, that mantles o'er their cottage roof,
Gives them a shade no tyrant dares to spoil.

Mark! how the sturdy peasant breasts the storm,
The white snow sleeting o'er his brawny chest;
He heeds it not, but carols as he goes
Some jocund measure or love-ditty, soon
In sprightlier key and happier accent sung
To the kind wench at home, whose ruddy cheeks
Shall thaw the icy winter on his lips,
And melt his frozen features into joy.
But who, that ever heard the hunter's shout,
When the shrill fox-hound doubles on the scent,
Which of you, sons and fathers of the chase,
Which of your hardy, bold, adventurous band
Will pine and murmur for Italian skies?
Hark! from the covert-side your game is view'd!
Music, which none but British dryads hear,
Shouts, which no foreign echoes can repeat,
Ring through the hollow wood and sweep the vale.
Now, now, ye joyous sportsmen, ye, whose hearts
Are unison'd to the extatic cry
Of the full pack, now give your steeds the rein!
Yours is the day—mine was, and is no more:
Yet ever as I hear you in the wind,
Though chill'd and hovering o'er my winter hearth,
Forth, like some Greenwich veteran, if chance
The conqu'ring name of Rodney meets his ear,
Forth I must come to share the glad'ning sound,
To shew my scars and boast of former feats.

They say our clime's inconstant, changeful—True!
It gives the lie to all astrology,
Makes the diviner mad and almost mocks
Philosophy itself; Cameleon-like
Our sky puts on all colours, blushing now,
Now lowering like a froward pettish child;
This hour a zephyr, and the next a storm,
Angry and pleas'd by fits—Yet take our clime,
Take it for all in all and day by day
Through all the varying seasons of the year,
For the mind's vigour and the body's strength,
Where is its rival?—Beauty is its own:
Not the voluptuous region of the Nile,
Not aromatic India's spicy breath,
Nor evening breeze from Tagus, Rhone, or Loire
Can tinge the maiden cheek with bloom so fresh.
Here too, if exercise and temperance call,
Health shall obey their summons; every fount,
Each rilling stream conveys it to our lips;

In every zephyr we inhale her breath ;
The shepherd tracks her in the morning dew,
As o'er the grassy down or to the heath
Streaming with fragrance he conducts his flock.
But oh ! defend me from the baneful east,
Screen me ye groves ! ye interposing hills,
Rise up and cover me ! Agues and rheums,
All Holland's marshes strike me in the gale !
Like Egypt's blight his breath is all alive :
His very dew is poison, honey-sweet,
Teeming with putrefaction ; in his fog
The locust and the caterpillar swarm,
And vegetable nature falls before them :
Open, all quarters else, and blow upon me,
But bar that gate, O regent of the winds !
It gives the food that melancholy dotes on,
The quick'ner that provokes the slanderer's spleen,
Makes green the eye of Jealousy, and feeds
The swelling gorge of Envy till it bursts :
'Tis now the poet's unpropitious hour ;
The student trims his midnight lamp in vain,
And beauty fades upon the painter's eye :
Hang up thy pallet, Romney ! and convene
The gay companions of thy social board ;
Apelles' self would throw his pencil by,
And swear the skies conspir'd against his art.
　　But what must Europe's softer climes endure,
Thy coast, Calabria ! or the neighbouring isle,
Of ancient Ceres once the fruitful seat ?
Where is the bloom of Enna's flowery field,
Mellifluous Hybla, and the golden vale
Of rich Panormus, when the fell Siroc,
Hot from the furnace of the Lybian sands,
Breathes all its plagues upon them ? Hapless isle,
Why must I call to mind thy past renown ?
Is it this desolating blast alone
That strips thy verdure ? Is it in the gulf
Of yawning earthquakes that thy glory sinks ?
Or hath the flood that thund'ring Ætna pours
From her convuls'd and flaming entrails whelm'd
In one wide ruin every noble spark
Of pristine virtue, genius, wisdom, wit ?
Ah no ! the elements are not in fault ;
Nature is still the same : 'Tis not the blast
From Afric's burning sands, it is the breath
Of Spain's despotic master lays thee low ;

'Tis not alone the quaking earth that reels
Under thy tottering cities, 'tis the fall
Of freedom, 'tis the pit which slavery digs,
That buries every virtue ; 'tis the flood
Of superstition, the insatiate fires
Of persecuting zealots that devour thee ;
These are the Titans who disturb thy peace,
This is thy grave, O Sicily ! the hell
Deeper than that, which heathen poets feign'd
Under thy burning mountain, that engulfs
Each grace and every muse, arts, arms, and all
That elegance inspires or fame records.

　　Return, ye victims of caprice and spleen,
Ye summer friends, daughters more fitly call'd
Than sons of Albion, to your native shores
Return, self-exiles as you are, and face
This only tyrant which our isle endures,
This hoary-headed terror of the year,
Stern Winter—What, tho' in his icy chains
Imprison'd for a time e'en Father Thames
Checks his imperial current and beholds
His wealthy navigation in arrest,
Yet soon, like Perseus, on his winged steed,
Forth from the horns of the celestial ram
Spring, his deliverer, comes—down, down at once
The affrighted monster dives into the earth,
Or bursts asunder with a hideous crash,
As thro' his stubborn ribs th' all-conqu'ring sun
Drives his refulgent spear : the ransomed floods,
As at a signal, rise and clap their hands;
The mountains shout for joy ; the laughing hours
Dance o'er the eastern hills, and in the lap
Of marriageable earth their odours fling,
Wreaths of each vernal flowret, whilst the choir
Of feather'd songsters make the groves resound
With Nature's hymenæals—all is joy.

　　Hail, bounteous Spring ! primæval season, hail !
Nature's glad herald ! who to all the tribes
That link creation's scale from lordly man
To the small insect, that eludes his sight,
Proclaims that universal law of life,
The first great blessing of the new-born world,
' Increase and multiply !'—No sooner heard
By sultry climes, than straight the rebel sun
Mounts his bright throne, and o'er the withering earth
Scatters his bold Titanian fires around,

And cancels Heaven's high edict; Nature feels
Quick growth and quick decay; the verdant scene
Glitters awhile, and vanishes at once.
Not such the tints that Albion's landscape wears,
Her mantle dipt in never-fading green,
Keeps fresh its vernal honours thro' the year;
Soft dew-drops nurse her rose's maiden bloom,
And genial showers refresh her vivid lawn.
Thro' other lands indignant of delay
Spring travels homeward with a stranger's haste;
Here he reposes, dwells upon the scene
Enamour'd, native here prolongs his stay,
And when his fiery successor at length
Warns him from hence, with ling'ring step and slow,
And many a stream of falling tears he parts,
Like one, whom surly creditors arrest
In a fond consort's arms, and force him thence.

But now, my Muse, to humbler themes descend!
'Tis not for me to paint the various gifts
Which freedom, science, art, or fav'ring Heav'n
Shower on my native isle; quench'd are the fires
Which young ambition kindled in my breast;
Morning and noon of life's short day are past,
And what remains for me ere night comes on,
But one still hour perchance of glimmering eve
For sober contemplation? Come, my Muse,
Come then! and as from some high mountain's top
The careful shepherd counts his straggling flock,
So will we take one patient last survey
Of this unquiet, babbling, anxious world;
We'll scan it with a calm but curious eye;
Silence and solitude are all our own;
Their's is the tumult, their's the throng; my soul
Is fitted to the task—for, oh fair truth!
Yet I am thine, on thy perennial base
I will inscribe my monumental verse;
And tho' my heart with kindred ardour beats
To every brave compatriot, yet no ties,
Tho' dignified with friendship's specious name,
Shall shackle my free mind, nor any space
Less than the world's wide compass bound my love.

No more; for now the hospitable gates
Of wealthy Attalus invite their guest;
I paus'd and look'd, and yielding to the wish
That fortune had bequeath'd me such a lot,
A momentary sigh surpris'd my heart:

Flocks, herds, and fields of golden grain, of these
I envied not the owner; but I saw
The curling smoke from cottages ascend,
And heard the merry din of childish sports;
I saw the peasant stooping to his plough
And whistling time away; I met a form
Fair as a fabled nymph; Nature had spread
Her toilette, Health her handmaid dealt the bloom,
Simplicity attir'd her; by the copse
Skirting the horn-beam row, where violets bud
And the first primrose opens to the spring.
With her fond lover arm and arm she walk'd,
Not with the stealthy step and harlot leer
Of guilty assignation, nor unnerv'd
By midnight feast or revel, but in prime
Of youth and health and beauty's genuine glow:
I mark'd the conscious look of honest truth,
That greets the passenger with eye direct,
Nor fears nor meditates surprise; my heart
Yearn'd at the sight, and as they pass'd I cried—
' Why was it not my fortune to have said
Go, and be happy?'—On a rising slope
Full to the south the stately mansion stands,
Where dwells the master of this rich domain;
Plain and of chaste proportion the device,
Not libell'd and bedawb'd with tawdry frize
Or lac'd pilaster, patch'd with refuse scraps,
Like that fraternal pile on Thames's bank,
Which draws its title not its taste from Greece.
Happy! if there in rural peace he dwells,
Untortur'd by ambition, and enjoys
An eye for nature and a heart for man.

---

# NUMBER LVIII.

Οὔτ' ἔραμαι πλουτεῖν, οὔτ' εὔχομαι· ἀλλά μοι εἴη
Ζῆν ἀπὸ τῶν ὀλίγων, μηδὲν ἔχοντι κακόν.—THEOGNIS.

I ask not wealth; let me enjoy
An humble lot without annoy!

Upon my arrival at the house I was shewn into a
small room in the base-story, which the owner of

this fine place usually occupied, and in which he now received me : here I had been but a very few minutes before he proposed to shew me the house, and for that purpose conducted me up stairs to the grand apartment, and from thence made the entire tour, without excepting any one of the bed-chambers, offices, or even closets in the house ; I cannot say my friend Attalus consulted times and seasons in choosing so early a moment after my arrival for parading me about in this manner ; some of the apartments were certainly very splendid ; a great deal of rich furniture and many fine pictures solicited my notice, but the fatigue of so ill-timed a perambulation disabled me from expressing that degree of admiration, which seemed to be expected on this occasion, and which on any other I should have been forward to bestow : I was sorry for this, because I believe he enjoyed little other pleasure in the possession of his house, besides this of shewing it ; but it happened to my host, as it does too frequently to the owners of fine places, that he missed the tribute of flattery by too great eagerness in exacting it.

It appeared to me that Attalus was no longer the gay lively man he was formerly ; there was a gloom upon his countenance, and an inquietude in his manner, which seemed to lay him under a constraint that he could not naturally get rid of : time hung heavy on our hands till the hour of dinner, and it was not without regret I perceived he had arranged his family meals upon the fashionable system of London hours, and at the distance of two hundred miles from the capital had by choice adopted those very habits, which nothing but the general custom of late assemblies and long sittings in parliament can excuse upon the plea of necessity : it was now the midst of summer, which made the absurdity of

such a disposition of our time more glaring, for
whilst the best hours of the afternoon were devoted
to the table, all exercise and enjoyment out of doors
were either to be given up, or taken only in the
meridian heat of the day. I discovered a farther
bad consequence of these habits upon society and
good fellowship, for such of the neighbouring gentry, who had not copied his example, were deterred
from making him any visits, not presuming to disturb him at unsuitable hours, and yet not able,
without a total disarrangement of their own comforts, to make their time conform to his. Attalus
himself, I must acknowledge, both saw and confessed
the bad system he was upon: he found himself
grown unpopular amongst his country neighbours
on this very score, and was piqued by their neglect
of him: ' it was a villanous custom,' he observed,
' and destructive both of health and pleasure; but
all people of fashion dined at five, and what could
he do? he must live as other great families lived; if
indeed he was a mere private gentleman, he might
do as he liked best.' If it be so, thought I, this
man's great fortune is an encumbrance to him: if it
robs him of health and pleasure, what does it give
him, nay what can it give him, in compensation for
the loss of such blessings? if fashion takes away
from Attalus the liberty of doing what he best likes,
and is best for him, I must have been mistaken in
supposing independence was the result of affluence;
I suspect there are not all the advantages in his condition which I supposed there were—I will examine
this more narrowly.

The next morning after a late breakfast, the consequence I had foreseen ensued, for we were advanced into the hottest hours of the day, when Attalus,
being impatient to shew me the beauties of his park
and grounds, gave orders for the equipages and

horses to be made ready, and we were to set out
upon the survey in a burning sun. When the train
was in waiting at the door, we sallied forth, but here
a discussion began, in which so many things required
a new arrangement, that a long stop was put to our
march, whilst the scrutinizing eye of Attalus was
employed in a minute examination of every thing
appertaining to the cavalry and carriages: the horses
were wrong harnessed, they were to be changed from
the off-side to the near-side, saddles were to be altered, and both groom and coachman were heartily
recommended to repeated damnation for their stupidity and inattention.—' Never any man was so
plagued with rascally servants as I am,' cried Attalus; ' they are the curse and vexation of my life;
I wish I could live without them : no man can be
happy, who has to do with them.'—Is it so ? (said I
within myself) then I have the advantage over you
in that respect, for I have but one man and one
horse, and both are always ready at a moment's
warning.

I mounted a phaeton with Attalus, and we set
forward in a broiling day : my conductor immediately began to vent his angry humour upon the wrong
object, and plied his thong at such a furious rate
upon his unoffending horses, that the high mettled
animals so resented the unjust correction, that after
struggling and kicking under the lash for some time,
one of them reared across the pole of the chaise,
and snapped it : this produced a storm of passion
more violent than the first, and though it was evident the servant had put the horses on their proper
sides at first, the fault was charged upon him with
vehement imprecations, and this produced a second
halt longer and more disagreeable than our setting
out had been : our purpose however was not to be
defeated and we must positively proceed; Attalus

was not in a humour to submit with patience to disappointments, so that having ordered two of his
servants to dismount, we took their horses and set
off upon our tour: the beauties of nature were before us, but that serenity of mind, which should
ever accompany the contemplation of those beauties,
was wanting; Attalus was one of fortune's spoilt
children, and his temper, grown irritable by indulgence and humorsome by prosperity, had lost its
relish for simplicity, and was wholly given up to a
silly passion for ostentation and parade; he immediately began to harangue upon the many evil qualities of servants, a topic at the best unedifying and
commonly most disgusting to the hearers; he be-
wailed his own ill-fortune in that respect very bit-
terly, and so much of the way passed off before this
philippic was concluded, that I began to think I had
been carried out for no better purpose than to hear
a declamation in the open air : I brought him at last
to a stop, by observing, he had a paradise about
him, and that it was a pity his vexations did not
suffer him to enjoy it—Upon this hint he seemed to
recollect himself, and proceeded to expatiate upon
his own improvements, pointing out to me what he
had done, and what he had more in mind to do, if
his overseer had obeyed his instructions, and proper
people had been found to execute his designs.

I took notice of a group of neat cottages, which
had a very picturesque and pleasing appearance, for
they were deliciously situated, and had all the air,
as I observed, of happy habitations—' No matter
for that,' replied Attalus, ' down they must all come,
for they are cruelly in my eye, and I purpose to
throw all that hill into wilderness with plantations
of pine, where you see the rock and broken ground,
which will be a bold and striking contrast to the ornamented grounds about it—I am surprised,' added

he, ' you can see any beauty in those paltry huts.'
—Before I could make reply, an old peasant had
approached us, and humbly inquired of Attalus,
when he was to be dislodged from his cottage—' I
have ordered the workmen to take it down next
week,' said he, ' the season is favourable for your
removal, and you must seek out elsewhere.' The
decree was heard without an effort to reply ; a sigh
was all the plea the poor man offered, and with that
sigh he sent a look to heaven that in its passage rent
my heart ; I determined to be gone next morning.

We proceeded in our circuit till we were crossed
by a high enclosure, which awkwardly enough separated a pasture of about three acres, in which was
a brick-kiln too conspicuously placed not to annoy
the sight, and at that very moment too furiously
employed in the act of duty, not to be excessively
offensive to the smell ; we found ourselves involved
in columns of thick smoke, which were not of the
most grateful odour in the world ; I confess I was
not a little surprised at the location of this flaming
nuisance, and as we were making our way through
the smothering cloud, remarked to Attalus that ornament must give place to use.—' I brought you
hither,' says he, ' purposely to shew you how I am
treated by a surly obstinate fellow in my neighbour-
hood, who has not another foot of land in the world,
but this cursed patch of ground, and which the rascal keeps on purpose to spite me, though I have
bidden three times the value of it : indeed it is indispensably necessary to me, as you may well believe by the annoyance it produces in his hands ; I
have tried all means to get it from him, rough and
smooth, and if a prosecution would have laid against
it, I would have driven him out of it by the expenses
of a suit ; but all to no purpose ; I am so tormented
by the fellow's obstinacy, and my comforts are so

sacrificed by the nuisance, that I have no longer
any enjoyment in my place; nay I have stopped
most of my works and discharged my labourers,
for what signifies carrying on improvements, when
I can no longer live in my house with that cursed
brick-kiln for ever in my eye, and with little intermission in my nostrils also?'

A new theme of discontent was now started,
which the unhappy Attalus pursued with heavy
complaints as we travelled down a stream of smoke,
which seemed as if maliciously to pursue us, determined not to quit its execrator, till he left off his ex-
ecrations; at last they both ceased in the same moment and parted by consent. As soon as Attalus
desisted from his invectives I took up my reflections,
and if a wish could have purchased his possessions,
encumbered with the vexations of their owner, I
would not have taken them at the price. Down sunk
the vision of prosperity; swifter than the shifting of
a playhouse-scene vanished all the enchanting prospect; a naked lodge in a warren with content had
been more enviable in my eye than his palace haunted with disgust; I saw Attalus, the veriest darling
of fortune, sickening and surfeited with prosperity;
peevish with his servants, unsociable to his neighbours, a slave to fashions, which he obeyed and dis-
approved, unfeeling to the poor, tired with the splendour of a magnificent house, and possessing an ex-
tensive territory, yet sighing after a small nook of
land, the want of which poisoned all his comforts.
—And what then are riches? said I within myself.
The disturbers of human happiness; the corrupters
of human nature. I remember this Attalus in his
youth; I knew him intimately at school and college;
he was of a joyous, social temper; placid, accommodating, full of resource; always in good humour
with himself and the world, and he had a heart as

liberal and compassionate as it was sincere and
open; this great estate was then out of sight: it
must be this estate then, which has wrought the unhappy change in his manners and disposition; and
if riches operate thus upon a nature like his, where
is the wonder if we meet so many wretches, who
derive their wants from their abundance.

How beautiful is the maxim of Menander!—
Ψυχὴν ἔχειν δεῖ πλουσίαν—enrich your mind!
‘ Riches,’ says the same elegant and moral dramatist,
‘ are no better than an actor’s wardrobe,’ the paltry
tinsel, that enables him to glitter for a few minutes
in a counterfeited character—

> To fret and strut his hour upon the stage,
> And then be heard no more.

In another place he says, ‘ they transform a man
into a different kind of being from what he was originally’—

Εἰς ἕτερον ἦθος οὐκ ἐν ᾧ τὸ πρόσθεν ἦν,

and then concludes with that Attic simplicity, so
neatly turned and elegantly expressed as to distance
all translation :

Κρεῖττον γάρ ἐστιν ἂν σκοπῇ τὶς κατὰ λόγον,
Μὴ πολλ᾽ ἀπλῶς, ὀλίγα δ᾽ ἡδέως ἔχειν.

> Better to choose, if you would choose the best,
> A cheerful poverty, than wealth unblest.

## NUMBER LIX.

Omnes eodem cogimur; omnium
Versatur urnâ seriùs ociùs
   Sors exitura.—— HORAT. Carm.

All to the same last home are bound ;
Time's never-weary wheel runs round :
And life at longest or at shortest date
Snaps like a thread betwixt the shears of Fate.

I REMEMBER to have been told of a certain humorist, who set up a very singular doctrine upon the subject of death, asserting that he had discovered it to be not a necessary and inevitable event, but an act of choice and volition; he maintained that he had certain powers and resources within himself sufficient to support him in his resolution of holding out against the summons of death, till he became weary of life ; and he pledged himself to his friends, that he would in his own person give experimental proof of his hypothesis.

What particular address death made use of, when this ingenious gentleman was prevailed upon to step out of the world, I cannot take upon myself to say; but certain it is, that in some weak moment he was over persuaded to lay his head calmly on the pillow and surrender up his breath.

Though an event, so contrary to the promise he had given, must have been a staggering circumstance to many, who were interested in the success of his experiment, yet I see good reason to suspect that his hypothesis is not totally discredited, and that he has yet some surviving disciples, who are acting such a part in this world as nobody would act but upon a strong presumption, that they shall not be compelled to go out of it, and enter upon another.

Mortality, it must be owned, hath means of providing for the event of death, though none have yet been discovered of preventing it. Religion and virtue are the great physicians of the soul; patience and resignation are the nursing-mothers of the human heart in sickness and in sorrow; conscience can smooth the pillow under an aching-head, and Christian hope administers a cordial even in our last moments, that lulls the agonies of death : but where is the need of these, had this discovery been established? Why call in physicians and resort to cordials, if we can hold danger at a distance without their help? I am to presume, therefore, that every human being, who makes his own will his master, and goes all lengths in gratifying his guilty passions without restraint, must rely upon his own will for keeping him out of all danger of future trouble, or he would never commit himself so confidentially and entirely to a master, which can give him no security in return for his blind obedience and devotion. All persons of this description I accordingly set down in the lump as converts to the doctrine of the learned gentleman, who advanced the interesting discovery above-mentioned, but who unluckily missed some step in the proof, that was to have established it.

To what lengths of credulity they may really go is hard to say, but some such hopes as these must buoy them up, because I cannot think that any man would be wilfully wicked, fraudulent, perfidious, avaricious, cruel, or whatever else is detestable in the eye of God, if he saw death, his messenger, at the door; and I am even unwilling to believe, that he would be wantonly guilty, was he only convinced that when death shall come to the door, he must be obliged to admit him: for if this be so, and if ad-

mission may not be denied, then hath death a kind
of visitorial power over us, which makes him not a
guest to be invited at our pleasure, but a lord and
master of the house, to enter it as his own, and
(which is worst of all) without giving notice to us to
provide for his entertainment. What man is such a
fool in common life, as to take up his abode in a te-
nement, of which he is sure to be dispossessed, and
yet neglect to prepare himself against a surprise,
which he is subject to every moment of the day and
night? We are not apt to overlook our own interests
and safety in worldly concerns, and therefore when
the soul is given up to sin, I must suspect some error
in the brain.

What shall I say to persuade the inconsiderate
that they exist upon the precarious sufferance of
every moment, that passes over them in succession?
How shall I warn a giddy fool not to play his antic
tricks, and caper on the very utmost edge of a precipice? Who will guide the reeling drunkard in his
path, and teach him to avoid the gravestones of his
fellow-sots, set up by death as marks and signals to
apprize him of his danger? If the voice of nature,
deposing to the evidence of life's deceitful tenure
from the beginning of things to the moment present,
will neither gain audience nor belief, what can the
moralist expect?

Which of all those headlong voluptuaries, who
seem in such haste to get to the end of life, is possessed of the art of prolonging it at pleasure? To
whom has the secret been imparted? Either they
are deceived by a vain hope of evading death, or
there is something in a life of dissipation not worth
preserving. I am astonished at the stupidity of any
man, who can deny himself the gratification of conscious integrity: the proud man must be a consummate blockhead to take such wearisome pains

for a little extorted flattery of the most servile sort,
and overlook the ready means of gaining general
respect upon the noblest terms: is it not an abuse
of language and an insult to common sense for a
silly fellow to announce himself to the world as a
man of pleasure, when there is not an action in his
life, but leaves a sting behind it to belie the character he professes? Can one fellow-creature find
amusement in tormenting another? Is it possible
there can be a recreation in malice, when it slanders
the innocent; in fraud, when it cheats the unsus-
pecting; in perfidy, when it betrays a benefactor?
If any being, who does me wrong, will justify himself against the wrong by confessing that he takes
delight in injury, I will own to one instance of human depravity, which till that shall happen I will
persist to hope is not in existence. The fact is, that
all men have that respect for justice, that they attempt to shelter their very worst actions under its
defence; and even those contemptible pilferers of
reputation, who would be as much unknown by
their names as they are by the concealment of them,
qualify (I am persuaded) the dirty deed they are
about by some convenient phantom of offence in the
character they assault; even their hands cannot be
raised to strike without prefacing the blow by saying
to themselves—This man deserves to die.—Foolish
wretches, what computation must they make of life,
who devote so great a portion of it to miseries and
reproaches of their own creating!

Let a rational creature for once talk common sense
to himself, and if no better words than the following
occur to his thoughts, let him make use of them:
he is heartily welcome to the loan.

‘ I know there is a period in approach, when I
must encounter an enemy to my life, whose power
is irresistible: this is a very serious thing for me to

reflect upon, and knowing it to be a truth infallible,
I am out of hope, that I can so far forget the terms
of my existence, as totally to expel it from my
thoughts : if I could foresee the precise hour, when
this enemy will come, I would provide against it as
well as I am able, and fortify my mind to receive
him with such complacency as I could muster but
of this hour I have, alas ! no foresight ; it may be
this moment, or the next, or years may intervene
before it comes to pass. It behoves me then to be
upon my guard : he may approach in terrors, that
agonize me to think of ; he may seize my soul in
the commission of some dreadful act, and transport
it to a place whose horrors have no termination ; I
will not then commit that dreadful act, because I
will not expose myself to that dreadful punishment :
it is in my own choice to refrain from it, and I am
not such a desperate fool to make choice of misery.
If I act with this precaution, will he still appear in
this shape of terror ! Certainly he will not, nor can
he in justice transport me to a place of punishment,
when I have committed nothing to deserve it : Whither then will he convey me ? To the mansions of
everlasting happiness : Where are my fears ? What
is now become of his terrors ? He is my passport,
my conductor, my friend : I will welcome him with
embraces : I will smile upon him with gratitude, and
accompany him with exultation.

---

## NUMBER LX.

I WOULD wish no man to deceive himself with opinions, which he has not thoroughly reflected upon

in his solitary hours : till he has communed with his own heart in his chamber, it will be dangerous to commit himself to its impulses amidst the distractions of society: in solitude he will hear another voice than he has been used to hear in the colloquial scenes of life; for conscience, though mute as the ancient chorus in the bustle of the drama, will be found a powerful speaker in soliloquy. If I could believe that any man in these times had seriously and deliberately reasoned himself into an absolute contempt of things sacred, I should expect that such a being should uniformly act up to his principles in all situations, and, having thrown aside all the restraints of religion, should discharge from his mind all those fears, apprehensions, and solicitudes, that have any connexion with the dread of futurity. But, without knowing what passes in the private thoughts of men, who profess these daring notions, I cannot help observing, that, if noisy clamour be a mark of cowardice, they also have the symptoms strongly upon them of belying their own conscience : they are bold in the crowd, and loudest in the revels of the feast; there they can echo the insult, dash the ridicule in the very face of Heaven, and stun their consciences in the roar of the carousal.

Let me picture to myself a man of this description surprised into unexpected solitude after the revels of an evening, where he has been the wit of the company, at the expense of decency and religion ; here his triumphs are over ; the plaudits of his comrades no longer encourage him; the lights of the feast are extinguished, and he is surrendered to darkness and reflection : place him in the midst of a desert heath, a lonesome traveller in some dark tempestuous night, and let the elements subscribe their terrors to encounter this redoubted champion—

Who durst defy the Omnipotent.

If consistency be the test of a man's sincerity, he ought now to hold the same language of defiance, and with undaunted spirit cry out to the elements— 'Do your worst, ye blind tools of chance! Since there can be neither intelligence nor direction in your rage, I set you at nought. You may indeed subject me to some bodily inconvenience, but you can raise no terrors in my mind, for I have said you have no master: there is no hand to point the lightning, and the stroke of its flash is directed to no aim: if it smites the oak, it perishes; if it penetrates my breast, it annihilates my existence, and there is no soul within me to resume it. What have I to fear? The worst you threaten is a momentary extinction without pain or struggle: and as I only wait on earth till I am weary of life, the most you can do is to forestall me in the natural rights of suicide. I have lived in this world as the only world I have to live in, and have done all things therein as a man, who acts without account to an Hereafter. The moral offices, as they are called, I have sometimes regarded as a system of worldly wisdom, and where they have not crossed my purposes, or thwarted my pleasures, I have occasionally thought fit to comply with them: my proper pride in some instances, and self-interest in others, have dissuaded me from the open violation of a trust, for it is inconvenient to be detected; and though I acknowledge no remonstrances from within upon the score of infamy, I do not like the clamours of the crowd. As for those mercenary inducements, which a pretended revelation holds forth as lures for patience under wrongs and tame resignation to misfortune, I regard them as derogatory to my nature; they sink the very character of virtue by meanly tendering a reversionary happiness as the bribe for practising it: the doctrine therefore of a future life, in which the obedient are to expect rewards, and the disobedient are threatened with punishments, confutes itself by its own internal weakness, and is a system so sordid in its principle, that it can only be calculated to dupe us into mental slavery, and frighten us out of that generous privilege, which is our universal birth-right, the privilege of dismissing ourselves out of existence, when we are tired with its conditions.'

Had I fabricated this language for infidelity with the purpose of stamping greater detestation upon its audacity, I had rather bear the blame of having overcharged the character, than to be able (as I now am) to point out a recent publication, which openly avows this shameless doctrine: but as I do not wish to help any anonymous blasphemer into notice, let the toleration of the times be his shelter, and their contempt his answer! In the mean time I will take leave to oppose to it a short passage from a tract, lately translated into English, entitled Philosophical and Critical Inquiries concerning Christianity, by Mr. Bonnet, of Geneva; a work well deserving an attentive perusal :—

' Here I invite that reader, who can elevate his mind to the contemplation of the ways of Providence, to meditate with me on the admirable methods of divine wisdom in the establishment of Christianity; a religion, the universality of which was to comprehend all ages, all places, nations, ranks, and situations in life; a religion, which made no distinction between the crowned head and that of the lowest subject; formed to disengage the heart from terrestrial things, to ennoble, to refine, to sublime the thoughts and affections of man; to render him conscious of the dignity of his nature, the importance of his end, to carry his hopes even to eternity, and thus associate him with superior intelligences; a religion, which gave every thing to the spirit and nothing to the flesh; which called its disciples to the greatest sacrifices, because men who are taught to fear God alone, can undergo the severest trials; a religion, in short (to conclude my weak conceptions on so sublime a subject), which was the perfection or completion of natural law, the science of the truly wise, the refuge of the humble, the consolation of the wretched; so majestic in its simplicity, so sublime in its doctrine, so great in its object, so astonishing in its effects. I have endeavoured (says this excellent author in his conclusions) to explore the inmost recesses of my heart, and having discovered no secret motive there, which should induce me to reject a religion so well calculated to supply the defects of my reason, to comfort me under affliction, and to advance the perfection of my nature, I receive this religion as the greatest blessing Heaven in its goodness could confer upon mankind; and I should still receive it with gratitude, were I to consider it only as the very best and most perfect system of practical philosophy.'—BONNET.

That man, hurried away by the impetuosity of his passions, is capable of strange and monstrous irregularities, I am not to learn; even vanity and the mean ambition of being eccentric may draw out very wild expressions from him in his unguarded hours; but that any creature should be deliberately blasphemous, and reason himself (if I may so express it) into irrationality, surpasses my conception, and is a species of desperation for which I have no name.

If the voice of universal nature, the experience of all ages, the light of reason, and the immediate evidence of my senses, cannot awaken me to a dependance upon my God, a reverence for his religion, and a humble opinion of myself, what a lost creature am I!

Where can we meet a more touching description of God's omnipresence and providence than in the

139th psalm? And how can I better conclude this paper, than by the following humble attempt at a translation of that most beautiful address to the Creator of mankind!

## PSALM CXXXIX.

1  O Lord, who by thy mighty power
    Hast search'd me out in every part,
    Thou know'st each thought at every hour,
    Or e'er it rises to my heart.

2  In whatsoever path I stray,
    Where'er I make my bed at night,
    No maze can so conceal my way,
    But I stand open to thy sight.

3  Nor can my tongue pronounce a word,
    How secretly soe'er 'twere said,
    But in thine ear it shall be heard,
    And by thy judgment shall be weigh'd.

4  n every particle I see
    The fashion of thy plastic hand :

5  Knowledge too excellent for me,
    Me, wretched man, to understand.

6  Whither, ah! whither then can I
    From thine all-present Spirit go?

7  To Heaven? 'tis there thou'rt thron'd on high.
    To Hell? 'tis there thou rul'st below.

8  Lend me, O Morning, lend me wings!
    On the first beam of op'ning day
    To the last wave, that ocean flings
    On the world's shore, I'll flit away.

9  Ah fool! if there I meant to hide,
    For thou, my God, shalt reach me there
    Ev'n there thy hand shall be my guide,
    Thy right hand hold me in its care.

10  Again, if calling out for night,
    I bid it shroud me from thine eyes,
    Thy presence makes a burst of light,
    And darkness to the centre hies.

11  Nay, darkness cannot intervene
    Betwixt the universe and Thee :

Light or no light, there's nought I ween,
God self-illumin'd cannot see.

12  Thine is each atom of my frame;
    Thy fingers strung my inmost reins,
    E'en in the womb, or e'er I came
    To life, and caus'd a mother's pains.

13  Oh! what a fearful work is man!
    A wonder of creative art!
    My God, how marvellous thy plan!
    'Tis character'd upon my heart.

14  My very bones, tho' deep conceal'd
    And buried in this living clay,
    Are to thy searching sight reveal'd
    As clear as in the face of day.

15  That eye, which thro' creation darts,
    My substance, yet imperfect, scann'd,
    And in thy books my embryo parts
    Were written and their uses plann'd.

16  Ere time to shape and fashion drew
    These ductile members one by one,
    Into man's image ere they grew,
    Thy great prospective work was done.

17  O God! how gracious, how divine,
    How dear thy counsels to my soul!
    Myriads to myriads could I join,
    They'd fail to number up the whole.

18  I might as well go tell the sand,
    And count it over grain by grain:
    No; in thy presence let me stand,
    And walking with my God remain.

19  Wilt thou not, Lord, avenge the good?
    Shall not blasphemers be destroy'd?
    Depart from me, ye men of blood,
    Hence murderer, and my sight avoid!

20  Loud are their hostile voices heard
    To take thy sacred name in vain:
21  Am I not griev'd? Doth not each word
    Wring my afflicted heart with pain?

    Doth not my zealous soul return
    Hatred for hatred to thy foes?
22  Yea, Lord! I feel my bosom burn,
    As tho' against my peace they rose.

23 Try me, dread power! and search my heart;
   Lay all its movements in thy view!
   Explore it to the inmost part,
   Nor spare it, if 'tis found untrue.

24 If devious from thy paths I stray,
   And wickedness be found with me,
   Oh! lead me back the better way
   To everlasting life and Thee.

# NUMBER LXI.

THE deistical writers, who would fain persuade us
that the world was in possession of as pure a system
of morality before the introduction of Christianity
as since, affect to make a great display of the virtues
of many eminent heathens, particularly of the philosophers, Socrates, Plato, and some others.

When they set up these characters as examples of
perfection, which human nature, with the aids of revelation, either has not attained to, or not exceeded,
they put us upon an invidious task, which no man
would voluntarily engage in, and challenge us to
discuss a question, which, if thoroughly agitated,
cannot fail to strip the illustrious dead of more than
half the honours which the voice of ages has agreed
to give them.

It is therefore to be wished that they had held the
argument to its general terms, and shewn us where
that system of ethics is to be found, which they
are prepared to bring into comparison with the moral
doctrines of Christ. This I take to be the fair ground
whereon the controversy should have been decided,
and here it would infallibly have been brought to

issue; but they knew their weapons better than to trust them in so close a conflict.

The maxims of some heathen philosophers, and the moral writings of Plato, Cicero, and Seneca, contain many noble truths, worthy to be held in veneration by posterity; and if the deist can from these produce a system of morality as pure and perfect as that which claims its origin from divine revelation, he will prove that God gave to man a faculty of distinguishing between right and wrong with such correctness, that his own immediate revelation added no lights to those, which the powers of reason had already discovered. Let us grant therefore for a moment, that Christ's religion revealed to the world no new truths in morality, nor removed any old errors, and what triumph accrues to the deist by the admission? The most he gains is, to bring reason to a level with revelation, as to its moral doctrines: in so doing he dignifies man's nature, and shews how excellent a faculty God gave his creatures in their original formation, to guide their judgments and control their actions; but will this diminish the importance of revealed religion? Certainly not, unless he can prove one or both of the following positions: viz.

First, That the moral tenets of Christianity either fall short of, or run counter to, the moral tenets of natural religion; or,

Secondly, That Christ's mission was nugatory and superfluous, because the world was already in possession of as good a system of morality as he imparted to mankind.

As to the first, I believe it has never been attempted by any heathen or deistical advocate to convict the Gospel system of false morality, or to allege that it is short and defective in any one particular duty, when compared with that system which the world was possessed of without its aid. No man, I believe, has controverted its truths, though many have disputed its discoveries. No man has been hardy enough to say of any of its doctrines—*This we ought not to practise!* though many have been vain enough to cry out—*All this we knew before.*—Let us leave this position therefore for the present, and pass to the next, viz. Whether Christ's mission was nugatory and superfluous, because the world already knew as much morality as he taught them.

This will at once be answered, if the Gospel assertion be established, that life and immortality were brought to light. We need not adduce any other of the mysteries of revelation : we may safely rest the question here, and say with the apostle to the Gentile world—' Behold ! I shew you a mystery : We shall not all sleep, but we shall all be changed ; in a moment, in the twinkling of an eye, at the last trump (for the trumpet shall sound), and the dead shall be raised incorruptible, and we shall be changed.' Mark to how short an issue the argument is now brought ! Either the apostle is not warranted in calling this a *mystery*, or the deist is not warranted in calling Christ's mission nugatory and superfluous.

It now rests with the deist to produce from the writings and opinions of mankind antecedent to Christianity, such a revelation of things to come, as can fully anticipate the Gospel revelation, or else to admit with the apostle that a *mystery was shewn*; and if the importance of this *mystery* be admitted, as it surely must, the importance of Christ's mission can no longer be disputed ; and though revelation shall have added nothing to the heathen system of morality, still it does not follow that it was superfluous and nugatory.

Let the deist resort to the heathen Elysium and the realms of Pluto in search of evidences, to set in

competition with the Christian revelation of a future
state; let him call in Socrates, Plato, and as many
more as he can collect in his cause; it is but lost
labour to follow the various tracks of reason through
the pathless ocean of conjecture, always wandering,
though with different degrees of deviation. What
does it avail, though Seneca had taught as good morality as Christ himself preached from the Mount?
How does it affect revealed religion, though Tully's
Offices were found superior to Saint Paul's Epistles?
Let the deist indulge himself in declaiming on the
virtues of the heathen heroes and philosophers; let
him ransack the annals of the Christian world, and
present us with legions of crusaders drenched in human blood, furious fanatics rushing on each other's
throats for the distinction of a word, massacring
whole nations, and laying nature waste for a metaphysical quibble, it touches not religion; let him
array a host of persecuting inquisitors, with all their
torturing engines, the picture indeed is terrible, but
who will say it is the picture of Christianity?

When we consider the ages which have elapsed
since the introduction of Christianity, and the events
attending its propagation, how wonderful is the history we contemplate! we see a mighty light spread-
ing over all mankind from one spark kindled in an
obscure corner of the earth: a humble persecuted
teacher preaches a religion of peace, of forgiveness
of injuries, of submission to temporal authorities, of
meekness, piety, brotherly love, and universal benevolence; he is tried, condemned, and executed, for
his doctrines; he rises from the tomb, and, breaking
down the doors of death, sets open to all mankind
the evidence of a life to come, and at the same time
points out the sure path to everlasting happiness in
that future state: a few unlettered disciples, his ad-
herents and survivors, take up his doctrines, and go-

ing forth amongst the provinces of the Roman empire, then in its zenith, preach a religion to the Gentiles, directly striking at the foundation of the most splendid fabric Superstition ever reared on earth. These Gentiles are not a rude and barbarous race, but men of illuminated minds, acute philosophers, eloquent orators, powerful reasoners, eminent in arts and sciences, and armed with sovereign power. What an undertaking for the teachers of Christianity! What a conflict for a religion, holding forth no temporal allurements! On the contrary, promising nothing but mortification in this world, and referring all hope of a reward for present sufferings, to the unseen glories of a life to come.

The next scene which this review presents to us, shews the followers of Christianity suffering under persecution by the heathen, whom their numbers had alarmed, and who began to tremble for their gods: in the revolution of ages the church becomes triumphant, and, made wanton by prosperity, degenerates from its primitive simplicity, and running into idle controversies and metaphysical schisms, persecutes its seceding brethren with unremitting fury; whilst the popes, thundering out anathemas and hurling torches from their throne, seem the vicegerents of the furies, rather than of the author of a religion of peace: the present time affords a different view; the temper of the church grown milder, though its zeal less fervent; men of different communions begin to draw nearer to each other: as refinement of manners becomes more general, toleration spreads; we are no longer slaves to the laws of religion, but converts to the reason of it; and being allowed to examine the evidence and foundation of the faith that is in us, we discover that Christianity is a religion of charity, toleration, reason, and peace, enjoining us to have compassion one of another, love as brethren, be pitiful, be courteous, not rendering railing for railing, but contrariwise blessing; knowing that we are thereunto called, that we should inherit a blessing.'

## NUMBER LXII.

Dark and erroneous as the minds of men in general were before the appearance of Christ, no friend to revelation ever meant to say, that all the gross and glaring absurdities of the heathen system, as vulgarly professed, were universally adopted, and that no thinking man amongst them entertained better conceptions of God's nature and attributes, juster notions of his superintendence and providence, purer maxims of morality, and more elevated expectations of a future state, than are to be found in the extravagant accounts of their established theology: no thinking man could seriously subscribe his belief to such fabulous and chimerical legends; and indeed it appears that opinions were permitted to pass without censure, very irreconcilable to the popular faith, and great latitude given to speculation in their reasonings upon natural religion; and what can be more gratifying to philanthropy, than to trace these efforts of right reason, which redound to the honour of man's nature, and exhibit to our view the human understanding, unassisted by the lights of revelation, and supported only by its natural powers, emerging from the darkness of idolatry, and breaking forth into the following description of the Supreme Being, which is faithfully translated from the fragment of an ancient Greek tragic poet :—

' Let not mortal corruption mix with your idea of

God, nor think of him as of a corporeal being, such as thyself; he is inscrutable to man, now appearing like fire, implacable in his anger; now in thick darkness, now in the flood of waters; now he puts on the terrors of a ravening beast, of the thunder, the winds, the lightning, of conflagrations, of clouds: him the seas obey, the savage rocks, the springs of fresh water, and the rivers that flow along their winding channels; the earth herself stands in awe of him: the high tops of the mountains, the wide expanse of the cœrulean ocean tremble at the frown of their Lord and Ruler.'

This is a strain in the sublime style of the Psalmist, and similar ideas of the Supreme Being may be collected from the remains of various heathen writers.

Antiphanes, the Socratic philosopher, says, 'That God is the resemblance of nothing upon earth, so that no conception can be derived from any effigy or likeness of the Author of the Universe.'

Xenophon observes, 'That a Being, who controls and governs all things, must needs be great and powerful; but being by his nature invisible, no man can discern what form or shape he is of.'

Thales, being asked to define the Deity, replied, that 'He was without beginning and without end.' Being farther interrogated, 'If the actions of men could escape the intelligence of God?' he answered, 'No, nor even their thoughts.'

Philemon, the comic poet, introduces the following question and answer in a dialogue: 'Tell me, I beseech you, what is your conception of God? As of a Being, who, seeing all things, is himself unseen.'

Menander says, that 'God, the Lord and Father of all things, is alone worthy of our humble adoration, being at once the maker and the giver of all blessings.'

Melanippidas, a writer also of comedy, introduces this solemn invocation to the Supreme Being, 'Hear me, O Father, whom the whole world regards with wonder, and adores! to whom the immortal soul of man is precious.'

Euripides, in a strain of great sublimity, exclaims, 'Thee I invoke, the self-created Being, who framed all nature in thy ethereal mould, whom light and darkness, and the whole multitude of the starry train encircle in eternal chorus.'

Sophocles also, in a fragment of one of his tragedies, asserts the unity of the Supreme Being; 'Of a truth there is one, and only one God, the maker of heaven and earth, the sea, and all which it contains.'

These selections, to which, however, many others might be added, will serve to shew what enlightened ideas were entertained by some of the nature of God. I will next adduce a few passages to shew what just conceptions some had formed of God's providence and justice, of the distribution of good and evil in this life, and of the expectation of a future retribution in the life to come.

Ariston, the dramatic poet, hath bequeathed us the following part of a dialogue :—

' Take heart : be patient ! God will not fail to help the good, and especially those who are as excellent as yourself; where would be the encouragement to persist in righteousness, unless those, who do well, are eminently to be rewarded for their welldoing ?

' I would it were as you say ! but I too often see men who square their actions to the rules of rectitude, oppressed with misfortunes ; whilst they, who have nothing at heart but their own selfish interest and advantage, enjoy prosperity unknown to us.

' For the present moment it may be so, but we must look beyond the present moment, and await the issue, when this earth shall be dissolved; for to think that chance governs the affairs of this life, is a notion as false as it is evil, and is the plea which vicious men set up for vicious morals; but be thou sure that the good works of the righteous shall meet a reward, and the iniquities of the unrighteous a punishment; for nothing can come to pass in this world, but by the will and permission of God.'

Epicharmus, the oldest of the comic poets, says, in one of the few fragments which remain of his writings, ' If your life hath been holy, you need have no dread of death, for the spirit of the blest shall exist for ever in heaven.'

Euripides has the following passage: ' If any mortal flatters himself that the sin which he commits, can escape the notice of an avenging Deity, he indulges a vain hope, deceiving himself in a false presumption of impunity, because the divine justice suspends for a time the punishment of his evil actions; but hearken to me, ye who say there is no God, and by that wicked infidelity enhance your crimes, There is, there is a God! let the evil doer then account the present hour only as gain, for he is doomed to everlasting punishment in the life to come.'

The Sybilline verses hold the same language; but these I have taken notice of in a former paper.

I reserve myself for one more extract, which I shall recommend to the reader as the finest which can be instanced from any heathen writer, exhibiting the most elevated conceptions of the being and superintendence of one supreme, all-seeing, ineffable God, and of the existence of a future state of rewards and punishments, by the just distribution of which to the good and evil, all the seeming irregularities of moral justice in this life shall hereafter be set straight; and this, if I mistake not, is the summary of all that natural religion can attain to. The following is a close translation of this famous fragment:—

'Thinkest thou, O Niceratus, that those departed spirits, who are satiated with the luxuries of life, shall escape as from an oblivious God? the eye of justice is wakeful and all-seeing; and we may truly pronounce that there are two several roads conducting us to the grave; one proper to the just, the other to the unjust; for if just and unjust fare alike, and the grave shall cover both to all eternity—Hence! get thee hence at once! destroy, lay waste, defraud, confound at pleasure! but deceive not thyself; there is a judgment after death, which God, the lord of all things, will exact, whose tremendous name is not to be uttered by my lips, and he it is who limits the appointed date of the transgressor.'

It is curious to discover sentiments of this venerable sort in the fragment of a Greek comedy, yet certain it is, that it has either Philemon or Diphilus for its author, both writers of the New Comedy and contemporaries. Justin Clemens and Eusebius have all quoted it, the former from Philemon, both the latter from Diphilus: Grotius and Le Clerc follow the authority of Justin, and insert it in their collection of Philemon's fragments: Hertelius, upon the joint authorities of Clemens and Eusebius, gives it to Diphilus, and publishes it as such in his valuable and rare remains of the Greek comic writers. I conceive there are now no *data*, upon which criticism can decide for either of these two claimants, and the honour must accordingly remain suspended between them.

Sentences of this sort are certainly very precious relics, and their preservation is owing to a happy custom which the Greeks had of marking the margins of their books, opposite to any passage which particularly struck them, and this mark was generally χ, the initial χρηστὸν (useful), and the collection afterward made of these distinguished passages they called χρηστομάθειαν.

It would be a curious and amusing collection of moral and religious sentences, extracted from heathen writers, with corresponding texts selected from the Holy Scriptures: Grotius hath done something towards it in his preface to the *Collectanea* of Stobæus; but the quotations already given will suffice to shew, in a general point of view, what had been the advances of human reason, before God enlightened the world by his special revelation.

## NUMBER LXIII.

If the deist, who contends for the all-sufficiency of natural religion, shall think that in these passages, which I have quoted in the preceding number, he has discovered fresh resources on the part of human reason as opposed to divine revelation, he will find himself involved in a very false conclusion. Though it were in my power to have collected every moral and religious sentence, which has fallen from the pens of the heathen writers antecedent to Christianity, and although it should thereby appear that the morality of the gospel had been the morality of right reason in all ages of the world, he would still remain as much unfurnished as ever for establishing his favourite position, that the Scriptures reveal nothing more than man's understanding had discovered without their aid. We may therefore console ourselves without scruple, in discovering that the heathen world was not immersed in total darkness, and the candid mind, however interested for Christianity, may be gratified with the reflection that the human understanding was not so wholly enslaved, but that in certain instances it could surmount the prejudices of system, and, casting off the shackles of idolatry, argue up to that supreme of all things, which the historian Tacitus emphatically defines, *summum illud et æternum, neque mutabile, neque interiturum.*

Now when the mind is settled in the proof of One Supreme Being, there are two several modes of reasoning, by which natural religion may deduce the probability of a future state: one of these results from an examination of the human soul, the other from reflecting on the unequal distribution of happiness in the present life.

Every man who is capable of examining his own faculties, must discern a certain power within him, which is neither coeval with, nor dependent upon his body and its members; I mean that power of reflection, which we universally agree to seat in the soul: it is not coeval with the body, because we were not in the use and exercise of it, when we were infants; it is not dependent on it, because it is not subject to the changes which the body undergoes in its passage from the womb to the grave; for instance, it is not destroyed, or even impaired, by amputation of the limbs or members, it does not evaporate by the continual flux and exhalation of the corporeal humours, is not disturbed by motion of the limbs, nor deprived of its powers by their inaction; it is not necessarily involved in the sickness and infirmity of the body, for whilst that is decaying and dissolving away by an incurable disease, the intellectual faculties shall in many cases remain perfect and unimpaired: why, then, should it be supposed the soul of a man is to die with his body, and accompany it into the oblivious grave, when it did not make its entrance with it into life, nor partook of its decay, its fluctuations, changes, and casualties?

If these obvious reflections upon the nature and properties of the soul, lead to the persuasion of a future state, the same train of reasoning will naturally discover that the condition of the soul in that future state must be determined by the merits or demerits of its antecedent life. It has never been the notion of heathen or of deist, that both the good and the evil shall enter upon equal and undistinguished felicity or punishment: no reasoning man could ever conceive that the soul of Nero and the soul of Antoninus in a future state partook of the same common lot: and thus it follows upon the evidence of reason, that the soul of man shall be rewarded or punished hereafter, according to his good or evil conduct here; and this consequence is the more obvious, because it does not appear in the moral government of the world, that any such just and regular distribution of rewards and punishments obtains on this side the grave; a circumstance no otherwise to be reconciled to our suitable conceptions of divine justice, than by referring things to the final decision of a judgment to come.

Though all these discoveries are open to reason, let no man conclude that what the reason of a few discovered, were either communicated to, or acknowledged by all: No, the world was dark and grossly ignorant, some indeed have argued well and clearly; others confusedly, and the bulk of mankind not at all: the being of a God, and the unity of that Supreme Being, struck conviction to the hearts of those, who employed their reason coolly and dispassionately in such sublime inquiries; but where was the multitude meanwhile? Bewildered with a mob of deities, whom their own fables had endowed with human attributes, passions, and infirmities; whom their own superstition had deified and enrolled amongst the immortals, till the sacred history of Olympus became no less impure than the journals of a brothel: many there were, no doubt, who saw the monstrous absurdity of such a system, yet not every one who discerned error, could discover truth: the immortality of the soul, a doctrine so harmonious to man's nature, was decried by system, and opposed by subtilty; the question of a future state was hung up in doubt, or bandied between conflicting disputants through all the quirks and evasions of sophistry and logic: philosophy, so called, was split into a variety of sects, and the hypothesis of each enthusiastic founder became the standing creed of his school, which it was an inviolable point of honour never to desert. In this confusion of systems men chose for themselves, not according to conviction, but by the impulse of passion, or from motives of convenience: the voluptuary was interested to dismiss the gods to their repose, that his might not be interrupted by them; and all who wished to have their range of sensuality in this world, without fear or control, readily enlisted under the banners of Epicurus till his followers out-numbered all the rest! this was the court-creed under the worst of the Roman emperors, and the whole body of the nation, with few exceptions, adopted it; for what could be more natural, than for the desperate to bury conscience in the grave of atheism, or rush into annihilation by the point of the poniard, when they were weary of existence, and discarded by fortune? With some it was the standard principle of their sect to doubt, with others to argue every thing; and when we recollect that Cicero himself was of the New Academy, we have a clue to unravel all the seeming contradictions of his moral and metaphysical sentiments, amidst the confusion of which we are never to expect his real opinion, but within the pale of his own particular school, and that school professed controversy upon every point. I will instance one passage which would have done honour to his sentiments, had he spoke his own language as well as that of the Platonists, whom he is here personating —*Nec verò Deus, qui intelligitur à nobis, alio modo intelligi potest, quàm mens soluta quædam et libera, segregata ab omni concretione mortali, omnia sentiens et movens.* Whilst the purest truths were thrown out only as themes for sophistry to cavil at, the mass of mankind resembled a chaos, in which, if some few sparks of light glimmered, they only served to cast the general horror into darker shades.

It must not, however, be forgotten, that there was a peculiar people then upon earth, who professed to worship that one Supreme Being, of whose nature and attributes certain individuals only amongst the Gentile nations entertained suitable conceptions. Whilst all the known world were idolaters by establishment, the Jews alone were Unitarians upon system. Their history was most wonderful, for it undertook to give a relation of things, whereof no human records could possibly be taken, and all who received it for truth, must receive it as the relation of God himself; for how else should men obtain a knowledge of the Creator's thoughts and operations in the first formation of all things? Accordingly we find their inspired historian, after he has brought down his narration to the journal of his own time, holding conferences with God himself, and receiving through his immediate communication, certain laws and commandments, which he was to deliver to the people, and according to which they were to live and be governed. In this manner Moses appears as the commissioned legislator of a Theocracy, empowered to work miracles in confirmation of his vicegerent authority, and to denounce the most tremendous punishments upon the nation, so highly favoured, if in any future time they should disobey and fall off from these sacred statutes and ordinances.

A people under such a government, set apart and distinguished from all other nations by means so supernatural, form a very interesting object for our contemplation, and their history abounds in events no less extraordinary and miraculous than the revelation itself of those laws, upon which their constitution was first established: their tedious captivities, their wonderful deliverances, the administration of their priests and prophets, their triumphs and successes, whilst adhering to God's worship, and their deplorable condition, when they corrupted his service with the impurities of the idolatrous nations, whom they drove from their possessions, form a most surprising chain of incidents, to which the annals of no other people upon earth can be said to bear resemblance.

Had it suited the all-wise purposes of God, when he revealed himself to this peculiar people, to have made them the instruments for disseminating the knowledge of his true religion and worship over the Gentile world, their office and administration had been glorious indeed; but this part was either not allotted to them, or justly forfeited by their degenerate and abandoned conduct: disobedient and rebellious against God's ordinances, they were so far from propagating these imparted lights to the neighbouring nations, that they themselves sunk into their darkness, and whilst all the land was overrun with idols, few were the knees which bowed to the living, true, and only God.

Moses, their inspired lawgiver, judge, and prophet, is generally said to have delivered to them no doctrine of a future state: I am aware there is a learned author now living, one of their nation, *David Levi* by name, who controverts this assertion; it is fit, therefore, I should leave it in reference to his future proofs, when he shall see proper to produce them; in the mean time I may fairly state it upon this alternative, that if Moses did not impart the doctrine above-mentioned, it was wholly reserved for future special revelation; if he did impart it, there must have been an obstinate want of faith in great part of the Jewish nation, who knowingly professed a contrary doctrine, or else there must have been some obscurity in Moses's account, if they innocently misunderstood it: the Sadducees were a great portion of the Jewish community, and if they were instructed by their lawgiver to believe and expect a future state, it is high matter of offence in them to have disobeyed their teacher; on the other hand, if they were not instructed to this effect by Moses, yet having been taught the knowledge of one all-righteous God, it becomes just matter of surprise, how they came to overlook a consequence so evident.

## NUMBER LXIV.

FROM the review we have taken of the state of mankind, in respect to their religious opinions at the Christian era, it appears that the Gentile world was systematically devoted to idolatry, whilst the remnant of the Jewish tribes professed the worship of the true God; but at the same time there did not exist on earth any other temple dedicated to God's service, save that at Jerusalem. The nation so highly favoured by him, and so enlightened by his immediate revelations, was in the lowest state of political and religious declension; ten out of their twelve tribes had been carried away into captivity, from which there has to this hour been no redemption, and the remaining two were brought under the Roman yoke, and divided into sects, one of which opposed the opinion of the other, and maintained that there was to be no resurrection of the dead; the controversy was momentous, for the eternal welfare of mankind was the object of discussion, and who was to decide upon it? the worshippers of the true God had one place only upon earth, wherein to call upon his name; the groves and altars of the idols occupied all the rest: who was to restore his worship? who was to redeem mankind from almost total ignorance and corruption? Where was *the light* that was *to lighten the Gentiles?* reason could do no more; it could only argue for the probability of a future state of rewards and punishments, but demonstration was required; an evidence that might remove all doubts, and this was not in the power of man to furnish: some Being therefore must appear, of more than human talents, to instruct mankind; of more than human authority, to reform them: the world was lost, unless it should please God to interpose, for the work was above human hands, and nothing but the power which created the world, could save the world.

Let any man cast his ideas back to this period, and ask his reason if it was not natural to suppose that the Almighty Being, to whom this general ruin and disorder must be visible, would in mercy to his creatures send some help amongst them; unless it had been his purpose to abandon them to destruction, we may presume to say he surely would: is it then with man to prescribe in what particular mode and form that redemption should come? Certainly it is not with man, but with God only; he, who grants the vouchsafement will direct the means: be these what they may, they must be preternatural and miraculous, because we have agreed that it is beyond the reach of man by any natural powers of his own to accomplish: a special inspiration then is requisite; some revelation, it should seem, we know not what, we know not how, nor where, nor whence, except that it must come from God himself: what if he sends a Being upon earth to tell us his immediate will, to teach us how to please him, and to convince us of the reality of a future state? that Being then must come down from him, he must have powers miraculous, he must have qualities divine and perfect, he must return on earth from the grave, and personally shew us that he has survived it, and is corporeally living after death: will this be evidence demonstrative? who can withstand it? he must be of all men most obstinately bent upon his own destruction, who should attempt to hold out against it; he must prefer darkness to light, falsehood to truth, misery to happiness, hell to heaven, who would not thankfully embrace so great salvation.

Let us now apply what has been said to the appearance of that person, whom the Christian church believes to have been the true Messias of God, and let us examine the evidences upon which we assert the divinity of his mission, and the completion of its purposes.

In what form, and after what manner, was he sent amongst us? was it by natural or preternatural means? if his first appearance is ushered in by a miracle, will it not be an evidence in favour of God's special revelation? If he is presented to the world in some mode superior to, and different from, the ordinary course of nature, such an introduction must attract to his person and character a more than ordinary attention: if a miraculous and mys-

terious Being appears upon earth, so compounded of
divine and human nature, as to surpass our compre-
hension of his immediate essence, and at the same
time so levelled to our earthly ideas, as to be visibly
born of a human mother, not impregnated after the
manner of the flesh, but by the immediate spirit of
God, in other words, the son of a pure virgin, shall
we make the mysterious incarnation of such a preternatural being, a reason for our disbelief in that
revelation, which without a miracle we had not given
credit to? We are told that the birth of Christ was
in this wise; the fact rests upon the authority of the
evangelists who describe it: the Unitarians, who
profess Christianity with this exception, may dispute
the testimony of the sacred writers in this particular,
and the Jews may deny their account *in toto*, but
still if Christ himself performed miracles, which the
Jews do not deny, and if he rose from the dead after
his crucifixion, which the Unitarians admit, I do not
see how either should be staggered by the miracle
of his birth: for of the Jews I may demand whether
it were not a thing as credible for God to have
wrought a miracle at the birth of Moses for instance,
as that he should afterward empower that prophet
to perform, not one only, but many miracles? To
the Unitarians I would candidly submit, if it be not
as easy to believe the incarnation of Christ as his
resurrection, the authorities for each being the same?
Let the authorities therefore be the test.

I am well aware that the silence of two of the
evangelists is stated by the Unitarians amongst
other objections against the account, and the non-
accordance of the genealogies given by Saint
Matthew and Saint Luke is urged against the
Christian church by the author of *Lingua Sacra*,
in a pamphlet lately published in the following
words:—' The evangelist Saint Matthew in the first

chapter of his gospel gives us the genealogy of
Christ, and Luke in the third chapter of his gospel
does the same; but with such difference, that an
unprejudiced person would hardly think they belonged to one and the same person; for the latter
not only differs from the former in almost the whole
genealogy from Joseph to David, but has also added
a few more generations, and likewise made Jesus to
descend from Nathan the son of David instead of
Solomon.'—(Levi's Letter to Dr. Priestley, p. 81.)
    The learned Jew is founded in his observation
upon the non-accordance of these pedigrees, but not
in applying that to Christ which relates only to
Joseph. Saint Matthew gives the genealogy of
Joseph, whom he denominates ' the husband of
Mary, of whom was born Jesus, who is called
Christ,' chap. i. v. 16. Saint Luke, with equal precision, says, that ' Jesus himself began to be about
thirty years of age, being, as was supposed, the son
of Joseph.' Now when it is thus clear that both
these genealogies apply to Joseph, and both these
evangelists expressly assert that Jesus was born of
an immaculate virgin, I do not think it a fair statement to call it the genealogy of Christ for the purpose of discrediting the veracity of these evangelists
in points of faith or doctrine, merely because they
differ in a family catalogue of the generations of
Joseph, one of which is carried up to Adam, and the
other brought down from Abraham. The gospel historians, as I understand them, profess severally to
render a true account of Christ's mission, comprising
only a short period of his life; within the compass
of this period they are to record the doctrines he
preached, the miracles he performed, and the circumstances of his death, passion, and resurrection;
to this undertaking they are fairly committed; this
they are to execute as faithful reporters, and if their

reports shall be found in any essential matter contradictory to each other or themselves, let the learned author late mentioned, or any other opponent to Christianity, point it out, and candour must admit the charge ; but in the matter of a pedigree, which appertains to Joseph, which our Church universally omits in its service, which comprises no article of doctrine, and which being purely matter of family record, was copied probably from one roll by Matthew, and from another by Luke, I cannot in truth and sincerity see how the sacred historians are impeached by the non-agreement of their accounts. We call them the *inspired* writers, and when any such trivial contradictions as the above can be fixed upon them by the enemies of our faith, the word is retorted upon us with triumph ; but what has inspiration to do with the genealogy of Joseph, *the supposed*, not the real father of Jesus? And indeed what more is required for the simple narration of any facts than a faithful memory, and sincere adherence to truth?

Let this suffice for what relates to the birth of Christ, and the different ways in which men argue upon that mysterious event : if his coming was foretold, and if his person and character fully answer to those predictions, no man will deny the force of such an evidence : if we are simply told that ' a virgin did conceive and bear a son,' it is a circumstance so much out of the ordinary course of nature to happen, that it requires great faith in the veracity of the relater to believe it; but if we are possessed of an authentic record of high antecedent antiquity, wherein we find it expressly predicted, that such a circumstance shall happen, and that a ' virgin shall conceive and bear a son,' it is such a confirmation of the fact, that wonderful as it is, we can no longer doubt the truth of the historians who attest it. Now it is not one but many prophets who concur in foretelling the coming of the Messias; his person, his office, his humility and sufferings, his ignominious death, and the glorious benefits resulting from his atonement, are not merely glanced at with enigmatic obscurity, but pointedly and precisely announced. Had such evidences met for the verification of any historical event unconnected with religion, I suppose there is no man who could compare the one with the other, but would admit its full concordance and completion; and is it not a strange perverseness of mind, if we are obstinate in doubting it, only because we are so deeply interested to believe it?

I have said there was but one temple upon earth, where the only true and living God was worshipped, the temple at Jerusalem: the Jews had derived and continued this worship from the time of Abraham, and to him the promises were made, that ' in his seed all the nations of the world should be blessed.' Where then are we naturally to look for the Messias but from the stock of Abraham, from the descendants of that family, in which alone were preserved the knowledge and worship of the only true God? If therefore the religion, which Christ founded, does in fact hold forth that blessing to all the nations of the world, then was that promise fulfilled in the person of Christ, ' who took upon him the seed of Abraham.'

## NUMBER LXV.

WE are next to inquire if the character and commission of the Messias were marked by such performances, as might well be expected from a person, whose introduction into the world was of so extraordinary a nature.

We are told by one of the sacred historians, that 'the Jews came round about him and said unto him, how long dost thou make us to doubt? If thou be the Christ, tell us plainly: Jesus answered them, I told you, and ye believed not; the works that I do in my Father's name, they bear witness of me.'

In this passage Christ himself appeals to his works done in the name of God, to witness against all cavils for his being the true Messias. The same question was put to him by the disciples of the Baptist, 'Art thou he that should come, or do we look for another?' The same appeal is made to his works in the reply he gives to these inquirers.

It follows next in order that we should ask what these works were, and it so happens, that the person who performed them, has himself enumerated them in the following words: ' The blind receive their sight and the lame walk, the lepers are cleansed and the deaf hear, the dead are raised up and the poor have the gospel preached unto them.' These are works, it must be acknowledged, of a most benevolent sort; they are not indeed so splendid as the miraculous act of dividing the Red Sea for the people of Israel to march through it, and again commanding it to close upon their pursuers in the rear and swallow up the army of Pharaoh;' they are not of so tremendous a character as those afflicting plagues with which Moses punished the Egyptians : but would these, or such as these, have been characteristic of a mediator? Christ came to save and not to destroy the world, and the works above described are no less merciful in their nature, than miraculous.

When the Jews therefore tauntingly assert the superior magnificence of the miracles wrought by Moses, which we admit to have been in all respects suitable to the commission which Moses was encharged with, they should with equal candour admit, that the less splendid, but more salutary, miracles of Christ, were no less suited to the merciful commission, which he came amongst us to perform. There is indeed more horrible grandeur in the spectacle of a vast army swallowed up by the sea, miraculously divided into a wall on each side of those who passed through it; but who will say that God's power is not as wonderfully and conspicuously displayed in restoring dead Lazarus to life, as in drowning Pharaoh and his host? Surely it is as great a miracle to give life to the dead, as it is to put the living to death.

The miracles of Christ were performed without ostentation and display, yet they were of such general notoriety that the Jews themselves did not, and do not even now, deny their being wrought by him, but ascribed them to the aid and agency of the devil: a miserable subterfuge indeed! But this is not all; a contemporary writer of that nation, David Levi, in his letter to Dr. Priestley, asserts, that there was not only 'no such necessity' for the miracles of Jesus as for those of Moses, but 'that they were scarcely just or rational, and consequently cannot be offered as proofs of his divine mission in comparison with that of Moses.' p. 67, 68.

In support of this assertion the learned controversialist observes, 'that as to the miracles of Moses, there was the greatest necessity for them; for instance, the plagues he brought upon the Egyptians were necessary for the redemption of the Jewish nation; as was the dividing of the Red Sea, and the drowning the Egyptians for their farther deliverance from them; the manna from heaven and the water from the rock were necessary for their subsistence in the wilderness; the same of all the rest.'

This we may admit in its full force; but as the

miracles which Christ wrought were altogether as *necessary* for the proof of his divine mission, as these of Moses for the proof of his; a man must be very partial to his own nation, who will assert, that the deliverance of the Jews from their captivity in Egypt, was a more important object than the redemption of lost mankind. We will not doubt but it was *necessary* the Egyptian host should be drowned, because it seemed good to God so to punish their obduracy, and extricate the Jewish tribes; but it is no less *necessary*, that mankind should believe in Christ, if they are to be saved through his means, and for the confirmation of that *necessary* faith, these miracles were performed : the author of the objection, who himself asserts that Moses delivered the important doctrine of a future state, will not deny that the belief of a future state is a *necessary* belief; and if it be so, it must follow that Christ's resurrection and appearance upon earth after his crucifixion (a miracle I presume as great and striking as any wrought by the hand of Moses) was as pertinent to that general end, as the wonders in the land of Egypt and at the Red Sea were to the particular purpose of rescuing the Jews out of their captivity.

If we grant that Moses, as this objector intimates, did impart the doctrine of a future state, Christ did more by exemplifying it in his own person, and against such evidence we might presume even a Sadducee would not hold out. Now as so large a portion of the Jewish nation were still in the avowed disbelief of that doctrine, which our opponent believes was taught them by their great prophet and lawgiver himself, surely he must of course allow, that the resurrection of Christ was to them at least, and to all who like them did not credit the doctrine of a life to come, a *necessary* miracle.

Where such a teacher as Moses had failed to persuade, what less than a miracle could conquer their infidelity? Unless, indeed, our author shall join issue with Abraham in his reply to Dives, as recorded in the words of Christ, and maintain with him, that as they would not believe the word of Moses, ' neither would they be persuaded, though one actually rose from the dead.'

And now I will more closely animadvert upon the bold assertion of David Levi, the Jew (whose hostile opinions we tolerate), that the miracles of Christ, the Saviour of the world (whose religion we profess) were ' scarcely just or rational.'

Our faith is at issue, our established church falls to the ground, our very sovereign becomes no longer the *defender of our faith*, but rather the defender of our folly, if this contemner of Christ, this alien, who assaults our religion, whilst he is living under the protection of our laws, shall with one stroke of an audacious pen, undermine the strong foundation of our belief.

Let us hear how this modern caviller confutes those miracles, which his forefathers saw and did not dare to deny.

He takes two out of the number, and if there is any merit in the selection, he is beholden to his correspondent for it; these are, first, ' the driving the devils out of the man possessed, and sending them into the herd of swine;' Mat. viii. 28. Secondly, ' the curse pronounced upon the barren fig-tree;' Mark xi. 13.

Upon the first of these he has the following stricture :—' This I think was not strictly just, for as, according to your (Dr. Priestley's) opinion, he was but a man and a prophet, I would willingly be informed what right he had to destroy another man's property in the manner he did by sending the devils

XXXIX.       K

into them, and so causing them to run violently into
the sea and perish?'

This miracle is recorded also by Saint Mark, v. 1,
and again by Saint Luke, viii. 26. What Saint
Matthew calls the country of the Gergesenes, the
other two evangelists call the country of the Gada-
renes, and Saint Luke adds that it is over against
Galilee; this country, as I conceive, was within the
boundaries of the half tribe of Manasseh, on the
other side of Jordan, and is by Strabo called Gada-
rida, lib. 16. Now Moses both in Leviticus xi. and
Deuteronomy xiv. prohibits swine, as one of the
unclean beasts : 'Of their flesh ye shall not eat, and
their carcass shall ye not touch ; they are unclean
to you.' Isaiah also states it as a particular sin and
abomination in the Jews, whom he calleth a ' rebellious people, a people that provoketh me to anger
continually to my face ; which remain among the
graves and lodge in the monuments, which eat
swine's flesh.' lxv. 2—4. And again, ' They that
sanctify themselves and purify themselves in the
gardens, behind one tree in the midst, eating swine's
flesh, &c. shall be consumed together, saith the
Lord.' lxvi. 17. Eleazar the scribe, ' when con-
strained to open his mouth and eat swine's flesh,
chose rather to die gloriously, than to live stained
with such an abomination.' 2 Macc. vi. 18, 19.
The seven brethren also, who were compelled to the
like abomination, declared, ' they were ready to die
rather than to transgress the laws of their fathers.'
This being the law of Moses with respect to this
proscribed animal, and such being the corruptions
of the people in violating that law, I am at a loss
to discover the *injustice* of the miracle ; seeing
what abominations these creatures had occasioned
amongst the Jews, so as to draw down the denun-
ciations of the prophet Isaiah, repeatedly urged in

the passages above quoted; and it is with particular surprise I meet the charge from one, who is himself a Jew, and who, I must presume, would die the death of Eleazar rather than be defiled with such abominable food. It would be hard indeed if Christ, whom he arraigns for abolishing the Mosaical dispensation in one part of his argument, should in another be accused of wrong and injury for conforming to it: but any wretched shift shall be resorted to for matter of railing against Christ, and rather than not feed his spleen at all, he will feed it upon swine's flesh: let the learned Jew first prove to me that a hog was not an abomination to his countrymen, and it will then be time enough to debate upon the *injustice* of destroying them; meanwhile I shall not be disposed to allow of any damages for the swine in question at the suit and prosecution of a Jew.

His second attack is pointed against the miracle of the fig-tree, which was blasted at the word of Christ.

Though Saint Matthew as well as Saint Mark records this miracle, yet, for reasons sufficiently obvious, he refers to the latter, who says, ' that when Christ came to it he found nothing but leaves; for the time of figs was not yet.' His argument upon this passage is as follows: ' Hence it is manifest, that he required the tree to produce fruit out of season, and which would have been contrary to the intent of its Creator; and therefore he, as a dutiful son, curses the innocent and guiltless tree for doing that, which his Father had commanded it to do, viz. to bear fruit in its proper season.' In this paragraph our Jew has quickened his argument with some facetious irony, and he follows it with an air of exultation as well as insult: ' If, after this, Christians should still persist in the miracle, according to the letter of the story, much good may it do them; but I am sure it will never be the means of converting the unbelieving Jews to the Christian faith.'

I close with him in opinion that this miracle will not be the means of converting his unbelieving brethren to Christianity; for how can I hope, that what their fathers saw and yet believed not, should at this distant period gain belief from their posterity? I also join with him in saying (and I suspect I say it with somewhat more sincerity), *much good may it do* to all those Christians, who persist in their belief of it! A descendant of those who murdered Christ, may act in character, when he insults his miracles and ridicules his person, but a believer in Christ will be an imitator of his patience.

It is now time to dismiss the irony and apply to the argument. This simply turns upon St. Mark's interjectional observation, not noticed by St. Matthew in his account, viz. ' that the time of figs was not yet.' He says, that Jesus being hungry saw a fig-tree afar off, having leaves, and came if haply he might find any thing thereon. By this it appears that the tree was in leaf, and Jesus approached it with the expectation of finding something thereon; but when he found nothing but leaves he said unto it, ' No man eat fruit of thee hereafter for ever!' And his disciples heard it: these came again the next morning, and passing by the fig-tree saw it dried up from the roots; which when Peter remarked as a completion of the miracle, Jesus said to them all, ' Have faith in God!'

In these important words we have the moral of the act. The tree, which this reviler takes upon himself to say, was *commanded* by God *to bear fruit in its proper season*, was on the contrary commanded by God to bear fruit no more, but serve a nobler purpose by witnessing to the miraculous power of Christ: and now if *an innocent and guiltless tree was* blasted out of season by the word of Christ for the purpose of inspiring the beholders with *Faith in God*, the benefit conferred upon human nature may well atone for the injury done to vegetable nature; though I am free to acknowledge to its pathetic advocate, that, as a Jew, he has undertaken a more cleanly cause, than when he before stood forth in defence of the hogs: as well may he bewail the *innocent and guiltless trees* and grain of Egypt, which were smitten by the hail, when Moses called it down upon the land, if such be his tender feelings towards the productions of the earth, as this single fig-tree: till he can convince us that the deliverance of the Jews from their Egyptian bondage was a more important object than the redemption of the world, he will find it hard to make a reasoning man allow, that this single fig-tree, even though it had no right to bear fruit, hath a stronger appeal to justice against the miracle of Christ, *than every herb of the field that was smitten*, every guiltless and innocent *tree of the field that was broken* by the stretching forth of the rod of Moses.

Thus then stands the account between Christ and his accuser; the Jewish nation lost a tree, and mankind gained—a Saviour!

## NUMBER LXVI.

IF it were necessary to enter into a more literal defence of the miracle of the blasted fig-tree, I see no absolute reason to conclude with the caviller, that Christ required the tree to produce fruit out of season, and act against its nature; for *if the time of figs*

be the gathering or harvest of figs, it was more reasonable to expect fruit from this tree before the time
of plucking, than after it; and as this fruit was no
small article in the produce and traffic of Judea, we
may well conclude *the time of figs*, mentioned by
Saint Mark, was like the vintage in the wine countries; and I apprehend it would not be an unreason-
able expectation to find a cluster of grapes on a vine,
before the time of vintage was come. This construction of the words will seem the more reasonable,
when we remark that Saint Matthew, who records
the miracle, takes no account of this circumstance,
and that Saint Mark, who states it, states also that
Christ in his hunger applied to the tree, ' if haply he
might find any thing thereon,' which implies expectation.

But our Jew hath suggested a better method of
performing the miracle, by commanding fruit from
a withered tree instead of blasting a living one;
which, says he, ' if Jesus had done, it would have
been such an instance of his power, as to have rendered the proof of the miracle indisputable.'

Here let him stand to his confession, and I take
him at his word: I agree with him in owning that
the miracle, as he states it, would have been indisputable, had Christ given life and fruit to a withered
tree; and I demand of him to agree with me, that
the miracle was indisputable, when the same Christ
gave breath and life to dead Lazarus.

But, alas! I can hardly expect that the raising a
dead tree to life would have been thus successful,
though even infidelity asserts it, when the miracle of
restoring a dead man to life hath not silenced his
cavils, but left him to quibble about hogs and figs,
and even in the face of his own confession to arraign
the Saviour of the world as ' unjust and irrational'
through the channel of a Christian press: neither

am I bound to admit, that his correction of the miracle would in any respect have amended it; for as an instance of Christ's miraculous power, I can see no greater energy in the act of enlivening a dead tree, than in destroying a living one by the single word of his command.

I must yet ask patience of the reader, whilst I attend upon this objector to another cavil started against this miracle of the fig-tree, in the account of which he says there is a contradiction of dates between Saint Matthew and Saint Mark, for that in the former it appears ' Christ first cast the buyers and sellers out of the temple, and on the morrow cursed the fig-tree; whereas, according to Saint Mark, it was transacted before the driving them out of the temple; and such a manifest contradiction must greatly affect the credibility of the history.'

Whether or not a day's disagreement in the dates would so ' greatly affect the credibility of the history,' we are not called upon to argue, because it will be found that no such contradiction exists.

Saint Mark agrees with Saint Matthew in saying that ' Jesus entered into Jerusalem, and into the temple,' and on the morrow cursed the fig-tree; he then adds, that he returned to Jerusalem, and drove the buyers and sellers out of the temple. Again, the next morning, he and his disciples passed by the fig-tree, and saw it dried up from the roots: this is told in detail.

Saint Matthew agrees with St. Mark in saying Jesus went into the temple the day before he destroyed the fig-tree, but he does not break the narrative into detail, as Saint Mark does; for as he relates the whole miracle of the fig-tree at once, comprising the events of two days in one account, so doth he give the whole of what passed in the temple at once also.

Both evangelists agree in making Christ's entrance into the temple antecedent to his miracle; but Saint Matthew with more brevity puts the whole of each incident into one account; Saint Mark more circumstantially details every particular: and this is the mighty contradiction which David Levi hath discovered in the sacred historians, upon which he exultingly pronounces, that ' he is confident there are a number of others as glaring as this; but which he has not, at present, either time or inclination to point out.'

These menaces I shall expect he will make good, for when his time serves to point them out, I dare believe his inclination will not stand in the way.

In the mean time, let it be remembered, that David Levi stands pledged as the author of an unsupported charge against the veracity of the Evangelists; and let every faithful Christian to whom those holy records are dear, but most of all the proper guardians of our Church, be prepared to meet their opponent and his charge.

But our caviller hath not yet done with the Evangelists, for he asserts that ' they are not only contradictory to each other, but are inconsistent with themselves; for what can be more so than Matthew i. 18. with Matthew xiii. 55?'

Now mark the contradiction! ' The birth of Jesus was on this wise; when as his mother Mary was espoused to Joseph, before they came together, she was found with child of the Holy Ghost,' chap. i. 18. The other text is found in chap. xiii. 55: ' Is not this the carpenter's son? is not his mother Mary? and his brethren James and Joses and Simon and Judas?'

Need any child be told, that in the first text Saint Matthew speaks, and in the second the cavilling Jews? Who then can wonder if they disagree? As well we might expect agreement between truth and falsehood, between the Evangelist and David Levi, as between two passages of such opposite characters. Is this the man who is to confute the Holy Scriptures? Weak champion of an unworthy cause!

What he means by an inconsistency between Luke i. 34, 35, and Luke xiv. 22, I cannot understand, and conclude there must be an error of the press, of which I think no author can have less reason to complain than David Levi.

These two unprosperous attacks being the whole of what he attempts upon the inconsistency of the sacred historians with themselves, I shall no longer detain my readers than whilst I notice one more cavil, which this author points against the divine mission of Christ, as compared with that of Moses, viz. ' That God speaking with Moses face to face in the presence of six hundred thousand men, besides women and children, as mentioned in Exod. xix. 9, was such an essential proof of the divine mission of Moses, as is wanting on the part of Jesus;' and therefore he concludes, that taking the miracles of Moses and this colloquy with the Supreme Being together, the evidences for him are much stronger than for Christ.

A man, who does not instantly discern the futility of this argument, must forget all the several incidents in the history of Christ, where the voice of God audibly testifies to his divine mission: for instance, Matt. iii. 16, 17 : ' And Jesus, when he was baptized, went up straightway out of the water, and lo! the heavens were opened unto him, and he saw the Spirit of God descending like a dove, and lighting upon him; and lo! a voice from heaven, saying, This is my beloved Son, in whom I am well pleased.' The same is repeated by Mark, i. 10, 11; again by Luke, iii. 21, 22; again by John, i. 32, 33, 34.

If these supernatural signs and declarations do not evince the superiority of Christ's mission above that of Moses; if Christ, to whom angels ministered, when the devil in despair departed from him, Christ, who was transfigured before his disciples, ' and his face did shine as the sun, and his raiment was white as the light, and behold! there appeared unto them Moses and Elias talking with him : *Christ, at whose death* the vail of the temple was rent in twain from the top to the bottom, and the earth did quake, and the rocks rent, and the graves were opened, and many bodies of saints, which slept, arose, and came out of the graves after his resurrection, and went into the holy city, and appeared unto many :' in conclusion, if Christ, whose resurrection was declared by angels, seen and acknowledged by many witnesses, and whose ascension into heaven crowned and completed the irrefragable evidence of his divine mission; if Christ, whose prophecies of his own death and resurrection, of the destruction of Jerusalem and the subsequent dispersion of the Jews, have been and are now so fully verified, cannot, as our caviller asserts, meet the comparison with Moses, then is the Redeemer of lost mankind a less sublime and important character than the legislator of the Jews.

I have now attempted in the first place to discover how far the world was illuminated by right reason before the revelation of Christ took place; for had men's belief been such, and their practice also such as Christianity teaches, the world had not stood in need of a Redeemer.

The result of this inquiry was, that certain persons have expressed themselves well and justly upon the subject of God and religion in times antecedent to the Christian era, and in countries where idolatry was the established worship.

That the nation of the Jews was a peculiar nation,

and preserved the worship of the true and only God, revealed in very early time to their fathers, but that this worship, from various circumstances and events, in which they themselves were highly criminal, had not been propagated beyond the limits of a small tract, and that the temple of Jerusalem was the only church in the world, where God was worshipped, when Christ came upon earth:

That from the almost universal diffusion of idolatry, from the unworthy ideas men had of God and religion, and the few faint notions entertained amongst them of a future state of rewards and punishments, the world was in such deplorable error, and in such universal need of an instructor and redeemer, that the coming of Christ was most seasonable and necessary to salvation:

That there were a number of concurrent prophecies of an authentic character in actual existence, which promised this salvation to the world, and depicted the person of the Messias, who was to perform this mediatorial office in so striking a manner, that it cannot be doubted but that all those characteristics meet and are fulfilled in the person of Christ:

That his birth, doctrines, miracles, prophecies, death, and passion, with other evidences, are so satisfactory for the confirmation of our belief in his divine mission, that our faith as Christians is grounded upon irrefragable proofs:

Lastly, that the vague opinions of our own dissenting brethren, and the futile cavils of a recent publication by a distinguished writer of the Jewish nation, are such weak and impotent assaults upon our religion, as only serve to confirm us in it the more.

If I have effected this to the satisfaction of the serious reader, I shall be most happy; and as for

those who seek nothing better than amusement in
these volumes, I will apply myself without delay to
the easier task of furnishing them with matter more
suited to their taste.

## NUMBER LXVII.

Musa dedit fidibus Divos, puerosque Deorum,
    Et pugilem victorem, et equum certamine primum
    Et juvenum curas, et libera vina referre.—HORAT.

IN times of very remote antiquity, when men were
not so lavish of their wit as they have since been,
poetry could not furnish employment for more than
*three Muses;* but as business grew upon their hands
and departments multiplied, it became necessary to
enlarge the commission, and a board was constituted,
consisting of *nine* in number, who had their several
presidencies allotted to them, and every branch of
the art poetic thenceforth had its peculiar patroness
and superintendant.

As to the specific time when these three senior
goddesses called in their six new assessors, it is matter of conjecture only; but if the poet Hesiod was,
as we are told, the first who had the honour of an-
nouncing their names and characters to the world,
we may reasonably suppose this was done upon the
immediate opening of their new commission, as they
would hardly enter upon their offices without ap-
prising all those, whom it might concern, of their accession.

Before this period, the three elder sisters condescended to be *maids of all work;* and if the work became more than they could turn their hands to, they

have nobody but themselves and their fellow-deities to complain of; for had they been content to have let the world go on in its natural course, mere mortal poets would not probably have overburdened either it or them; but when Apollo himself (who being their president should have had more consideration for their ease) begot the poet Linus in one of his terrestrial frolics, and endowed him with hereditary genius, he took a certain method to make work for the muses: accordingly, we find the chaste Calliope herself, the eldest of the sisterhood, and who should have set a better example to the family, could not hold out against this heavenly bastard, but in an unguarded moment yielded her virgin honours to Linus, and produced the poet Orpheus: such an instance of celestial incontinence could not fail to shake the morals of the most demure; and even the cold goddess Luna caught the flame, and smuggled a bantling into the world, whom, maliciously enough, she named Musæus, with a sly design no doubt of laying her child at the door of the Parnassian nunnery.

Three such high-blooded bards as Linus, Orpheus, and Musæus, so fathered and so mothered, were enough to people all Greece with poets and musicians; and in truth they were not idle in their generation, but like true patriarchs spread their families over all the shores of Ionia and the islands of the Archipelago: it is not therefore to be wondered at, if the three sister muses, who had enough to do to nurse their own children and descendants, were disposed to call in other helpmates to the task, and, whilst Greece was in its glory, it may well be supposed that all the nine sisters were fully employed in bestowing upon every votary a portion of their attention, and answering every call made upon them for aid and inspiration: much gratitude is due

to them from their favoured poets, and much hath
been paid; for even to the present hour they are in-
voked and worshipped by the sons of verse, whilst
all the other deities of Olympus have either abdi-
cated their thrones, or been dismissed from them
with contempt; even Milton himself in his sacred
epic invokes the *heavenly muse*, who inspired Moses
*on the top of Horeb or of Sinai;* by which he ascribes
great antiquity as well as dignity to the character he
addresses.

The powers ascribed to Orpheus were, under the
veil of fable, emblems of his influence over savage
minds, and of his wisdom and eloquence in reclaim-
ing them from that barbarous state: upon these impressions civilization and society took place: the
patriarch, who founded a family or tribe, the legislator who established a state, the priest, prophet,
judge, or king, are characters which, if traced to
their first sources, will be found to branch from that
of poet: the first prayers, the first laws, and the
earliest prophecies, were metrical; prose hath a later
origin, and before the art of writing was in existence,
poetry had reached a very high degree of excellence,
and some of its noblest productions were no otherwise preserved than by tradition. As to the sacred
quality of their first poetry, the Greeks are agreed,
and to give their early bards the better title to inspiration, they feign them to be descended from the
gods; Orpheus must have profited by his mother's
partiality, and Linus may well be supposed to have
had some interest with his father Apollo. But to
dwell no longer on these fabulous legends of the
Greeks, we may refer to the books of Moses for the
earliest and most authentic examples of sacred
poetry: every thing that was the immediate effusion
of the prophetic spirit seems to have been chanted
forth in dithyrambic measure: the valedictory bless-

ings of the patriarchs, when dying, the songs of
triumph and thanksgiving after victory, are metrical,
and high as the antiquity of the sacred poem of Job
undoubtedly is, such nevertheless is its character
and construction, as to carry strong internal marks
of its being written in an advanced state of the art.

The poet therefore, whether Hebrew or Greek,
was in the earliest ages a sacred character, and his
talent a divine gift, a celestial inspiration: men regarded him as the ambassador of heaven and the
interpreter of its will. It is perfectly in nature, and
no less agreeable to God's providence, to suppose
that even in the darkest times some minds of a
more enlightened sort should break forth, and be
engaged in the contemplation of the universe and its
Author: from meditating upon the works of the
Creator, the transition to the act of praise and
adoration follows as it were of course: these are
operations of the mind, which naturally inspire it
with a certain portion of rapture and enthusiasm,
rushing upon the lips in warm and glowing language,
and disdaining to be expressed in ordinary and vulgar phrase; the thoughts become inflated, the breast
labours with a passionate desire to say something
worthy of the ear of Heaven, something in a more
elevated tone and cadence, something more harmonious and musical; this can only be effected by
measured periods, by some chant, that can be repeated in the strain again and again, grateful at
once to the ear and impressive on the memory;
and what is this but poetry? Poetry then is the
language of prayer, an address becoming of the
Deity; it may be remembered, it may be repeated
in the ears of the people called together for the purpose of worship; this is a form that may be fixed
upon their minds, and in this they may be taught
to join.

The next step in the progress of poetry from the praise of God is to the praise of men: illustrious characters, heroic actions, are singled out for celebration: the inventors of useful arts, the reformers of savage countries, the benefactors of mankind, are extolled in verse, they are raised to the skies: and the poet, having praised them as the first of men whilst on earth, deifies them after death, and, conscious that they merit immortality boldly bestows it, and assigns to them a rank and office in heaven appropriate to the character they maintained in life: hence it is that the merits of a Bacchus, a Hercules, and numbers more, are amplified by the poet, till they become the attributes of their divinity, altars are raised and victims immolated to their worship. These are the fanciful effects of poetry in its second stage: religion overheated turns it into enthusiasm; enthusiasm forces the imagination into all the visionary regions of fable, and idolatry takes possession of the whole Gentile world. The Egyptians, a mysterious, dogmatizing race, begin the work with symbol and hieroglyphic; the Greeks, a vain, ingenious people, invent a set of tales and fables for what they do not understand, embellish them with all the glittering ornaments of poetry, and spread the captivating delusion over all the world.

In the succeeding period we review the poet in full possession of this brilliant machinery, and with all Olympus at his command: surrounded by Apollo and the muses, he commences every poem with an address to them for protection; he has a deity at his call for every operation of nature; if he would roll the thunder, Jupiter shakes Mount Ida to dignify his description; Neptune attends him in his car, if he would allay the ocean; if he would let loose the winds to raise it, Æolus unbars his cave; the spear of Mars and the ægis of Minerva arm him for the battle; the arrows of Apollo scatter pestilence through the air! Mercury flies upon the messages of Jupiter; Juno raves with jealousy, and Venus leads the Loves and Graces in her train. In this class, we contemplate Homer and his inferior brethren of the epic order; it is their province to form the warrior, instruct the politician, animate the patriot; they delineate the characters and manners; they charm us with their descriptions, surprise us with their incidents, interest us with their dialogue; they engage every passion in its turn, melt us to pity, rouse us to glory, strike us with terror, fire us with indignation; in a word, they prepare us for the drama, and the drama for us.

A new poet now comes upon the stage; he stands in person before us: he no longer appears as a blind and wandering bard, chanting his rhapsodies to a throng of villagers collected in a group about him, but erects a splendid theatre, gathers together a whole city as his audience, prepares a striking spectacle, provides a chorus of actors, brings music, dance, and dress to his aid, realizes the thunder, bursts open the tombs of the dead, calls forth their apparitions, descends to the very regions of the damned, and drags the Furies from their flames to present themselves personally to the terrified spectators: such are the powers of the drama; here the poet reigns and triumphs in his highest glory.

The fifth denomination gives us the lyric poet chanting his ode at the public games and festivals, crowned with olive and encompassed by all the wits and nobles of his age and country: here we contemplate Stesichorus, Alcæus, Pindar, Callistratus: sublime, abrupt, impetuous, they strike us with the shock of their electric genius; they dart from earth to heaven; there is no following them in their flights; we stand gazing with surprise, their boldness awes us, their brevity confounds us: their sudden transitions and ellipses escape our apprehension; we are charmed we know not why, we are pleased with being puzzled, and applaud although we cannot comprehend. In the lighter lyric we meet Anacreon, Sappho, and the votaries of Bacchus and Venus; in the grave, didactic, solemn class we have the venerable names of a Solon, a Tyrtæus, and those, who may be styled the demagogues in poetry: Is liberty to be asserted, licentiousness to be repressed? Is the spirit of a nation to be roused? It is the poet not the orator must give the soul its energy and spring: Is Salamis to be recovered? It is the elegy of Solon must sound the march to its attack. Are the Lacedemonians to be awakened from their lethargy? It is Tyrtæus, who must sing the war-song and revive their languid courage.

Poetry next appears in its pastoral character; it affects the garb of shepherds and the language of the rustic: it represents to our view the rural landscape and the peaceful cottage. It records the labours, the amusements, the loves, of the village nymphs and swains, and exhibits nature in its simplest state: it is no longer the harp or the lyre, but the pipe of the poet, which now invites our attention; Theocritus, leaning on his crook in his russet mantle and *clouted brogues*, appears more perfectly in character than the courtly Maro, who seems more the shepherd of the theatre than of the field. I have yet one other class in reserve for the epigrammatist, but I will shut up my list without him, not being willing that poetry, which commences with a prayer, should conclude with a pun.

# NUMBER LXVIII.

TASTE may be considered either as sensitive or mental; and under each of these denominations is sometimes spoken of as natural, sometimes as acquired; I propose to treat of it in its intellectual construction only, and in this sense Mr. Addison defines it to be that faculty of the soul, which discerns the beauties of an author with pleasure, and the imperfections with dislike.

This definition may very properly apply to the faculty which we exercise in judging and deciding upon the works of others; but how does it apply to the faculty exercised by those who produced those works? How does it serve to develope the taste of an author, the taste of a painter, or a statuary? And yet we may speak of a work of taste with the same propriety, as we do of a man of taste. It should seem therefore as if this definition went only to that denomination of taste, which we properly call an acquired taste; the productions of which generally end in imitation, whilst those of natural taste bear the stamp of originality. Another characteristic of natural taste will be simplicity; for how can nature give more than she possesses, and what is nature but simplicity? Now when the mind of any man is endued with a fine natural taste, and all means of profiting by other men's ideas are out of the question, that taste will operate by disposing him to select the fairest subjects out of what he sees either for art or imagination to work upon: Still his production will be marked with simplicity; but as it is the province of taste to separate deformity or vulgarity from what is merely simple, so according to the nature of his mind who possesses it, beauty or sublimity will be the result of the operation : if his taste inclines him to what is fair and elegant in nature, he will produce beauty ; if to what is lofty, bold, and tremendous, he will strike out sublimity.

Agreeably to this, we may observe in all literary and enlightened nations, their earliest authors and artists are the most simple : First, adventurers represent what they see or conceive with simplicity, because their impulse is unbiassed by emulation, having nothing in their sight either to imitate, avoid, or excel : on the other hand, their successors are sensible that one man's description of nature must be like another's, and in their zeal to keep clear of imitation, and to outstrip a predecessor, they begin to compound, refine, and even to distort. I will refer to the Venus de Medicis and the Laöcoon for an illustration of this : I do not concern myself about the dates or sculptors of these figures : but in the former we see beautiful simplicity, the fairest form in nature, selected by a fine taste, and imitated without affectation or distortion, and as it should seem without even an effort of art : in the Laöcoon we have a complicated plot ; we unravel a maze of ingenious contrivance, where the artist has compounded and distorted nature in the ambition of surpassing her.

Virgil possessed a fine taste according to Mr. Addison's definition, which I before observed applies only to an *acquired taste :* he had the ' faculty of discerning the beauties of an author with pleasure, and the imperfections with dislike :' he had also the faculty of *imitating* what he *discerned ;* so that I cannot verify what I have advanced by any stronger instance than his. I should think there does not exist a poet, who has gone such lengths in imitation as Virgil; for to pass over his pastoral and bucolic poems, which are evidently drawn from Theocritus and Hesiod, with the assistance of Aratus in every thing that relates to the scientific part of the signs and seasons, it is supposed that his whole narrative of the destruction of Troy, with the incident of the wooden horse and the episode of Sinon, are an almost literal translation of Pisander the epic poet, who in his turn perhaps might copy his account from the Ilias Minor (but this last is mere suggestion). As for the Æneid, it does little else but reverse the order of Homer's epic, making Æneas's voyage precede his wars in Italy, whereas the voyage of Ulysses is subsequent to the operations of the Iliad. As Apollo is made hostile to the Greeks, and the cause of his offence is introduced by Homer in the opening of the Iliad, so Juno in the Æneid stands in his place with every circumstance of imitation. It would be an endless task to trace the various instances throughout the Æneid, where scarce a single incident can be found which is not copied from Homer. Neither is there greater originality in the executive parts of the poem, than in the constructive; with this difference only, that he has copied passages from various authors, Roman as well as Greek, though from Homer the most. Amongst the Greeks, the dramatic poets Æschylus, Sophocles, and principally Euripides, have had the greatest share of his attention; Aristophanes, Menander, and other comic authors, Callimachus and some of the lyric writers, also may be traced in his imitations. A vast collection of passages from Ennius chiefly, from Lucretius, Furius, Lucilius, Pacuvius, Suevius, Nævius, Varius, Catullus, Accius, and others of his own nation, has been made by Macrobius in his Saturnalia, where Virgil has done little else but put their sentiments into more elegant verse; so that in strictness of speaking we may say of the Æneid, 'that it is a miscellaneous compilation of poetical passages, composing altogether an epic poem, formed upon the model of Homer's Iliad and Odyssey: abounding in beautiful versification, and justly to be admired for the fine *acquired taste* of its author, but devoid of originality either of construction or execution.' Besides its general inferiority as being a copy from Homer, it particularly falls off from its original in the conception and preservation of character: it does not reach the sublimity and majesty of its model, but it has in a great degree adopted the simplicity, and entirely avoided the rusticity, of Homer.

Lucan and Claudian in later ages were perhaps as good versifiers as Virgil, but far inferior to him in that fine acquired taste in which he excelled: they are ingenious but not simple; and execute better than they contrive. A passage from Claudian, which I shall beg the reader's leave to compare with one from Virgil (where he personifies the evil passions and plagues of mankind, and posts them at the entrance of hell, to which Æneas is descending), will exemplify what I have said: for at the same time that it will bear a dispute, whether Claudian's description is not even superior to Virgil's in poetical merit, yet the judicious manner of introducing it in one case, and the evident want of judgment in the other, will help to shew, that the reason why we prefer Virgil to Claudian, is more on account of his superiority of taste than of talents.

Claudian's description stands in the very front of his poem on Ruffinus; Virgil's is woven into his fable, and will be found in the sixth book of his Æneid, as follows:

> Vestibulum ante ipsum, primisque in faucibus Orci,
> Luctus, et ultrices posuere cubilia Curæ;
> Pallentesque habitant Morbi, tristisque Senectus,

Et Metus, et malesuada Fames, et turpis Egestas,
Terribiles visu formæ; Lethumque, Laborque;
Tum consanguineus Lethi Sopor, et mala mentis
Gaudia, mortiferumque adverso in limine Bellum,
Ferreique Eumenidum thalami, et Discordia demens
Vipereum crinem vittis innexa cruentis.—VIRGIL.

Just in the gates and in the jaws of Hell
Revengeful Cares and sullen Sorrows dwell,
And pale Diseases, and repining Age;
Want, Fear, and Famine's unresisted rage:
Here Toils, and Death, and Death's half-brother, Sleep,
Forms terrible to view, their sentry keep:
With anxious Pleasures of a guilty mind,
Deep Frauds before, and open Force behind:
The Furies' iron beds, and Strife that shakes
Her hissing tresses, and unfolds her snakes.—DRYDEN.

Protinùs infernas ad limina tetra sorores,
Concilium deforme, vocat; glomerantur in unum
Innumeræ pestes Erebi, quascunque sinistro
Nox genuit fœtu: Nutrix Discordia belli;
Imperiosa Fames; leto vicina Senectus;
Impatiensque sui Morbus; Livorque secundis
Anxius, est scisso mœrens velamine Luctus,
Et Timor, et cæco præceps Audacia vultu;
Et luxus populator opum; cui semper adhærens
Infelix humili gressu comitatur Egestas;
Fœdaque Avaritiæ complexæ pectora matris
Insomnes longo veniunt examine Curæ.—CLAUDIAN.

The infernal council, at Alecto's call
Conven'd, assemble in the Stygian hall;
Myriads of ghastly plagues that shun the light,
Daughters of Erebus and gloomy Night:
Strife war-compelling; Famine's wasting rage;
And Death just hovering o'er decrepit Age;
Envy, Prosperity's repining foe,
Restless Disease, and self-dishevell'd Woe,
Rashness, and Fear, and Poverty, that steals
Close as the shadow at the Spendthrift's heels;
And Cares that clinging to the Miser's breast,
Forbid his sordid soul to taste of rest.

The productions of the human genius will borrow
their complexion from the times in which they originate.  Ben Jonson says, 'that the players often

mentioned it as an honour to Shakspeare, that in his
writing (whatsoever he penned) he never blotted out
a line. My answer hath been, adds he, Would he
had blotted out a thousand! which they thought a
malevolent speech. I had not told posterity this
but for their ignorance, who chose that circumstance
to commend their friend by, wherein he most faulted;
and to justify mine own candour, for I loved the
man, and do honour his memory on this side idolatry
as much as any: he was indeed honest, and of an
open and free nature; had an excellent phantasie,
brave notions, and gentle expressions, wherein he
flowed with that facility, that sometime it was necessary he should be stopped; *Sufflaminandus erat,*
as Augustus said of Haterius: his wit was in his
own power; would the rule of it had been so too!'

I think there can be no doubt but this kind of indignant negligence with which Shakspeare wrote,
was greatly owing to the slight consideration he had
for his audience. Jonson treated them with the dictatorial haughtiness of a pedant: Shakspeare with
the carelessness of a gentleman who wrote at his
ease, and gave them the first flowings of his fancy
without any dread of their correction. These were
times in which the poet indulged his genius without
restraint; he stood alone and supereminent, and
wanted no artificial scaffold to raise him above the
heads of his contemporaries; he was natural, lofty,
careless, and daringly incorrect. Place the same
man in other times, amongst a people polished almost into general equality, and he shall begin to hesitate and retract his sallies; for in this respect
poetical are like military excursions, and it makes a
wide difference in the movements of a skilful general, whether he is to sally into a country defended
by well-disciplined troops, or only by an irregular
mob of unarmed barbarians. Shakspeare might

vault his Pegasus without a rein; mountains might rise and seas roll in vain before him; Nature herself could neither stop nor circumscribe his career. The modern man of verse mounts with the precaution of a riding-master, and prances round his little circle full-bitted and caparisoned in all the formality of a review. Whilst he is thus pacing and piaffering with every body's eyes upon him, his friends are calling out every now and then—' Seat yourself firm in the saddle! Hold your body straight! Keep your spurs from his sides for fear he sets a kicking! Have a care he does not stumble: there lies a stone, here runs a ditch; keep your whip still, and depend upon your bit, if you have not a mind to break your neck!' —On the other quarter his enemies are bawling out—' How like a tailor that fellow sits on horse-back! Look at his feet, look at his arms! Set the curs upon him; tie a cracker to his horse's tail, and make sport for the spectator!'—All this while per-haps the poor devil could have performed passably well, if it were not for the mobbing and hallooing about him: whereas Shakspeare mounts without fear, and starting in the jockey phrase at *score*, cries out, ' Stand clear, ye sons of earth! or by the beams of my father Apollo, I'll ride over you and trample you into dust!'

---

# NUMBER LXIX.

> Nil intentatum nostri liquere poetæ :
> Nec minimum meruere decus, vestigia Græca
> Ausi deserere, et celebrare domestica facta.—HORAT.

THERE are two very striking characters delineated by our great dramatic poet, which I am desirous of bringing together under one review, and these are *Macbeth* and *Richard the Third*.

The parts which these two persons sustain in their respective dramas, have a remarkable coincidence: both are actuated by the same guilty ambition in the opening of the story: both murder their lawful sovereign in the course of it: and both are defeated and slain in battle at the conclusion of it: yet these two characters under circumstances so similar, are as strongly distinguished in every passage of their dramatic life by the art of the poet, as any two men ever were by the hand of nature.

Let us contemplate them in the three following periods; viz. The premeditation of their crime; the perpetration of it; and the catastrophe of their death.

Duncan, the reigning king of Scotland, has two sons: Edward the Fourth of England has also two sons; but these kings and their respective heirs do not affect the usurpers Macbeth and Richard in the same degree, for the latter is a prince of the blood royal, brother to the king, and next in consanguinity to the throne after the death of his elder brother the Duke of Clarence: Macbeth, on the contrary, is not in the succession—

> And to be king
> Stands not within the prospect of belief.

His views therefore being farther removed and more out of hope, a greater weight of circumstances should be thrown together to tempt and encourage him to an undertaking so much beyond *the prospect of his belief.* The art of the poet furnishes these circumstances, and the engine which his invention employs, is of a preternatural and prodigious sort. He introduces in the very opening of his scene a troop of sibyls or witches, who salute Macbeth with their divinations, and in three solemn prophetic gratulations hail him Thane of Glamis, Thane of Cawdor, and King hereafter!

> By Sinel's death I know I'm Thane of Glamis;
> But how of Cawdor?

One part of the prophecy therefore is true; the remaining promises become more deserving of belief. This is one step in the ladder of his ambition, and mark how artfully the poet has laid it in his way: no time is lost; the wonderful machinery is not suffered to stand still, for behold a verification of the second prediction, and a courtier thus addresses him from the king—

> And for an earnest of a greater honour,
> He bade me from him call thee Thane of Cawdor.

The magic now works to his heart, and he cannot wait the departure of the royal messenger before his admiration vents itself aside—

> Glamis, and Thane of Cawdor!
> The greatest is behind.

A second time he turns aside, and unable to repress the emotions, which this second confirmation of the predictions has excited, repeats the same secret observation—

> Two truths are told
> As happy prologues to the swelling act
> Of the imperial theme.

A soliloquy then ensues, in which the poet judiciously opens enough of his character to shew the spectator that these preternatural agents are not superfluously set to work upon a disposition prone to evil, but one that will have to combat many compunctious struggles, before it can be brought to yield even to oracular influence. This alone would demonstrate (if we needed demonstration) that Shakspeare, without resorting to the ancients, had the judgment of ages as it were instinctively. From this

instant we are apprized that Macbeth meditates an
attack upon our pity as well as upon our horror, when
he puts the following question to his conscience—

> Why do I yield to that suggestion,
> Whose horrid image doth unfix my hair,
> And make my seated heart knock at my ribs
> Against the use of nature?

Now let us turn to Richard, in whose cruel heart
no such remorse finds place: he needs no tempter:
there is here no *dignus vindice nodus*, nor indeed
any *knot* at all, for he is already practised in murder; ambition is his ruling passion, and a crown is
in view, and he tells you at his very first entrance
on the scene—

> I am determined to be a villain.

We are now presented with a character full formed
and complete for all the savage purposes of the
drama.

> Impiger, iracundus, inexorabilis, acer.

The barriers of conscience are broken down, and
the soul, hardened against shame, avows its own
depravity—

> Plots have I laid, inductions dangerous,
> To set my brother Clarence and the king
> In deadly hate the one against the other.

He observes no gradations in guilt, expresses no
hesitation, practises no refinements, but plunges into
blood with the familiarity of long custom, and gives
orders to his assassins to dispatch his brother Clarence with all the unfeeling tranquillity of a Nero or
Caligula. Richard, having no longer any scruples
to manage with his own conscience, is exactly in
the predicament, which the dramatic poet Diphilus
has described with such beautiful simplicity of expression—

Ὅστις γὰρ αὐτὸν αὑτὸν οὐκ αἰσχύνεται,
Συνειδός᾽ αὑτῷ φαῦλα διαπεπραγμένος,
Πῶς τόν γε μηδὲν εἰδότ᾽ αἰσχυνθήσεται.

The wretch who knows his own vile deeds, and yet fears not
himself, how should he fear another, who knows them not.

It is manifest therefore that there is an essential
difference in the developement of these characters,
and that in favour of Macbeth: in his soul cruelty
seems to dawn; it breaks out with faint glimmer-
ings, like a winter morning, and gathers strength by
slow degrees: in Richard it flames forth at once,
mounting like the sun between the tropics, and enters
boldly on its career without a herald.  As the character of Macbeth has a moral advantage in this
distinction, so has the drama of that name a much
more interesting and affecting cast: the struggles of
a soul, naturally virtuous, whilst it holds the guilty
impulse of ambition at bay, affords the noblest theme
for the drama, and puts the creative fancy of our
poet upon a resource, in which he has been rivalled
only by the great father of tragedy Æschylus in the
prophetic effusions of Cassandra, the incantations of
the Persian Magi for raising the ghost of Darius,
and the imaginary terrific forms of his furies; with
all which our countryman probably had no acquaintance, or at most a very obscure one.

When I see the names of these two great lumi-
naries of the dramatic sphere, so distant in time but
so nearly allied in genius, casually brought in con-
tact by the nature of my subject, I cannot help
pausing for awhile in this place to indulge so interesting a contemplation, in which I find my mind
balanced between two objects, that seem to have
equal claims upon me for my admiration.  Æschylus
is justly styled the father of tragedy, but this is not
to be interpreted as if he was the inventor of it:
Shakspeare with equal justice claims the same title,

and his originality is qualified with the same exception : the Greek tragedy was not more rude and undigested when Æschylus brought it into shape, than the English tragedy was when Shakspeare began to write : if therefore it be granted that he had no aids from the Greek theatre (and I think this is not likely to be disputed), so far these great masters are upon equal ground. Æschylus was a warrior of high repute, of a lofty generous spirit, and deep as it should seem in the erudition of his times : in all these particulars he has great advantage over our countryman, who was humbly born, of the most menial occupation, and, as it is generally thought, unlearned. Æschylus had the whole epic of Homer in his hands, the Iliad, Odyssey, and that prolific source of dramatic fable, the Ilias Minor; he had also a great fabulous creation to resort to amongst his own divinities, characters ready defined, and an audience, whose superstition was prepared for every thing he could offer; he had therefore a firmer and broader stage (if I may be allowed the expression) under his feet, than Shakspeare had : his fables in general are Homeric, and yet it does not follow that we can pronounce for Shakspeare that he is more original in his plots, for I understand that late researches have traced him in all or nearly all : both poets added so much machinery and invention of their own in the conduct of their fables, that whatever might have been the source, still their streams had little or no taste of the spring they flowed from. In point of character we have better grounds to decide, and yet it is but justice to observe, that it is not fair to bring a mangled poet in comparison with one who is entire : in his divine personages, Æschylus has the field of heaven, and indeed of hell also, to himself; in his heroic and military characters he has never been excelled; he had too good a model within his own bosom to fail of making those delineations natural: in his imaginary being also he will be found a respectable, though not an equal rival of our poet; but in the variety of character, in all the nicer touches of nature, in all the extravagances of caprice and humour, from the boldest feature down to the minutest foible, Shakspeare stands alone: such persons as he delineates never came into the contemplation of Æschylus as a poet; his tragedy has no dealing with them; the simplicity of the Greek fable, and the great portion of the drama filled up by the chorus, allow of little variety of character; and the most which can be said of Æschylus in this particular is, that he never offends against nature or propriety, whether his cast is in the terrible or pathetic, the elevated or the simple. His versification, with the intermixture of lyric composition, is more various than that of Shakspeare; both are lofty and sublime in the extreme, abundantly metaphorical, and sometimes extravagant:—

—— Nubes et inania captat.

This may be said of each poet in his turn; in each the critic, if he is in search for defects, will readily enough discover—

In scenam missus magno cum pondere versus.

Both were subject to be hurried on by an uncontrollable impulse, nor could nature alone suffice for either: Æschylus had an apt creation of imaginary beings at command—

He could call spirits from the vasty deep,

and they *would come*—Shakspeare, having no such creation in resource, boldly made one of his own; if Æschylus therefore was invincible, he owed it to his armour, and that, like the armour of Æneas, was the work of the gods: but the unassisted invention of Shakspeare seized all and more than superstition supplied to Æschylus.

# NUMBER LXX.

Ille profecto
Reddere personæ scit convenientia cuique.—HORAT.

WE are now to attend Macbeth to the perpetration of the murder, which puts him in possession of the crown of Scotland; and this introduces a new personage on the scene, his accomplice and wife: she thus developes her own character—

Come, all you spirits,
That tend on mortal thoughts, unsex me here,
And fill me from the crown to the toe topful
Of direst cruelty; make thick my blood,
Stop up the access and passage to remorse,
That no compunctious visitings of nature
Shake my fell purpose, nor keep peace between
Th' effect and it. Come to my woman's breasts,
And take my milk for gall, you murth'ring ministers,
Wherever in your sightless substances
You wait on nature's mischief: come, thick night,
And pall thee in the dunnest smoke of hell!

Terrible invocation! Tragedy can speak no stronger language, nor could any genius less than Shakspeare's support a character of so lofty a pitch, so sublimely terrible at the very opening.

The part which Lady Macbeth fills in the drama has a relative as well as positive importance, and serves to place the repugnance of Macbeth in the strongest point of view; she is in fact the auxiliary of the witches, and the natural influence, which so high and predominant a spirit asserts over the tamer qualities of her husband, makes those witches but secondary agents for bringing about the main action of the drama. This is well worth a remark; for if they, which are only artificial and fantastic instruments, had been made the sole or even principal movers of the great incident of the murder, nature would have been excluded from her share in the drama, and Macbeth would have become the mere machine of an uncontrollable necessity, and his character, being robbed of its free agency, would have left no moral behind: I must take leave therefore to anticipate a remark, which I shall hereafter repeat, that when Lady Macbeth is urging her Lord to the murder, not a word is dropt by either of the witches or their predictions. It is in these instances of his conduct that Shakspeare is so wonderful a study for the dramatic poet. But I proceed—

Lady Macbeth in her first scene, from which I have already extracted a passage, prepares for an attempt upon the conscience of her husband, whose nature she thus describes—

> Yet do I fear thy nature;
> It is too full o'th' milk of human kindness
> To catch the nearest way.

He arrives before she quits the scene, and she receives him with consummate address—

> Great Glamis! worthy Cawdor!
> Greater than both by the All-hail hereafter!

These are the very gratulations of the witches; she welcomes him with confirmed predictions, with the tempting salutations of ambition, not with the softening caresses of a wife—

> *Macb.* Duncan comes here to-night.
> *Lady.* And when goes hence?
> *Macb.* To-morrow, as he purposes.
> *Lady.* Oh never
> Shall sun that morrow see!

The rapidity of her passion hurries her into imme-

diate explanation, and he, consistently with the
character she had described, evades her precipitate
solicitations with a short indecisive answer—

> We will speak further——

His reflections upon this interview, and the dreadful
subject of it, are soon after given in soliloquy, in
which the poet has mixed the most touching strokes
of compunction with his meditations : he reasons
against the villany of the act, and honour jointly
with nature assails him with an argument of double
force—

> He's here in double trust ;
> First as I am his kinsman and his subject,
> Strong both against the deed ; then as his host,
> Who should against the murtherer shut the door,
> Not bear the knife himself.

This appeal to nature, hospitality, and allegiance,
was not without its impression ; he again meets his
lady, and immediately declares—

> We will proceed no further in this business.

This draws a retort upon him, in which his tergi-
versation and cowardice are satirized with so keen
an edge, and interrogatory reproaches are pressed
so fast upon him, that, catching hold in his retreat
of one small but precious fragment in the wreck of
innocence and honour, he demands a truce from
her attack, and, with the spirit of a combatant who
has not yet yielded up his weapons, cries out—

> Pr'thee, peace ;

The words are no expletives ; they do not fill up a
sentence, but they form one : they stand in a most
important pass : they defend the breach her ambition
has made in his heart ; a breach in the very citadel
of humanity ; they mark the last dignified struggle
of virtue, and they have a double reflecting power,
which, in the first place, shews that nothing but the

voice of authority could stem the torrent of her invective, and in the next place announces that something, worthy of the solemn audience he had demanded, was on the point to follow—and worthy it is to be a standard sentiment of moral truth expressed with proverbial simplicity, sinking into every heart that hears it—

> I dare do all that may become a man,
> Who dares do more is none.

How must every feeling spectator lament that a man should fall from virtue with such an appeal upon his lips!

Οὐκ ἔστιν οὐδεὶς δειλὸς, ὁ δεδοικὼς νόμον.—PHILONIDES.

'A man is not a coward because he fears to be unjust,' is the sentiment of an old dramatic poet.

Macbeth's principle is honour; cruelty is natural to his wife; ambition is common to both; one passion favourable to her purpose has taken place in his heart: another still hangs about it, which being adverse to her plot, is first to be expelled, before she can instil her cruelty into his nature. The sentiment above quoted had been firmly delivered, and was ushered in with an apostrophe suitable to its importance; she feels its weight; she perceives it is not to be turned aside with contempt, or laughed down by ridicule, as she had already done where weaker scruples had stood in the way: but, taking sophistry in aid, by a ready turn of argument she gives him credit for his sentiment, erects a more glittering though fallacious logic upon it, and by admitting his objection cunningly confutes it—

> What beast was't then
> That made you break this enterprise to me?
> When you durst do it, then you were a man,
> And to be more than what you were, you wou'd
> Be so much more than man.

Having thus parried his objection by a sophistry calculated to blind his reason and inflame his ambition, she breaks forth into such a vaunting display of hardened intrepidity, as presents one of the most terrific pictures that was ever imagined—

> I have given suck, and know
> How tender 'tis to love the babe that milks me;
> I wou'd, whilst it was smiling in my face,
> Have pluckt my nipple from its boneless gums,
> And dasht its brains out, had I but so sworn
> As you have done to this.

This is a note of horror, screwed to a pitch that bursts the very sinews of nature; she no longer combats with a human weapon, but seizing the flash of the lightning extinguishes her opponent with the stroke: here the controversy must end, for he must either adopt her spirit, or take her life; he sinks under the attack, and offering nothing in delay of execution but a feeble hesitation, founded in fear— 'If we should fail'—he concludes with an assumed ferocity, caught from her and not springing from himself—

> I am settled, and bend up
> Each corporal agent to this terrible feat.

The strong and sublime strokes of a master impressed upon this scene make it a model of dramatic composition, and I must in this place remind the reader of the observation I have before hinted at, that no reference whatever is had to the auguries of the witches: it would be injustice to suppose that this was other than a purposed omission by the poet; a weaker genius would have resorted back to these instruments: Shakspeare had used and laid them aside for a time; he had a stronger engine at work, and he could proudly exclaim—

> We defy auguries!——

Nature was sufficient for that work, and to shew the

mastery he had over nature, he took his human agent from the weaker sex.

This having passed in the first act, the murder is perpetrated in the succeeding one. The introductory soliloquy of Macbeth, the chimera of the dagger, and the signal on the bell, are awful preludes to the deed. In this dreadful interim Lady Macbeth, the great superintending spirit, enters to support the dreadful work. It is done; and he returns appalled with sounds; he surveys his bloody hands with horror; he starts from her proposal of going back to besmear the guards of Duncan's chamber, and she snatches the reeking daggers from his trembling hands to finish the imperfect work—

> Infirm of purpose,
> Give me the daggers!

She returns on the scene, the deed which he revolted from is performed, and with the same unshaken ferocity she vauntingly displays her bloody trophies and exclaims—

> My hands are of your colour, but I shame
> To wear a heart so white.

Fancied noises, the throbbings of his own quailing heart, had shaken the constancy of Macbeth; real sounds, the certain signals of approaching visiters, to whom the situation of Duncan must be revealed, do not intimidate her; she is prepared for all trials, and coolly tells him—

> I hear a knocking
> At the south entry: Retire we to our chamber;
> A little water clears us of this deed.
> How easy is it then!

The several incidents thrown together in this scene of the murder of Duncan, are of so striking a sort as to need no elucidation: they are better felt than described, and my attempts points at passages of more obscurity, where the touches are thrown into shade, and the art of the author lies more out of sight.

Lady Macbeth being now retired from the scene, we may in this interval, as we did in the conclusion of the former paper, permit the genius of Æschylus to introduce a rival murderess on the stage.

Clytemnestra has received her husband Agamemnon, on his return from the capture of Troy, with studied rather than cordial congratulations. He opposes the pompous ceremonies she had devised for the display of his entry, with a magnanimous contempt of such adulation—

> Sooth me not with strains
> Of adulation, as a girl; nor raise
> As to some proud barbaric king, that loves
> Loud acclamations echoed from the mouths
> Of prostrate worshippers, a clamorous welcome:
> Spread not the streets with tapestry; 'tis invidious:
> These are the honours we should pay the gods;
> For mortal men to tread on ornaments
> Of rich embroidery—no; I dare not do it:
> Respect me as a man, not as a god.
>
> POTTER'S ÆSCHYLUS.

These are heroic sentiments, but in conclusion the persuasions of the wife overcome the modest scruples of the hero, and he enters his palace in the pomp of triumph; when soon his dying groans are echoed from the interior scene, and the adultress comes forth besprinkled with the blood of her husband to avow the murder—

> I struck him twice, and twice
> He groan'd; then died: a third time as he lay
> I gor'd him with a wound; a grateful present
> To the stern god, that in the realms below
> Reigns o'er the dead: there let him take his seat.
> He lay: and spouting from his wounds a stream
> Of blood, bedew'd me with these crimson drops.
> I glory in them, like the genial earth,
> When the warm showers of heav'n descend, and wake

The flowrets to unfold their vermeil leaves.
Come then, ye reverend senators of Argos,
Joy with me, if your hearts be turn'd to joy,
And such I wish them.—— POTTER.

## NUMBER LXXI.

Ille per extentum funem mihi posse videtur
Ire poeta, meum qui pectus inaniter angit,
Irritat, mulcet, falsis terroribus implet,
Ut magus; et modò me Thebis, modò ponit Athenis.
                                        HORAT.

RICHARD perpetrates several murders, but as the poet has not marked them with any distinguishing circumstances, they need not be enumerated on this occasion. Some of these he commits in his passage to power, others after he has seated himself on the throne. Ferociousness and hypocrisy are the prevailing features of his character, and as he has no one honourable or humane principle to combat, there is no opening for the poet to develope those secret workings of conscience, which he has so naturally done in the case of Macbeth.

The murder of Clarence, those of the queen's kinsmen, and of the young princes in the Tower, are all perpetrated in the same style of hardened cruelty. He takes the ordinary method of hiring ruffians to perform his bloody commissions and there is nothing which particularly marks the scenes, wherein he imparts his purposes and instructions to them; a very little management serves even for Tirrel, who is not a professional murderer, but is reported to be——

——a discontented gentleman,
Whose humble means match not his haughty spirit.

N 2

With such a spirit Richard does not hold it necessary to use much circumlocution, and seems more in
dread of delay than disappointment or discovery—

> R. Is thy name Tirrel?
> T. James Tirrel, and your most obedient subject.
> R. Art thou indeed?
> T. Prove me, my gracious lord.
> R. Dar'st thou resolve to kill a friend of mine?
> T. Please you, I had rather kill two enemies,
> R. Why then thou hast it; two deep enemies,
>    Foes to my rest and my sweet sleep's disturbers,
>    Are they that I would have thee deal upon:
>    Tirrel, I mean those bastards in the Tower.

If the reader calls to mind by what circumspect
and slow degrees King John opens himself to Hu-
bert under a similar situation with this of Richard,
he will be convinced that Shakspeare considered preservation of character too important to sacrifice on
any occasion to the vanity of fine writing; for the
scene he has given to John, a timorous and wary
prince, would ill suit the character of Richard. A
close observance of nature is the first excellence of
a dramatic poet, and the peculiar property of him
we are reviewing.

In these two stages of our comparison, Macbeth
appears with far more dramatic effect than Richard,
whose first scenes present us with little else than
traits of perfidiousness, one striking incident of successful hypocrisy practised on the Lady Anne, and
an open unreserved display of remorseless cruelty.
Impatient of any pause or interruption in his measures, a dangerous friend and a determined foe:—

> Effera torquebant avidæ præcordia curæ,
> Effugeret ne quis gladios;
> Crescebat scelerata sitis; prædæque recentis
> Incestus flagrabat amor, nullusque petendi
> Cogendive pudor: crebris perjuria nectit
> Blanditiis; sociat perituro fœdere dextras:
> Si semel et antis poscenti quisque negâsset,
> Effera prætumido quatiebat corda furore.—CLAUDIAN.

> The sole remorse his greedy heart can feel
> Is if one life escapes his murdering steel;
> That, which should quench, inflames his craving thirst,
> The second draught still deepens on the first;
> Shameless by force or fraud to work his way,
> And no less prompt to flatter than betray:
> This hour makes friendships which he breaks the next,
> And every breach supplies a vile pretext
> Basely to cancel all concessions past,
> If in a thousand you deny the last.

Macbeth has now touched the goal of his ambition—

> Thou hast it now; King, Cawdor, Glamis, all
> The weird sisters promised——

The auguries of the witches, to which no reference had been made in the heat of the main action, are now called to mind with many circumstances of galling aggravation, not only as to the prophecy, which gave the crown to the posterity of Banquo, but also of his own safety from the gallant and noble nature of that general

> Our fears in Banquo
> Stick deep, and in his royalty of nature
> Reigns that which would be fear'd.

Assassins are provided to murder Banquo and his son, but this is not decided upon without much previous meditation, and he seems prompted to the act more by desperation and dread, than by any settled resolution or natural cruelty. He convenes the assassins, and in a conference of some length works round to his point, by insinuations calculated to persuade them to dispatch Banquo for injuries done to them, rather than from motives which respect himself; in which scene we discover a remarkable preservation of character in Macbeth, who by this artifice strives to blind his own conscience and throw the guilt upon theirs: in this, as in the former action, there is nothing kingly in his cruelty; in one he acted under the controlling spirit of his wife, here he plays the sycophant with hired assassins, and confesses himself under awe of the superior genius of Banquo—

> ———Under him
> My genius is rebuk'd, as it is said
> Antony's was by Cæsar.

There is not a circumstance ever so minute in the conduct of this character, which does not point out to a diligent observer, how closely the poet has adhered to nature in every part of his delineation; accordingly we observe a peculiarity in the language of Macbeth, which is highly characteristic; I mean the figurative turn of his expressions, whenever his imagination strikes upon any gloomy subject—

> Oh! full of scorpions is my mind, dear wife!

And in this state of self-torment every object of solemnity, though ever so familiar becomes an object of terror! night, for instance, is not mentioned by him without an accompaniment of every melancholy attribute which a frighted fancy can annex—

> Ere the bat hath flown
> His cloister'd flight, ere to black Hecate's summons
> The shard-born beetle with his drowsy hums
> Hath rung Night's yawning peal, there shall be done
> A deed of dreadful note.

It is the darkness of his soul that makes the night so dreadful, the *scorpions in his mind*, convoke these images—but he has not yet done with it—

> Come sealing Night!
> Skarf up the tender eye of pitiful day;
> And with thy bloody and invisible hand
> Cancel and tear to pieces that great bond,
> Which keeps me pale.  Light thickens, and the crow
> Makes wing to the rooky wood.
> Good things of day begin to droop and drowse,
> Whilst night's black agents to their prey do rouse.

The critic of language will observe that here is a redundancy and crowd of metaphors, but the critic of nature will acknowledge that it is the very truth of character, and join me in the remark which points it out.

In a tragedy so replete with murder, and in the display of a character so tortured by the *scorpions of the mind*, as this of Macbeth, it is naturally to be expected that a genius like Shakspeare's will call in the dead for their share in the horror of the scene. This he has done in two several ways; first, by the apparition of Banquo, which is invisible to all but Macbeth; secondly, by the spells and incantations of the witches, who raise spirits, which in certain enigmatical predictions shadow out his fate; and these are followed by a train of unborn revelations, drawn by the power of magic from the womb of futurity before their time.

It appears that Lady Macbeth was not a party in the assassination of Banquo, and the ghost, though twice visible to the murderer, is not seen by her. This is another incident highly worthy a particular remark; for by keeping her free from any participation in the horror of the sight, the poet is enabled to make a scene aside, between Macbeth and her, which contains some of the finest speakings in the play. The ghost in *Hamlet*, and the ghost of Darius in Æschylus, are introduced by preparation and prelude, this of Banquo is an object of surprise as well as terror, and there is scarce an incident to be named of more striking and dramatic effect: it is one amongst various proofs, that must convince every man who looks critically into Shakspeare, that he was as great a master in art as in nature: how it strikes me in this point of view, I shall take the liberty of explaining more at length.

The murder of Duncan is the main incident of this tragedy; that of Banquo is subordinate: Duncan's blood was not only the first so shed by Macbeth, but the dignity of the person murdered, and the aggravating circumstances attending it, constitute a crime of the very first magnitude: for these reasons it might be expected, that the spectre most likely to haunt his imagination, would be that of Duncan; and the rather because his terror and compunction were so much more strongly excited by this first murder, perpetrated with his own hands, than by the subsequent one of Banquo, palliated by evasion, and committed to others. But when we recollect that Lady Macbeth was not only his accomplice, but in fact the first mover in the murder of the king, we see good reason why Duncan's ghost could not be called up, unless she who so deeply partook of the guilt, had also shared in the horror of the appearance; and as visitations of a peculiar sort were reserved for her in a later period of the drama, it was a point of consummate art and judgment to exclude her from the affair of Banquo's murder, and make the more susceptible conscience of Macbeth figure this apparition in his mind's eye, without any other witness to the vision.

I persuade myself these will appear very natural reasons why the poet did not raise the ghost of the king in preference, though it is reasonable to think it would have been a much more noble incident in his hands, than this of Banquo. It now remains to examine, whether this is more fully justified by the peculiar situation reserved for Lady Macbeth, to which I have before adverted.

The intrepidity of her character is so marked, that we may well suppose no waking terrors could shake it, and in this light it must be acknowledged a very natural expedient to make her vent the agonies of her conscience in sleep. Dreams have been a dramatic expedient ever since there has been a drama; Æschylus recites the dream of Clytemnestra imme-

diately before her son Orestes kills her; she fancies
she has given birth to a dragon—

> This new-born dragon like an infant child,
> Laid in the cradle seem'd in want of food;
> And in her dream she held it to her breast:
> The milk he drew was mixed with clotted blood.—POTTER.

This which is done by Æschylus, has been done by
hundreds after him; but to introduce upon the scene
the very person, walking in sleep, and giving vent
to the horrid fancies that haunt her dream, in broken
speeches expressive of her guilt, uttered before witnesses, and accompanied with that natural and expressive action of washing the blood from her defiled
hands, was reserved for the original and bold genius
of Shakspeare only. It is an incident so full of
tragic horror, so daring, and at the same time so
truly characteristic, that it stands out as a prominent
feature in the most sublime drama in the world, and
fully compensates for any sacrifices the poet might
have made in the previous arrangement of his incidents.

---

# NUMBER LXXII.

*Servetur ad imum*
*Qualis ab incepto processerit, et sibi constet.*—HORAT.

MACBETH now approaches towards his catastrophe;
the heir of the crown is in arms, and he must defend
valiantly what he has usurped villanously. His
natural valour does not suffice for this trial; he re-
sorts to the witches; he conjures them to give answer to what he shall ask, and he again runs into all
those pleonasms of speech which I before remarked:
the predictions he extorts from the apparitions are

so couched as to seem favourable to him, at the
same time that they correspond with events, which
afterward prove fatal. The management of this incident has so close a resemblance to what the poet
Claudian has done in the instance of Ruffinus's vision, the night before his massacre, that I am tempted
to insert the passage—

> Ecce videt diras alludere protinùs umbras,
> Quas dedit ipse neci ; quarum quæ clarior una
> Visa loqui—Proh ! surge toro ; quid plurima volvis
> Anxius ? hæc requiem rebus, finemque labori
> Allatura dies : Omni jam plebe redibis
> Altior, et læti manibus portabere vulgi—
> Has canit ambages.  Occulto fallitur ille
> Omine, nec capitis fixi præsagia sentit.

> A ghastly vision in the dead of night,
> Of mangled, murder'd ghosts appal his sight ;
> When hark ! a voice from forth the shadowy train
> Cries out—Awake ! what thoughts perplex thy brain ?
> Awake, arise ! behold the day appears,
> That ends thy labours, and dispels thy fears ;
> To loftier heights thy towering head shall rise,
> And the glad crowd shall lift thee to the skies—
> Thus spake the voice: he triumphs, nor beneath
> Th' ambiguous omen sees the doom of death.

Confiding in his auguries, Macbeth now prepares for
battle : by the first of these he is assured—

> That none of woman born
> Shall harm Macbeth.

By the second prediction he is told—

> Macbeth shall never vanquished be until
> Great Birnam-wood to Dunsinane's high hill
> Shall come against him.

These he calls *sweet boadments!* and concludes—

> To sleep in spite of thunder.

This play is so replete with excellences, that it
would exceed all bounds, if I were to notice every
one : I pass over therefore that incomparable scene
between Macbeth, the Physician, and Seyton, in

which the agitations of his mind are so wonderfully expressed, and, without pausing for the death of Lady Macbeth, I conduct the reader to that crisis, when the messenger has announced the ominous approach of Birnam-wood—A burst of fury, an exclamation seconded by a blow, is the first natural explosion of a soul so stung with *scorpions* as Macbeth's: the sudden gust is no sooner discharged, than nature speaks her own language, and the still voice of conscience, like reason in the midst of madness, murmurs forth these mournful words—

> I pall in resolution, and begin
> To doubt the equivocation of the fiend,
> That lies like truth.

With what an exquisite feeling has this darling son of nature here thrown in this touching, this pathetic sentence, amidst the very whirl and eddy of conflicting passions! Here is a study for dramatic poets : this is a string for an actor's skill to touch : this will discourse sweet music to the human heart, with which it is finely unisoned when struck with the hand of a master.

The next step brings us to the last scene of Macbeth's dramatic existence. Flushed with the blood of Siward he is encountered by Macduff, who crosses him like his evil genius—Macbeth cries out—

> Of all men else I have avoided thee.

To the last moment of character the faithful poet supports him; he breaks off from single combat, and in the tremendous pause, so beautifully contrived to hang suspense and terror on the moral scene of his exit, the tyrant driven to bay, and panting with the heat and struggle of the fight, vauntingly exclaims—

*Macb.* As easy may'st thou the intrenchant air
　　　　With thy keen sword impress, as make me bleed :

Let fall thy blade on vulnerable crests,
I bear a charm'd life, which must not yield
To one of woman born.
*Macd.*                    Despair thy charm!
And let the angel, whom thou still hast served,
Tell thee Macduff was from his mother's womb
Untimely ripp'd.
*Macb.*  Accursed be that tongue that tells me so?
For it hath cowed my better part of man.

There sinks the spirit of Macbeth—

Behold! where stands
Th' usurper's cursed head!

How completely does this coincide with the passage
already quoted!

Occulto fallitur ille
Omine, nec CAPITIS FIXI præsagia sentit.

Let us now approach the tent of Richard. It is
matter of admiration to observe how many incidents
the poet has collected in a small compass, to set the
military character of his chief personage in a brilliant point of view. A succession of scouts and
messengers report a variety of intelligence, all which,
though generally of the most alarming nature, he
meets not only with his natural gallantry, but sometimes with pleasantry, and a certain archness and
repartee, which is peculiar to him throughout the
drama.

It is not only a curious, but delightful task to
examine by what subtle and almost imperceptible
touches Shakspeare contrives to set such marks upon
his characters, as give them the most living like-
nesses that can be conceived. In this, above all
other poets that ever existed, he is a study and a
model of perfection: the great distinguishing passions every poet may describe; but Shakspeare gives
you their humours, their minutest foibles, those
little starts and caprices, which nothing but the
most intimate familiarity brings to light; other au-

thors write characters like historians: he like the
bosom friend of the person he describes. The following extracts will furnish an example of what I
have been saying.

Ratcliff informs Richard that a fleet is discovered
on the western coast, supposed to be the party of
Richmond—

> *K. Rich.* Some light-foot friend post to the Duke of Norfolk;
>    Ratcliff, thyself; or Catesby—Where is he?
> *Cates.* Here, my good lord.
> *K. Rich.* Catesby, fly to the Duke.
> *Cates.* I will, my lord, with all convenient haste.
> *K. Rich.* Ratcliff, come hither; post to Salisbury:
>    When thou com'st thither—*Dull unmindful villain!*
>                                    (To Catesby.
>    Why stay'st thou here, and go'st not to the Duke?
> *Cates.* First, mighty liege, tell me your highness' pleasure,
>    What from your grace I shall deliver to him.
> *K. Rich.* Oh, true, good Catesby!

I am persuaded I need not point out to the reader's
sensibility the fine turn in this expression, *Good
Catesby!* How can we be surprised if such a poet
makes us in love even with his villains?—Ratcliff
proceeds—

> *Rat.* What may it please you shall I do at Salisbury?
> *K. Rich.* Why, what wou'dst thou do there before I go?
> *Rat.* Your highness told me I should post before.
> *K. Rich.* My mind is chang'd.

These fine touches can escape no man, who has an
eye for nature. Lord Stanley reports to Richard—

> *Stanl.* Richmond is on the seas.
> *K. Rich.* There let him sink, and be the seas on him!
>    White-liver'd runagate, what doth he there?

This reply is pointed with irony and invective: there
are two causes in nature and character for this;
first, Richard was before informed of the news; his
person was not taken by surprise, and he was enough
at ease to make a play upon Stanley's words—*on the
seas*—and retort—*be the seas on him!*—Secondly

Stanley was a suspected subject, Richard was therefore interested to shew a contempt of his competitor, before a man of such doubtful allegiance. In the spirit of this impression he urges Stanley to give an explicit answer to the question—*What doth he there?* Stanley endeavours to evade by answering that he *knows not but by guess:* the evasion only strengthens Richard's suspicions, and he again pushes him to disclose what he only guesses—*Well as you guess*— Stanley replies—

> He makes for England here to claim the crown.
> *K. Rich.* Is the chair empty? Is the sword unsway'd?
> Is the king dead? the empire unpossess'd?
> What heir of York is there alive but we?
> And who is England's king but great York's heir?
> Then tell me what makes he upon the sea?

What a cluster of characteristic excellences are here before us! All these interrogatories are *ad hominem;* they fit no man but Stanley, they can be uttered by no man but Richard, and they can flow from the conceptions of no poet but the poet of nature.

Stanley's whole scene ought to be investigated, for it is full of beauties; but I confess myself exhausted with the task, and language does not suffice to furnish fresh terms of admiration, which a closer scrutiny would call forth.

Other messengers succeed Lord Stanley, Richard's fiery impatience does not wait the telling, but taking the outset of the account to be ominous, he strikes the courier, who proceeding with his report, concludes with the good tidings of Buckingham's dispersion—Richard instantly retracts and says—

> Oh! I cry thee mercy,
> There is my purse to cure that blow of thine.

This is another trait of the same cast with that of *Good Catesby.*

Battles are of the growth of modern tragedy; I am not learned enough in the old stage to know if Shakspeare is the inventor of this bold and bustling innovation; but I am sure he is unrivalled in his execution of it, and this of Bosworth-field is a masterpiece. I shall be less particular in my present description of it, because I may probably bring it under general review with other scenes of the like sort.

It will be sufficient to observe, that in the catastrophe of Richard nothing can be more glowing than the scene, nothing more brilliant than the conduct, of the chief character: he exhibits the character of a perfect general, in whom however ardent courage seems the ruling feature; he performs every part of his office with minute attention, he inquires if certain alterations are made in his armour, and even orders what particular horse he intends to charge with: he is gay with his chief officers, and even gracious to some he confides in: his gallantry is of so dazzling a quality, that we begin to feel the pride of Englishmen, and, overlooking his crimes, glory in our courageous king. Richmond is one of those civil, conscientious gentlemen, who are not very apt to captivate a spectator, and Richard, loaded as he is with enormities, rises in the comparison, and I suspect carries the good wishes of many of his audience into action, and dies with their regret.

As soon as he retires to his tent the poet begins to put in motion his great moral machinery of the ghosts. Trifles are not made for Shakspeare; difficulties, that would have plunged the spirit of any other poet, and turned his scenery into inevitable ridicule, are nothing in his way; he brings forward a long string of ghosts, and puts a speech into each of their mouths without any fear of consequences.

Richard starts from his couch, and before he has
shaken off the terrors of his dream, cries out—

> Give me another horse!—bind up my wounds!—
> Have mercy, Jesu!—Soft, I did but dream—
> O coward conscience—&c.

But I may conclude my subject; every reader can
go on with the soliloquy, and no words of mine can
be wanted to excite their admiration.

---

## NUMBER LXXIII.

---

WHEN it had entered into the mind of Shakspeare,
to form an historical play upon certain events in the
reign of Henry the Fourth of England, the character
of the Prince of Wales recommended itself to his
fancy, as likely to supply him with a fund of dramatic incidents; for what could invention have more
happily suggested than this character, which history
presented ready to his hands? a riotous disorderly
young libertine, in whose nature lay hidden those
seeds of heroism and ambition, which were to burst
forth at once to the astonishment of the world, and
to achieve the conquest of France.   This prince,
whose character was destined to exhibit a revolution
of so brilliant a sort, was not only in himself a very
tempting hero for the dramatic poet, who delights in
incidents of novelty and surprise, but also offered to
his imagination a train of attendant characters, in
the persons of his wild comrades and associates,
which would be of themselves a drama.   Here was
a field for invention wide enough even for the genius
of Shakspeare to range in.   All the humours, passions, and extravagances, of human life might be

brought into the composition, and when he had grouped and personified them to his taste and liking, he had a leader ready to place at the head of the train, and the truth of history to give life and interest to his drama.

With these materials ready for creation the great artist sat down to his work; the canvas was spread before him, ample and capacious as the expanse of his own fancy; nature put her pencil into his hand, and he began to sketch. His first concern was to give a chief or captain to this gang of rioters; this would naturally be the first outline he drew. To fill up the drawing of this personage he conceived a voluptuary, in whose figure and character there should be an assemblage of comic qualities: in his person he should be bloated and blown up to the size of a Silenus, lazy, luxurious, in sensuality a satyr, in intemperance a bacchanalian. As he was to stand in the post of a ringleader amongst thieves and cutpurses, he made him a notorious liar, a swaggering coward, vain-glorious, arbitrary, knavish, crafty, voracious of plunder, lavish of his gains, without credit, honour, or honesty, and in debt to every body about him. As he was to be the chief seducer and misleader of the heir-apparent of the crown, it was incumbent on the poet to qualify him for that part in such a manner as should give probability and even a plea to the temptation; this was only to be done by the strongest touches and the highest colourings of a master; by hitting off a humour of so happy, so facetious, and so alluring a cast, as should tempt even royalty to forget itself, and virtue to turn reveller in his company. His lies, his vanity, and his cowardice, too gross to deceive, were to be so ingenious as to give delight; his cunning evasions, his witty resources, his mock solemnity, his vapouring self-consequence, were to furnish a continual feast

of laughter to his royal companion; he was not only
to be witty himself, but the cause of wit in other
people; a whetstone for raillery; a buffoon, whose
very person was a jest. Compounded of these humours, Shakspeare produced the character of Sir
John Falstaff: a character, which neither ancient
nor modern comedy has ever equalled, which was
so much the favourite of its author as to be introduced
in three several plays, and which is likely to be the
idol of the English stage, as long as it shall speak
the language of Shakspeare.

This character almost singly supports the whole
comic plot of the first part of Henry the Fourth: the
poet has indeed thrown in some auxiliary humours
in the persons of Gadshill, Peto, Bardolph, and
Hostess Quickly; the two first serve for little else
except to fill up the action, but Bardolph as a butt
to Falstaff's raillery, and the hostess in her wran-
gling scene with him, when his pockets had been
emptied as he was asleep in the tavern, give occasion
to scenes of infinite pleasantry: Poins is contrasted
from the rest of the gang, and as he is made the
companion of the prince, is very properly represented as a man of better qualities and morals than Falstaff's more immediate hangers-on and dependants.

The humour of Falstaff opens into full display
upon his very first introduction with the prince; the
incident of the robbery on the highway, the scene in
Eastcheap in consequence of that ridiculous encounter, and the whole of his conduct during the
action with Percy, are so exquisitely pleasant, that
upon the renovation of his dramatic life in the second
part of Henry the Fourth, I question if the humour
does not in part evaporate by continuation; at least
I am persuaded that it flattens a little in the outset,
and though his wit may not flow less copiously, yet
it comes with more labour, and is farther fetched.

The poet seems to have been sensible how difficult it was to preserve the vein as rich as at first, and has therefore strengthened his comic plot in the second play with several new recruits, who may take a share with Falstaff, to whom he no longer intrusts the whole burden of the humour. In the front of these auxiliaries stands Pistol, a character so new, whimsical, and extravagant, that if it were not for a commentator now living, whose very extraordinary researches amongst our old authors have supplied us with passages to illuminate the strange rhapsodies which Shakspeare has put into his mouth, I should, for one, have thought Ancient Pistol as wild and imaginary a being as Caliban; but I now perceive, by the help of these discoveries, that the character is made up in great part of absurd and fustian passages from many plays, in which Shakspeare *was versed, and perhaps* had been a performer: Pistol's dialogue is a tissue of old tags of bombast, like the middle comedy of the Greeks, which dealt in parody. I abate of my astonishment at the invention and originality of the poet, but it does not lessen my respect for his ingenuity. Shakspeare founded his bully in parody, Jonson copied his from nature, and the palm seems due to Bobadil upon a comparison with Pistol; Congreve copied a very happy likeness from Jonson, and by the fairest and most laudable imitation produced his Noll Bluff, one of the pleasantest humorists on the comic stage.

Shallow and Silence are two very strong auxiliaries to the second part of Falstaff's humours, and though they do not absolutely belong to his family, they are nevertheless near of kin, and derivatives from his stock: surely two pleasanter fellows never trode the stage: they not only contrast and play upon each other, but Silence sober and Silence tipsy make the most comical reverse in nature;

never was drunkenness so well introduced or so happily employed in any drama: the dialogue between Shallow and Falstaff, and the description given by the latter of Shallow's youthful frolics, are as true nature and as true comedy as man's invention ever produced: the recruits are also in the literal sense the recruits of the drama. These personages have the farther merit of throwing Falstaff's character into a new cast, and giving it the seasonable relief of variety.

Dame Quickly also in this second part resumes her rôle with great comic spirit, but with some variation of character, for the purpose of introducing a new member into the troop in the person of Doll Tearsheet, the common trull of the times. Though this part is very strongly coloured, and though the scene with her and Falstaff is of a loose as well as ludicrous nature, yet if we compare Shakspeare's conduct of this incident with that of the dramatic writers of his time, and even since his time, we must confess he has managed it with more than common care, and exhibited his comic hero in a very ridiculous light, without any of those gross indecencies which the poets of his age indulged themselves in without restraint.

The humour of the Prince of Wales is not so free and unconstrained as in the first part: though he still demeans himself in the course of his revels, yet it is with frequent marks of repugnance and self-consideration, as becomes the conqueror of Percy, and we see his character approaching fast towards a thorough reformation; but though we are thus prepared for the change that is to happen when this young hero throws off the reveller and assumes the king, yet we are not fortified against the weakness of pity, when the disappointment and banishment of Falstaff takes place, and the poet executes justice upon his inimitable delinquent, with all the rigour of an unrelenting moralist. The reader or spectator, who has accompanied Falstaff through his dramatic story, is in debt to him for so many pleasant moments, that all his failings, which should have raised contempt, have only provoked laughter, and he begins to think they are not natural to his character, but assumed for his amusement. With these impressions we see him delivered over to mortification and disgrace, and bewail his punishment with a sensibility, that is only due to the sufferings of the virtuous.

As it is impossible to ascertain the limits of Shakspeare's genius, I will not presume to say he could not have supported his humour, had he chosen to have prolonged his existence through the succeeding drama of Henry the Fifth: we may conclude, that no ready expedient presented itself to his fancy, and he was not apt to spend much pains in searching for such: he therefore put him to death, by which he fairly placed him out of the reach of his contemporaries, and got rid of the trouble and difficulty of keeping him up to his original pitch, if he had attempted to carry him through a third drama, after he had removed the Prince of Wales out of his company, and seated him on the throne. I cannot doubt but there were resources in Shakspeare's genius, and a latitude of humour in the character of Falstaff, which might have furnished scenes of admirable comedy by exhibiting him in his disgrace, and both Shallow and Silence would have been accessories to his pleasantry: even the field of Agincourt, and the distress of the king's army before the action, had the poet thought proper to have produced Falstaff on the scene, might have been as fruitful in comic incidents as the battle of Shrewsbury: this we can readily believe from the humours of Fluellen and Pistol, which he has woven into his drama; the former of

whom is made to remind us of Falstaff, in his dialogue with Captain Gower, when he tells him that—
' As Alexander is kill his friend Clytus, being in
his ales and his cups, so also Harry Monmouth,
being in his right wits and his goot judgments, is
turn away the fat Knight with the great pelly-doublet :
he was full of jests and gypes and knaveries and
mocks ; I am forget his name.—Sir John Falstaff.—
That is he.'—This passage has ever given me a
pleasing sensation, as it marks a regret in the poet
to part with a favourite character, and is a tender
farewell to his memory : it is also with particular
propriety that these words are put into the mouth of
Fluellen, who stands here as his substitute, and
whose humour, as well as that of Nym, may be said
to have arisen out of the ashes of Falstaff.

## NUMBER LXXIV.

I was surprised the other day to find our learned
poet Ben Jonson had been poaching in an obscure
collection of love-letters, written by the sophist Philostratus in a very rhapsodical style, merely for the
purpose of stringing together a parcel of unnatural
far-fetched conceits, more calculated to disgust a
man of Jonson's classic taste, than to put him upon
the humble task of copying them, and then fathering the translation.  The little poem he has taken
from this despicable sophist is now become a very
popular song, and is the ninth in his collection, entitled, ' The Forest.'
    I will take the liberty of inserting Jonson's trans-

lation, and compare it with the original, stanza by stanza—

### I.

Drink to me only with thine eyes,
　　And I will pledge with mine,
Or leave a kiss but in the cup,
　　And I'll not look for wine.

PHILOSTRATUS, Letter XXIV.

Ἐμοὶ δὲ μόνοις πρόπινε τοῖς ὅμμασιν—‘ Drink to me with thine eyes only.’ Εἰ δὲ βούλει, τοῖς χείλεσι προσφέρουσα, πλήρου φιλημάτων τὸ ἔκπωμα καὶ οὕτως δίδου. ‘ Or if thou wilt, putting the cup to thy lips, fill it with kisses, and so bestow it upon me.’

### II.

The thirst that from the soul doth rise,
　　Demands a drink divine;
But might I of Jove's nectar sip,
　　I would not change for thine.

PHIL. Letter XXV.

Ἐγὼ ἐπειδὰν ἴδω σε, διψῶ, καὶ τὸ ἔκπωμα κατέχων, τὸ μὲν οὐ προσάγω τοῖς χείλεσι, σοῦ δὲ οἶδα πίνων. ‘ I, as soon as I behold thee, thirst, and taking hold of the cup, do not indeed apply that to my lips for drink, but thee.’

### III.

I sent thee late a rosy wreath,
　　Not so much honouring thee,
As giving it a hope that there
　　It might not wither'd be.

PHIL. Letter XXX.

Πέπομφά σοι στέφανον ῥόδων, οὐ σὲ τιμῶν (καὶ τοῦτο μὲν γὰρ) ἀλλ' αὐτοῖς τι χαριζόμενος τοῖς ῥόδοις, ἵνα μὴ μαρανθῇ. ‘ I send thee a rosy wreath, not so much honouring thee (though this also is in my thoughts) as bestowing favour upon the roses, that so they might not be withered.’

### IV.

But thou thereon didst only breathe,
　　And sent'st it back to me,
Since when it grows and smells, I swear,
　　Not of itself, but thee.

PHIL. Letter XXXI.

Εἰ δὲ βούλει τί φίλῳ χαρίζεσθαι, τὰ λείψανα αὐτῶν ἀντίπεμψον, μηκέτι πνέοντα ῥόδον μόνον, ἀλλὰ καὶ σοῦ. ‘ If thou wou'dst do a kindness to thy lover, send back the reliques of the roses (I gave thee), for they will smell no longer of themselves only, but of thee.

When the learned poet published this love-song without any acknowledgment to Philostratus, I hope the reason of his omitting it was because he did not choose to call the public curiosity to a perusal of such unseemly and unnatural rhapsodies, as he had condescended to copy from.

Now I am upon the subject of Ben Jonson, I shall take notice of two passages in The Induction on the Stage prefixed to his play of *Bartholomew Fair*, in which he gives a sly glance at Shakspeare—' And then a substantial watch to have stolen in upon them, and taken them away with mistaking words, as the fashion is in the stage practice.' It is plain he has Dogberry and Verges in his eye, and no less so in the following, that he points his ridicule against Caliban and the romance of the *Tempest*—' If there be never a servant monster in the fair who can help it (he says), nor a nest of antics? He is loath to make nature afraid of his plays, like those that beget tales, tempests, and such-like drolleries, to mix his head with other men's heels.' If any of our commentators upon Shakspeare have anticipated my remark upon these instances of Jonson's propensities to carp at their favourite poet, I have overlooked the annotation, but when I find him recommending to his audience such a farrago of vulgar ribaldry as *Bartholomew Fair*, by pretending to exalt it above such exquisite productions as *The Tempest* and *Much Ado about Nothing*, it is an act of warrantable retaliation to expose his vanity.

It is not always however that he betakes himself to these masked attacks upon that sublime genius which he professed to admire almost to idolatry, it must be owned he sometimes meets him upon equal ground, and nobly contends with laudable emulation for the chaplet of victory: what I now particularly have in my eye is his *Masque of the Queens*.

Many ingenious observations have been given to the public upon Shakspeare's Imaginary Beings; his Caliban, Ariel, and all his family of witches, ghosts, and fairies, have been referred to as examples of his creative fancy, and with reason has his superiority been asserted in the fabrication of these preternatural machines; and as to the art with which he has woven them into the fables of his dramas, and the incidents he has produced by their agency, he is in these particulars still more indisputably unrivalled; the language he has given to Caliban, and no less characteristically to his Ariel, is so original, so inimitable, that it is more like magic than invention, and his fairy poetry is as happy as it can be: it were a jest to compare Æschylus's ghost of Darius, or any ghost that ever walked, with the perturbed spirit of Hamlet; great and merited encomiums have also been passed upon the weird sisters in that wonderful drama, and a decided preference given them over the famous Erichtho of Lucan: preferable they doubtless are, if we contemplate them in their dramatic characters, and take into our account the grand and awful commission, which they bear in that scene of tragic terror; but of their poetical superiority, simply considered, I have some doubts; let me add to this, that when the learned commentator was instancing Lucan's Erichtho, it is matter of some wonder with me, how he came to overlook Jonson's witches, in the *Masque of the Queens*.

As he has not however prevented me the honour of bringing these two poetic champions together into the lists, I will avail myself of the occasion, and leave it with the spectators to decide upon the contest. I will only, as their herald, give notice that the combatants are enchanters, and he that has no

taste for necromancy, nor any science in the terms
of the art, has no right to give his voice upon the
trial of skill.

### SHAKSPEARE.

*1st Witch.* Where hast thou been, sister?

*2d* ——— Killing swine.

*3d* ——— A sailor's wife had chesnuts in her lap,

And mouncht, and mouncht, and mouncht——Give me,
     quoth I!

Aroint thee, witch, the rump-fed ronyon cries.

Her husband's to Aleppo gone, master o' th' Tyger;

But in a sieve I'll thither sail,

And like a cat without a tail,

I'll do—I'll do—I'll do.

*2d Witch.* I'll give thee a wind.

*3d* ——— Thou art kind.

*1st* ——— And I another.

*3d* ——— I myself have all the other,

And the very points they blow,

All the quarters that they know,

I' th' shipman's card.

I will drain him dry as hay,

Sleep shall neither night nor day

Hang upon his pent-house lid;

He shall live a man forbid;

Weary sev'n-nights nine times nine

Shall he dwindle, peak, and pine;

Tho' his bark cannot be lost,

Yet it shall be tempest tost,

Look, what I have.

*2d Witch.* ——— Shew me, shew me.

*3d* ——— Here I have a pilot's thumb,

Wreckt as homeward he did come.

*1st Witch.* A drum, a drum!

Macbeth doth come.

*All.*    The weird sisters hand in hand,

Posters of the sea and land,

Thus do go about, about,

Thrice to thine and thrice to mine,

And thrice again to make up nine,

Peace! the charm's wound up.

### JONSON.

*Dame.* Well done, my hags!——

But first relate me what you have sought,

Where you have been, and what you have brought.

*1st Hag.* I have been all day looking after
A raven feeding upon a quarter;
And soon as she turned her beak to the south,
I snatch'd this morsel out of her mouth.

*2d Hag.* I last night lay all alone
O' th' ground to hear the mandrake groan,
And pluckt him up though he grew full low,
And as I had done the cock did crow.

*6th Hag.* I had a dagger; what did I with that?
Kill'd an infant to have his fat;
A piper it got at a church ale,
I bade him again blow wind in its tail.

*7th Hag.* A murderer yonder was hung in chains,
The sun and the wind had shrunk his veins;
I bit off a sinew, I clipt his hair,
I brought off his rags that danc'd in the air.

*8th Hag.* The scrich-owl's eggs, and the feathers black,
The blood of the frog, and the bone in his back,
I have been getting, and made of his skin
A purset to keep Sir Cranion in.

*9th Hag.* And I ha' been plucking (plants among)
Hemlock, henbane, adder's tongue,
Night-shade, moon-wort, libbard's bane;
And twice by the dogs was like to be ta'en.

*11th Hag.* I went to the toad, breeds under the wall,
I charm'd him out, and he came at my call,
I scratcht out the eyes of the owl before,
I tore the bat's wing.—What would you have more?

*Dame.* Yes, I have brought (to help our vows)
Horned poppy, cypress boughs,
The fig-tree wild, that grows on tombs,
And juice that from the larch-tree comes,
The basilisk's blood, and the viper's skin—
And now our orgies let's begin!

## SHAKSPEARE'S CHARM.

*1st Witch.* Thrice the brinded cat hath mew'd.
*2d* ———— Twice and once the hedge-pig whin'd.
*3d* ———— Harper cries, ' 'tis time ! 'tis time !'
*1st* ———— Round about the cauldron go,
In the poison'd entrails throw.
———Toad, that under the cold stone
Days and nights has thirty-one
Swelter'd venom sleeping got,
Boil thou first i' th' charmed pot.

*All.* Double, double, toil and trouble,
Fire burn and cauldron bubble!

   *2d Witch.* Fillet of a fenny snake
In the cauldron boil and bake:
Eye of newt and toe of frog,
Wool of bat and tongue of dog,
Adder's fork and blind worm's sting,
Lizard's leg and owlet's wing,
For a charm of powerful trouble,
Like a hell broth, boil and bubble.

   *All.* Double, double, toil and trouble,
Fire burn and cauldron bubble!

   *3d Witch.* Scale of dragon, tooth of wolf,
Witch's mummy, maw and gulf
Of the ravening salt-sea shark,
Root of hemlock, digg'd i' th' dark;
Liver of blaspheming Jew,
Gall of goat, and slips of yew
Sliver'd in the moon's eclipse,
Nose of Turk and Tartar's lips,
Finger of birth-strangled babe
Ditch deliver'd of a drab,
Make the gruel thick and slab;
Add thereto a tiger's chawdron
For the ingredients of our cauldron.

   *All.* Double, double, toil and trouble,
Fire burn and cauldron bubble!

   *1st Witch.* Cool it with a baboon's blood—
Then the charm is firm and good.

### Jonson's Charm.

The owl is abroad, the bat and the toad,
   And so is the cat-a-mountain,
The ant and the mole sit both in a hole,
   And frog peeps out of the fountain,
The dogs they do bay and the timbrels play,
   The spindle is now a-turning,
The moon it is red and the stars are fled,
   And all the sky is a burning.

### 2nd Charm.

Deep, oh deep, we lay thee to sleep,
We leave thee drink by, if thou chance to be dry,
Both milk and blood, the dew and the flood.

We breathe in thy bed, at the foot and the head;
We cover thee warm, that thou take no harm,
And when thou dost wake, dame earth shall quake, &c.

### 3d Charm.

A cloud of pitch, a spur and a switch,
  To haste him away, and a whirlwind play
Before and after, with thunder for laughter,
  And storms of joy, of the roaring boy,
    His head of a drake, his tail of a snake.

### 4th Charm.

About, about and about!
Till the mists arise and the lights fly out:
The images neither be seen nor felt,
The woollen burn and the waxen melt;
Sprinkle your liquors upon the ground,
And into the air : Around, around !
    Around, around !
    Around, around !
    Till a music sound,
    And the pace be found
    To which we may dance
    And our charms advance.

I should observe that these quotations from Jonson are selected partially, and not given in continuation, as they are to be found in the Masque, which is much too long to be given entire ; they are accompanied with a commentary by the author, full of demonological learning, which was a very courtly study in the time of James the First, who was an author in that branch of superstitious pedantry.

I am aware there is little to gratify the reader's curiosity in these extracts, and still less to distract his judgment in deciding between them : they are so far curious however as they shew how strongly the characters of the poets are distinguished even in these fantastic specimens ; Jonson dwells upon authorities without fancy, Shakspeare employs fancy, and creates authorities.

# NUMBER LXXV.

Usus vetusto genere, sed rebus novis.
PROLOG. PHÆD. FAB. lib. v.

BEN JONSON in his prologue to the comedy of *The Fox* says that he wrote it in the short space of five weeks, his words are—

> To these there needs no lie but this his creature,
> Which was two months since no feature;
> And tho' he dares give them five lives to mend it,
> 'Tis known five weeks fully penn'd it.

This he delivers in his usual vaunting style, spurning at the critics and detractors of his day, who thought to convict him of dulness by testifying in fact to his diligence. The magic movements of Shakspeare's muse had been so noted and applauded for their surprising rapidity, that the public had contracted a very ridiculous respect for hasty productions in general, and thought there could be no better test of a poet's genius, than the dispatch and facility with which he wrote ; Jonson therefore affects to mark his contempt of the public judgment for applauding hasty writers, in the couplet preceding those above quoted—

> And when his plays come out, think they can flout 'em
> With saying, He was a year about them.

But at the same time that he shews his contempt very justly, he certainly betrays a degree of weakness in boasting of his poetical dispatch, and seems to forget that he had noted Shakspeare with something less than friendly censure, for the very quality he is vaunting himself upon.

Several comic poets since his age have seemed to

pride themselves on the little time they expended on
their productions; some have had the artifice to
hook it in as an excuse for their errors, but it is no
less evident what share vanity has in all such apologies: Wycherly is an instance amongst these, and
Congreve tells of his expedition in writing the *Old
Bachelor*, yet the same man afterward, in his letter
to Mr. Dryden, pompously pronounces, that to write
one perfect comedy should be the labour of one entire life, produced from a concentration of talents
which hardly ever met in any human person.

After all it will be confessed, that the production
of such a drama as *The Fox*, in the space of five
weeks, is a very wonderful performance; for it must
on all hands be considered as the master-piece of a
very capital artist, a work, that bears the stamp of
elaborate design, a strong and frequently a sublime
vein of poetry, much sterling wit, comic humour,
happy character, moral satire, and unrivalled erudition; a work—

> Quod non imber edax, non aquilo impotens
> Possit diruere, aut innumerabilis
> Annorum series, et fuga temporum.

In this drama the learned reader will find himself
for ever treading upon classic ground: the foot of
the poet is so fitted and familiarized to the Grecian
sock, that he wears it not with the awkwardness of
an imitator, but with all the easy confidence and
authoritative air of a privileged Athenian; exclusive
of Aristophanes, in whose volume he is perfect, it
is plain that even the gleanings and broken fragments of the Greek stage had not escaped him; in
the very first speech of Volpone's, which opens the
comedy, and in which he rapturously addresses
himself to his treasure, he is to be traced most decidedly in the fragments of Menander, Sophocles,
and Euripides, in Theognis and in Hesiod, not to

mention Horace. To follow him through every one
would be tedious, and therefore I will give a sample
of one passage only; Volpone is speaking to his
gold—

> Thou being the best of things and far transcending
> All style of joy in children, parents, friends—
> Thy looks when they to Venus did ascribe,
> They should have given her twenty thousand Cupids,
> Such are thy beauties and our loves.

Let the curious reader compare this with the following fragment of Euripides's Bellerophon, and he
will find it almost a translation.

> Ὦ χρυσέ, δεξίωμα κάλλιστον βροτοῖς,
> Ὡς οὐδὲ μήτηρ ἡδονὰς τοίας ἔχει,
> Οὐ παῖδες ἀνθρώποισιν, οὐ φίλος πατήρ,
> Εἰ δὴ Κύπρις τοιοῦτον ὀφθαλμοῖς ὁρᾷ,
> Οὐ θαῦμ᾽ ἔρωτας μυρίους αὐτὴν τρέφειν.

Cicero made a selection of passages from the
Greek dramatic authors, which he turned into Latin
verse for the purpose of applying them, as occasion
should offer, either in his writings or pleadings, and
our learned countryman seems on his part to have
made the whole circle of Greek and Roman poets
his own, and naturalized them to our stage. If any
learned man would employ his leisure in following
his allusions through this comedy only, I should
think it would be no unentertaining task.

*The Fox* is indubitably the best production of its
author, and in some points of substantial merit,
yields to nothing which the English stage can oppose to it : there is a bold and happy spirit in the
fable, it is of moral tendency, female chastity and
honour are beautifully displayed, and punishment is
inflicted on the delinquents of the drama with strict
and exemplary justice : the characters of the Here-
dipetæ, depicted under the titles of birds of prey,
Voltore, Corbaccio, and Corvino, are warmly colour-

ed, happily contrasted, and faithfully supported from
the outset to the end. Volpone, who gives his name
to the piece, with a fox-like craftiness, deludes and
gulls their hopes, by the agency of his inimitable
Parasite, or (as the Greek and Roman authors expressed it) by his Fly, his Mosca; and in this finished portrait Jonson may throw the gauntlet to the
greatest masters of antiquity; the character is of
classic origin; it is found with the contemporaries
of Aristophanes, though not in any comedy of his
now existing; the Middle Dramatists seem to have
handled it very frequently, and in the New Comedy
it rarely failed to find a place; Plautus has it again
and again, but the aggregate merit of all his Para-
sites will not weigh in the scale against this single
Fly of our poet: the incident of his concealing
Bonario in the gallery, from whence he breaks in
upon the scene to the rescue of Celia and the detection of Volpone, is one of the happiest contrivances
which could possibly be devised, because, at the
same time that it produces the catastrophe, it does
not sacrifice Mosca's character in the manner most
villains are sacrificed in comedy, by making them
commit blunders, which do not correspond with the
address their first representation exhibits, and which
the audience has a right to expect from them throughout, of which the *Double Dealer* is amongst others a
notable instance. But this incident of Bonario's interference does not only not impeach the adroitness of
the Parasite, but it furnishes a very brilliant occasion
for setting off his ready invention and presence of
mind in a new and superior light, and serves to introduce the whole machinery of the trial and condemnation of the innocent persons before the court
of advocates: in this part of the fable the contrivance is inimitable, and here the poet's art is a study,
which every votarist of the dramatic muses ought to

pay attention and respect to; had the same address
been exerted throughout, the construction would
have been a matchless piece of art, but here we are
to lament the haste of which he boasts in his prologue, and that rapidity of composition, which he
appeals to as a mark of genius, is to be lamented as
the probable cause of incorrectness, or at least the
best and most candid plea in excuse of it: for who
can deny that nature is violated by the absurdity of
Volpone's unseasonable insults to the very persons,
who had witnessed falsely in his defence, and even
to the very advocate who had so successfully defended him? Is it in character for a man of his deep
cunning and long reach of thought to provoke those,
on whom his all depended, to retaliate upon him,
and this for the poor triumph of a silly jest? Certainly this is a glaring defect which every body must
lament, and which can escape nobody. The poet
himself knew the weak part of his plot, and vainly
strives to bolster t up by making Volpone exclaim
against his own folly—

I am caught in my own noose—

And again—

To make a snare for mine own neck, and run
My head into it wilfully with laughter!
When I had newly 'scap'd, was free and clear,
Out of mere wantonness! Oh, the dull devil
Was in this brain of mine, when I devis'd it,
And Mosca gave it second————
————These are my fine conceits!
I must be merry, with a mischief to me!
What a vile wretch was I, that could not bear
My fortune soberly! I must have my crotchets,
And my conundrums!

It is with regret I feel myself compelled to protest
against so pleasant an episode, as that which is carried on by Sir Politic Would-be and Peregrine, which
in fact produces a kind of double plot and catas-

trophe; this is an imperfection in the fable, which criticism cannot overlook, but Sir Politic is altogether so delightful a fellow, that it is impossible to give a vote for his exclusion; the most that can be done against him is, to lament that he has not more relation to the main business of the fable.

The judgment pronounced upon the criminals in the conclusion of the play is so just and solemn, that I must think the poet has made a wanton breach of character, and gained but a sorry jest by the bargain, when he violates the dignity of his court of judges by making one of them so abject in his flattery to the Parasite upon the idea of matching him with his daughter, when he hears that Volpone has made him his heir; but this is an objection, that lies within the compass of two short lines, spoken aside from the bench, and may easily be remedied by their omission in representation; it is one only, and that a very slight one, amongst those venial blemishes—

————quas incuria fudit.

It does not occur to me that any other remark is left for me to make upon this celebrated drama, that could convey the slightest censure; but very many might be made in the highest strain of commendation, if there was need of any more than general testimony to such acknowledged merit. *The Fox* is a drama of so peculiar a species, that it cannot be dragged into a comparison with the production of any other modern poet whatsoever; its construction is so dissimilar from any thing of Shakspeare's writing, that it would be going greatly out of our way, and a very gross abuse of criticism to attempt to settle the relative degrees of merit, where the characters of the writers are so widely opposite: in one we may respect the profundity of learning, in the other we must admire the sublimity of genius; to one we pay the tribute of understanding, to the other we surrender up the possession of our hearts; Shakspeare, with ten thousand spots about him, dazzles us with so bright a lustre, that we either cannot or will not see his faults; he gleams and flashes like a meteor, which shoots out of our sight before the eye can measure its proportions, or analyze its properties—but Jonson stands still to be surveyed, and presents so bold a front, and levels it so fully to our view, as seems to challenge the compass and the rule of the critic, and defy him to find out an error in the scale and composition of his structure.

Putting aside therefore any farther mention of Shakspeare, who was a poet out of all rule, and beyond all compass of criticism, one whose excellencies are above comparison, and his errors beyond number, I will venture an opinion that this drama of *The Fox*, is, critically speaking, the nearest to perfection of any one drama, comic or tragic, which the English stage is at this day in possession of.

# NUMBER LXXVI.

In my foregoing paper, when I remarked that Jonson in his comedy of *The Fox* was a close copier of the ancients, it occurred to me to say something upon the celebrated drama of *The Samson Agonistes*, which, though less beholden to the Greek poets in its dialogue than the comedy above-mentioned, is in all other particulars as complete an imitation of the ancient tragedy, as the distance of times and the difference of languages will admit of.

It is professedly built according to ancient rule and example, and the author, by taking Aristotle's definition of tragedy for his motto, fairly challenges the critic to examine and compare it by that test. His close adherence to the model of the Greek tragedy is in nothing more conspicuous than in the simplicity of his diction: in this particular he has curbed his fancy with so tight a hand, that, knowing as we do the fertile vein of his genius, we cannot but lament the fidelity of his imitation; for there is a harshness in the metre of his chorus, which to a certain degree seems to border upon pedantry and affectation: he premises that the measure is indeed of all sorts, but I must take leave to observe that in some places it is no measure at all, or such at least as the ear will not patiently endure, nor which any recitation can make harmonious. By casting out of his composition the strophe and antistrophe, those stanzas which the Greeks appropriated to singing, or, in one word, by making his chorus monostrophic, he has robbed it of that lyric beauty, which he was capable of bestowing in the highest perfection; and why he should stop short in this particular, when he had otherwise gone so far in imitation, is not easy to guess: for surely it would have been quite as natural to suppose those stanzas, had he written any, might be sung, as that all the other parts, as the drama now stands with a chorus of such irregular measure, might be recited or given in representation.

Now it is well known to every man conversant in the Greek theatre, how the chorus, which in fact is the parent of the drama, came, in process of improvement, to be woven into the fable, and from being at first the whole, grew in time to be only a part; the fable being simple, and the characters few, the striking part of the spectacle rested upon the singing and dancing of the interlude, if I may so call it, and to these the people were too long accustomed and too warmly attached, to allow of any reform for their exclusion; the tragic poet therefore never got rid of his Chorus, though the writers of the Middle Comedy contrived to dismiss theirs, and probably their fable being of a more lively character, their scenes were better able to stand without the support of music and spectacle than the mournful fable and more languid recitation of the tragedians. That the tragic authors laboured against the Chorus will appear from their efforts to expel Bacchus and his Satyrs from the stage, in which they were long time opposed by the audience, and at last, by certain ingenious expedients, which were a kind of compromise with the public, effected their point; this in part was brought about by the introduction of a fuller scene and a more active fable, but the Chorus, with its accompaniments, kept its place, and the poet, who seldom ventured upon introducing more than three speakers in the scene at the same time, qualified the sterility of his business by giving to the Chorus a share of the dialogue, who, at the same time that they furnished the stage with numbers, were not counted among the speaking characters, according to the rigour of the usage above mentioned. A man must be an enthusiast for antiquity, who can find charms in the dialogue part of a Greek Chorus, and reconcile himself to their unnatural and chilling interruptions of the action and pathos of the scene; I am fully persuaded they came there upon motives of expediency only, and kept their post upon the plea of long possession, and the attractions of spectacle and music: in short, nature was sacrificed to the display of art, and the heart gave up its feelings that the ear and eye might be gratified.

When Milton therefore takes the Chorus into his dialogue, excluding from his drama the lyric strophe and antistrophe, he rejects what I conceive to be its only recommendation, and which an elegant contemporary, in his imitations of the Greek tragedy, is more properly attentive to: at the same time, it cannot be denied that Milton's Chorus subscribes more to the dialogues, and harmonises better with the business of the scene, than that of any Greek tragedy we can now refer to.

I would now proceed to a review of the performance itself, if it were not a discussion, which the author of the Rambler has very ably prevented me in: respect however to an authority so high in criticism must not prevent me from observing, that, when he says—' This is the tragedy, which ignorance has admired, and bigotry applauded,' he makes it meritorious in any future critic to attempt at following him over the ground he has trode, for the purpose of discovering what those blemishes are, which he has found out by superior sagacity, and which others have so palpably overlooked, as to merit the disgraceful character of ignorance and bigotry.

The principal, and in effect the only, objection, which he states, is, ' that the poem *wants a middle*, since nothing passes between the first act and the last, that either hastens or delays the death of Samson.' This demands examination: the death of Samson I need not describe: it is a sudden, momentary event ; what can hasten or delay it, but the will of the person, who, by an exertion of miraculous strength, was to bury himself under the ruins of a structure, in which his enemies were assembled? To determine that will depends upon the impulse of his own spirit, or it may be upon the inspiration of Heaven : if there are any incidents in the body of the drama, which lead to this determination, and indicate an impulse, either natural or preternatural, such must be called leading incidents, and those

leading incidents will constitute a middle, or, in
more diffusive terms, the middle business of the
drama. Manoah, in his interview with Samson,
which the author of the Rambler denominates the
second act of the tragedy, tells him

> This day the Philistines a popular feast
> Here celebrate in Gaza, and proclaim
> Great pomp and sacrifice and praises loud
> To Dagon, as their God—

Here is information of a meeting of his enemies to
celebrate their idolatrous triumphs; an incident of
just provocation to the servant of the living God, an
opportunity perhaps for vengeance, either human or
divine; if it passes without notice from Samson, it
is not to be styled an incident; if, on the contrary,
he remarks upon it, it must be one—but Samson
replies—

> Dagon must stoop, and shall ere long receive
> Such a discomfit as shall quite despoil him
> Of all these boasted trophies won on me,
> And with confusion blank his worshippers.

Who will say the expectation is not here prepared
for some catastrophe, we know not what, but awful
it must be, for it is Samson which denounces the
downfal of the idol, it is God who inspires the
denunciation; the crisis is important, for it is that
which shall decide whether God or Dagon is to
triumph, it is in the strongest sense of the expression
—*dignus vindice nodus*—and therefore we may boldly
pronounce *Deus intersit!*

That this interpretation meets the sense of the
author is clear from the remark of Manoah, who is
made to say that he receives these words as a prophecy. Prophetic they are, and were meant to be
by the poet, who, in this use of his sacred prophecy,
imitates the heathen oracles, on which several of
their dramatic plots are constructed, as might be

shewn by obvious examples. The interview with Manoah then is conducive to the catastrophe, and the drama is not in this scene devoid of incident.

Delilah next appears, and if whatever tends to raise our interest in the leading character of the tragedy, cannot rightly be called episodical, the introduction of this person ought not to be accounted such, for who but this person is the cause and origin of all the pathos and distress of the story? The dialogue of this scene is moral, affecting, and sublime; it is also strictly characteristic.

The next scene exhibits the tremendous giant Harapha, and the contrast thereby produced is amongst the beauties of the poem, and may of itself be termed an important incident: that it leads to the catastrophe I think will not be disputed, and if it is asked in what manner, the Chorus will supply us with an answer—

> He will directly to the Lords I fear,
> And with malicious counsel stir them up
> Some way or other farther to afflict thee.

Here is another prediction connected with the plot, and verified by its catastrophe, for Samson is commanded to come to the festival and entertain the revellers with some feats of strength: these commands he resists, but obeys an impulse of his mind by going afterward, and thereby fulfils the prophetic declaration he had made to his father in the second act. What incident can shew more management and address in the poet, than this of Samson's refusing the summons of the idolaters, and obeying the visitation of God's Spirit.

And now I may confidently appeal to the judicious reader, whether the *Samson Agonistes* is so void of incident between the opening and conclusion as fairly to be pronounced *to want a middle*. Simple it is from first to last, simple perhaps to a degree of coldness in some of its parts; but to say that nothing passes between the first act and the last, which hastens or delays the death of Samson, is not correct, because the very incidents are to be found, which conduce to the catastrophe, and but for which it could not have come to pass.

The author of the Rambler professes to examine the *Samson Agonistes* according to the rule laid down by Aristotle for the disposition and perfection of a tragedy, and this rule he informs us is, that it should have a *beginning, a middle, and an end.* And is this the mighty purpose for which the authority of Aristotle is appealed to? If it be thus the author of the Rambler has read the Poetics, and this be the best rule he can collect from that treatise, I am afraid he will find it too short a measure for the poet he is examining, or the critic he is quoting. Aristotle had said, ' that every whole hath not amplitude enough for the construction of a tragic fable; now by a whole (adds he in the way of illustration), I mean that, which hath beginning, middle, and end.' This and no more is what he says upon beginning, middle, and end; and this which the author of the Rambler conceives to be a rule for tragedy, turns out to be merely an explanation of the word *whole,* which is only one term amongst many employed by the critic in his professed and complete definition of tragedy. I should add, that Aristotle gives a further explanation of the terms, beginning, middle, and end, which the author of the Rambler hath turned into English, but in so doing, he hath inexcusably turned them out of their original sense as well as language; as any curious critic may be convinced of, who compares them with Aristotle's words in the eighth chapter of the Poetics.

Of the poetic diction of the *Samson Agonistes* I have already spoken in general; to particularize

passages of striking beauty would draw me into too
great length; at the same time, not to pass over so
pleasing a part of my undertaking in absolute silence, I will give the following reply of Samson to
the Chorus—

> Wherever fountain or fresh current flow'd
> Against the eastern ray, translucent, pure
> With touch æthereal of Heaven's fiery rod,
> I drank, from the clear milky juice allaying
> Thirst, and refresh'd; nor envy'd them the grape
> Whose heads that turbulent liquor fills with fumes.

Of the character I may say in few words, that
Samson possesses all the terrific majesty of Prometheus chained, the mysterious distress of Œdipus,
and the pitiable wretchedness of Philoctetes. His
properties, like those of the first, are something
above human; his misfortunes, like those of the second, are derivable from the displeasure of Heaven,
and involved in oracles; his condition like that of
the last, is the most abject, which human nature can
be reduced to from a state of dignity and splendour.

Of the catastrophe there remains only to remark,
that it is of unparalleled majesty and terror.

# NUMBER LXXVII.

Dr. Samuel Johnson, in his life of Rowe, pronounces of 'The *Fair Penitent*, that it is one of the
most pleasing tragedies on the stage, where it still
keeps its turns of appearing, and probably will long
keep them, for that there is scarcely any work of any
poet at once so interesting by the fable, and so delightful by the language. The story,' he observes,
' is domestic, and therefore easily received by the

imagination, and assimilated to common life; the diction is exquisitely harmonious, and soft or sprightly as occasion requires.' Few people, I believe, will think this character of the *Fair Penitent* too lavish on the score of commendation; the high degree of public favour in which this tragedy has long stood, has ever attracted the best performers in its display. As there is no drama more frequently exhibited, or more generally read, I propose to give it a fair and impartial examination, jointly with the more unknown and less popular tragedy from which it is derived.

The *Fair Penitent* is in fable and character so closely copied from the *Fatal Dowry*, that it is impossible not to take that tragedy along with it; and it is matter of some surprise to me that Rowe should have made no acknowledgment of his imitation either in his dedication or prologue, or any where else that I am apprised of.

This tragedy of the *Fatal Dowry* was the joint production of Massinger and Nathaniel Field; it takes a wider compass of fable than the *Fair Penitent*, by which means it presents a very affecting scene at the opening, which discovers young Charalois attended by his friend Romont, waiting with a petition in his hand to be presented to the judges, when they shall meet, praying the release of his dead father's body, which had been seized by his creditors, and detained in their hands for debts he had incurred in the public service, as field-marshal of the armies of Burgundy. Massinger, to whose share this part of the tragedy devolved, has managed this pathetic introduction with consummate skill and great expression of nature; a noble youth in the last state of worldly distress, reduced to the humiliating yet pious office of soliciting an unfeeling and unfriendly judge to allow him to pay the solemn rites of burial to the remains of an illustrious father, who had fought his country's battles with glory, and had sacrificed life and fortune in defence of an ungrateful state, impresses the spectator's mind with pity and respect, which are felt through every passage of the play: one thing in particular strikes meat the opening of the scene, which is the long silence that the poet has artfully imposed upon his principal character (Charalois) who stands in mute sorrow with his petition in his hand, whilst his friend Romont, and his advocate Charmi, urge him to present himself to the judges and solicit them in person: the judges now make their entrance, they stop upon the stage: they offer him the fairest opportunity for tendering his petition and soliciting his suit; Charalois remains fixed and speechless: Romont, who is all eagerness in his cause, presses him again and again—

> Now put on your spirits—
> Now, Sir, lose not this offered means : their looks,
> Fix'd on you with a pitying earnestness,
> Invite you to demand their furtherance
> To your good purpose.

The judges point him out to each other ; they lament the misfortunes of his noble house ; they observe,

> It is young Charalois
> Son to the Marshal, from whom he inherits
> His fame and virtues only.
>  *Romont.* Hah ! They name you.
>  *Dulroy.* His father died in prison two days since.
>  *Rochfort.* Yes, to the shame of this ungrateful state
> That such a master in the art of war,
> So nobly and so highly meriting
> From this forgetful country, should, for want
> Of means to satisfy his creditors
> The sum he took up for the general good,
> Meet with an end so infamous.
>  *Romont.* Dare you ever hope for like opportunity ?

It is in vain ; the opportunity passes off, and Charalois opens not his mouth, nor even silently tenders his petition.

I have, upon a former occasion, both generally
and particularly observed upon the effects of dramatic silence; the stage cannot afford a more beautiful
and touching instance than this before us : to say it
is not inferior to the silence of Hamlet upon his first
appearance, would be saying too little in its favour.
I have no doubt but Massinger had this very case
in his thoughts, and I honour him no less for the
imitating, than I should have done for striking out
a silence so naturally and so delicately preserved.
What could Charalois have uttered to give him that
interest in the hearts of his spectators, which their
own conclusions during his affecting silence have
already impressed? No sooner are the judges gone,
than the ardent Romont again breaks forth—

> This obstinate spleen
> You think becomes your sorrow, and sorts well
> With your black suits.

This is Hamlet nimself, his *inky cloak*, and *customary
suits of solemn black.* The character of Charalois is
thus fixed before he speaks; the poet's art has given
the prejudice that is to bear him in our affections
through all the succeeding events of the fable ; and
a striking contrast is established between the undis-
cerning fiery zeal of Romont, and Charalois' fine
sensibility and high-born dignity of soul.

A more methodical and regular dramatist would
have stopped here, satisfied that the impression already made was fully sufficient for all the purposes
of his plot; but Massinger, according to the busy
spirit of the stage for which he wrote, is not alarmed
by a throng of incidents, and proceeds to open the
court and discuss the pleadings on the stage : the
advocate Charmi in a set harangue moves the judges
for dispensing with the rigour of the law in favour of
creditors, and for rescuing the Marshal's corpse out
of their clutches ; he is brow-beaten and silenced by

the presiding judge, old Novall: the plea is then taken up by the impetuous Romont, and urged with so much personal insolence, that he is arrested on the spot, put in charge of the officers of the court, and taken to prison. This is a very striking mode of introducing the set oration of Charalois: a son recounting the military achievements of a newly deceased father, and imploring mercy from his creditors and the law towards his unburied remains, now claims the attention of the court, who had been hitherto unmoved by the feeble formality of a hired pleader, and the turbulent passion of an enraged soldier. Charalois' argument takes a middle course between both; the pious feelings of a son, tempered by the modest manners of a gentleman: the creditors however are implacable, the judge is hostile, and the law must take its course.

> *Creditor.* 'Tis the city's doctrine:
> We stand bound to maintain it.
>
>    *Charalois.* Be constant in it;
> And since you are as merciless in your natures,
> As base and mercenary in your means
> By which you get your wealth, I will not urge
> The court to take away one scruple from
> The right of their laws, or one good thought
> In you to mend your disposition with.
> I know there is no music in your ears
> So pleasing as the groans of men in prison,
> And that the tears of widows, and the cries
> Of famished orphans, are the feasts that take you:
> That to be in your danger with more care
> Should be avoided than infectious air,
> The loath'd embraces of diseased women,
> A flatterer's poison, or the loss of honour.
> Yet rather than my father's reverend dust
> Shall want a place in that fair monument,
> In which our noble ancestors lie entomb'd,
> Before the court I offer up myself
> A prisoner for it: load me with those irons
> That have worn out his life; in my best strength
> I'll run to the encounter of cold hunger,
> And choose my dwelling where no sun dares enter,
> So he may be releas'd.

There was yet another incident, which the poet's passion for business and spectacle induced him to avail himself of, viz. the funeral of the Marshal; this he displays on the stage, with a train of captains and soldiers following the body of their general: Charalois and Romont, under custody of their gaolers appear as chief mourners, and a party of creditors are concerned in the group.

After this solemnity is dispatched, the poet proceeds to develop the amiable generosity of old Rochfort, who, being touched with the gallant spirit of Romont, and still more penetrated with the filial piety of young Charalois, delivers them both from imprisonment and distress, by discharging the debts of the Marshal and dismissing the creditors: this also passes before the eyes of the spectators. Before Charalois has given full expression to his gratitude for this extraordinary benefaction, Rochfort follows it with a farther act of bounty, which he introduces in the style of a request—

> Call in my daughter—Still I have a suit to you,
> Would you requite me—
> This is my only child.

Beaumelle, Rochfort's daughter, is presented to Charalois; the scene is hurried on with a precipitation almost without example: Charalois asks the lady,

> Fair Beaumelle, can you love me?
> *Beaumelle.* Yes, my lord.
> *Charalois.* You need not question me if I can you:
> You are the fairest virgin in Dijon,
> And Rochfort is your father.

The match is agreed upon as soon as proposed, and Rochfort hastens away to prepare the celebration.

In this cluster of incidents I must not fail to remark, that the poet introduces young Novall upon the scene, in the very moment when the short dialogue above quoted was passing: this Novall had before been exhibited as a suitor to Beaumelle, and his vain frivolous character had been displayed in a very ridiculous and contemptible light; he is now again introduced to be a witness of his own disappointment, and his only observation upon it is—*What's this change?*—Upon the exit of the father however he addresses himself to the lady, and her reply gives the alarming hint, that makes discovery of the fatal turn which the plot is now about to take; for when Novall, turning aside to Beaumelle, by one word—*Mistress!*—conveys the reproach of inconstancy, she replies,

> Oh, Servant! Virtue strengthen me!
> Thy presence blows round my affection's vane:
> You will undo me if you speak again.    *Exit.*

Young Novall is left on the scene with certain followers and dependants, which hang upon his fortune, one of which (Pontalier by name) a man under deep obligations to him, yet of an honest nature, advises him to an honourable renunciation of all farther hopes or attempts to avail himself of the affections of Beaumelle—

> Though you have sav'd my life,
> Rescu'd me often from my wants, I must not
> Wink at your follies, that will ruin you.
> You know my blunt way, and my love to truth:
> Forsake the pursuit of this lady's honour,
> Now you do see her made another man's.

This honourable advice is rejected with contempt: Novall, in whose mean bosom there does not seem a trace of virtue, avows a determined perseverance; and the poet having in this hasty manner completed these inauspicious nuptials, closes the second act of his tragedy.

# NUMBER LXXVIII.

WE have now expended two entire acts of *The Fatal Dowry*, in advancing to that period in the fable, at which the tragedy of *The Fair Penitent* opens. If the author of this tragedy thought it necessary to contract Massinger's plot, and found one upon it of a more regular construction, I know not how he could do this any otherwise, than by taking up the story at the point where we have now left it, and throwing the antecedent matter into narration; and though these two prefatory acts are full of very affecting incidents, yet the pathos which properly appertains to the plot, and conduces to the catastrophe of the tragedy, does not in strictness take place before the event of the marriage. No critic will say that the pleadings before the judges, the interference of the creditors, the distresses of Charalois, or the funeral of the Marshal, are necessary parts of the drama; at the same time no reader will deny (and neither could Rowe himself overlook) the effect of these incidents: he could not fail to foresee that he was to sacrifice very much of the interest of his fable, when he was to throw that upon narration, which his original had given in spectacle; and the loss was more enhanced by falling upon the hero of the drama; for who that compares Charalois, at the end of the second act of Massinger's, with Rowe's Altamont at the opening scene of *The Fair Penitent*, can doubt which character has most interest with the spectators? We have seen the former in all the most amiable offices which filial piety could perform; enduring insults from his inveterate oppressors, and voluntarily surrendering himself to a prison to ransom the dead body of his father from unrelenting creditors. Altamont presents himself before us in his wedding-suit, in the splendour of fortune, and at the summit of happiness: he greets us with a burst of exultation—

> Let this auspicious day be ever sacred,
> No mourning, no misfortunes happen on it;
> Let it be mark'd for triumphs and rejoicings!
> Let happy lovers ever make it holy,
> Choose it to bless their hopes and crown their wishes;
> This happy day, that gives me my Calista!

The rest of the scene is employed by him and Horatio alternately in recounting the benefits conferred upon them by the generous Sciolto; and the very same incident of the seizure of his father's corpse by the creditors, and his redemption of it, is recited by Horatio—

> When his hard creditors,
> Urg'd and assisted by Lothario's father
> (Foe to thy house and rival of their greatness),
> By sentence of the cruel law forbade
> His venerable corpse to rest in earth,
> Thou gav'st thyself a ransom for his bones;
> With piety uncommon didst give up
> Thy hopeful youth to slaves who ne'er knew mercy.

It is not however within the reach of this, or any other description, to place Altamont in that interesting and amiable light, as circumstances have already placed Charalois; the happy and exulting bridegroom may be an object of our congratulation, but the virtuous and suffering Charalois engages our pity, love, and admiration. If Rowe would have his audience credit Altamont for that filial piety, which marks the character he copied from, it was a small oversight to put the following expression into his mouth—

> Oh, great Sciolto! Oh, my more than father!

A closer attention to character would have reminded him that it was possible for Altamont to express his gratitude to Sciolto, without setting him above a father, to whose memory he had paid such devotion.

From this contraction of his plot, by the defalcation of so many pathetic incidents, it became impossible for the author of the *Fair Penitent* to make his Altamont the hero of his tragedy, and the leading part is taken from him by Horatio, and even by Lothario throughout the drama. There are several other reasons which concur to sink Altamont upon the comparison with Charalois, the chief of which arises from the captivating colours in which Rowe has painted his libertine: on the contrary, Massinger gives a contemptible picture of his young Novall; he makes him not only vicious, but ridiculous; in foppery and impertinence he is the counterpart of Shakspeare's Osrick; vain-glorious, purse-proud, and overbearing amongst his dependants; a spiritless poltroon in his interview with Romont. Lothario (as Johnson observes) ' with gaiety which cannot be hated, and bravery which cannot be despised, retains too much of the spectator's kindness.' His high spirit, brilliant qualities, and fine person, are so described, as to put us in danger of false impressions in his favour, and to set the passions in opposition to the moral of the piece: I suspect that the gallantry of Lothario makes more advocates for Calista than she ought to have. There is another consideration, which operates against Altamont, and it is an indelicacy in his character, which the poet should have provided against: he marries Calista with the full persuasion of her being averse to the match; in his first meeting with Sciolto he says—

Oh! could I hope there was one thought of Altamont,
One kind remembrance in Calista's breast—
————I found her cold

As a dead lover's statue on his tomb;
A rising storm of passion shook her breast,
Her eyes a piteous shower of tears let fall,
And then she sigh'd as if her heart were breaking.
With all the tenderest eloquence of love
I begg'd to be a sharer in her grief;
But she, with looks averse and eyes that froze me,
Sadly replied, her sorrows were her own,
Nor in a father's power to dispose of.

I am aware that Sciolto attempts to parry these
facts, by an interpretation too gross and unbecoming
for a father's character, and only fit for the lips of a
Lothario; but yet it is not in nature to suppose that
Altamont could mistake such symptoms, and it fixes
a meanness upon him which prevails against his character throughout the play. Nothing of this sort
could be discovered by Massinger's bridegroom, for
the ceremony was agreed upon and performed at the
very first interview of the parties; Beaumelle gave
a full and unreserved assent, and though her character suffers on the score of hypocrisy on that account, yet Charalois is saved by it: less hypocrisy
appears in Calista, but her's is the deeper guilt, because she was already dishonoured by Lothario, and
Beaumelle's coquetry with Novall had not yet reached
the length of criminality. Add to this, that Altamont appears in the contemptible light of a suitor,
whom Calista had apprized of her aversion, and to
whom she had done a deliberate act of dishonour,
though his person and character must have been
long known to her. The case is far otherwise between Charalois and Beaumelle, who never met before, and every care is taken by the poet to save his
hero from such a deliberate injury, as might convey
contempt; with this view the marriage is precipitated; nothing is allowed to pass that might open
the character of Charalois to Beaumelle: she is hurried into an assignation with Novall immediately

upon her marriage; every art of seduction is employed by her confidante Bellaperte, and Aymer the parasite of Novall, to make this meeting criminal; she falls the victim of passion, and when detection brings her to a sense of her guilt, she makes this penitent and pathetic appeal to Charalois—

> Oh my fate!
> That never would consent that I should see
> How worthy thou wert both of love and duty,
> Before I lost you; and my misery made
> The glass in which I now behold your virtue——
> With justice therefore you may cut me off,
> And from your memory wash the remembrance
> That e'er I was; like to some vicious purpose,
> Which in your better judgment you repent of,
> And study to forget—
> ————Yet you shall find,
> Tho' I was bold enough to be a strumpet,
> I dare not yet live one: let those fam'd matrons,
> That are canoniz'd worthy of our sex,
> Transcend me in their sanctity of life,
> I yet will equal them in dying nobly,
> Ambitious of no honour after life,
> But that, when I am dead, you will forgive me.

Compare this with the conduct of Calista, and then decide which frail fair-one has the better title to the appellation of a *Penitent*, and which drama conveys the better moral by its catastrophe.

There is indeed a grossness in the older poet, which his more modern imitator has refined; but he has only sweetened the poison, not removed its venom; nay, by how much more palatable he has made it, so much more pernicious it is become in his tempting sparkling cup, than in the coarse deterring dose of Massinger.

Rowe has no doubt greatly outstepped his original in the striking character of Lothario, who leaves Novall as far behind him as Charalois does Altamont: it is admitted then that Calista has as good a plea as any wanton could wish, to urge for her cri-

minality with Lothario, and the poet has not spared
the ear of modesty in his exaggerated description of
the guilty scene; every luxurious image, that his
inflamed imagination could crowd into the glowing
rhapsody, is there to be found, and the whole is recited in numbers so flowing and harmonious, that
they not only arrest the passions, but the memory
also, and perhaps have been, and still can be, as generally repeated as any passage in English poetry.
Massinger, with less elegance, but not with less regard to decency, suffers the guilty act to pass within
the course of his drama; the greater refinement of
manners in Rowe's day did not allow of this, and he
anticipated the incident; but when he revived the
recollection of it by such a studied description, he
plainly shewed that it was not from moral principle
that he omitted it; and if he has presented his heroine to the spectators with more immediate delicacy during the compass of the play, he has at the
same time given her greater depravity of mind; her
manners may be more refined, but her principle is
fouler than Beaumelle's. Calista, who yielded to
the gallant gay Lothario, *hot with the Tuscan grape*,
might perhaps have disdained a lover who addressed
her in the holiday language which Novall uses to
Beaumelle—

> Best day to nature's curiosity!
> Star of Dijon, the lustre of all France!
> Perpetual Spring dwell on thy rosy cheeks,
> Whose breath is perfume to our continent;
> See Flora trimm'd in her varieties!—
> No Autumn, nor no Age ever approach
> This heavenly piece, which Nature having wrought,
> She lost her needle, and did then despair
> Ever to work so lively and so fair.

The letter of Calista (which brings about the discovery by the poor expedient of Lothario's dropping it
and Horatio's finding it) has not even the merit of

being characteristically wicked, and is, both in its matter and mode, below tragedy. It is *Lothario's cruelty has determined her to yield a perfect obedience to her father, and give her hand to Altamont, in spite of her weakness for the false Lothario.*——If the lady had given her *perfect obedience* its true denomination, she had called it a most dishonourable compliance; and if we may take Lothario's word (who seems full correct enough in describing facts and particulars), she had not much cause to complain of his being false; for he tells Rossano——

> I lik'd her, would have marry'd her,
> But that it pleas'd her father to refuse me,
> To make this honourable fool her husband.

It appears by this that Lothario had not been *false* to her in the article of marriage, though he might have been *cruel* to her on the score of passion, which indeed is confest on his part with as much *cold indifference*, as the most barefaced avowal could express.——But to return to the letter: she proceeds to tell him—' that she could almost wish she had that heart, and that honour to bestow with it which he has robbed her of.'——But, lest this half wish should startle him, she adds—' But oh! I fear, could I retrieve them, I should again be undone by the too faithless, yet too lovely Lothario.'——This must be owned as full a reason as she could give, why she should only *almost wish* for her lost honour, when she would make such a use of it, if she had it again at her disposal.   And yet the very next paragraph throws every thing into contradiction, for she tells him—' this is the last weakness of her pen, and to-morrow shall be the last in which she will indulge her eyes.'   If she could keep to that resolution, I must think the recovery of her innocence would have been worth a whole wish, and many a wish; unless we are to suppose she was so devoted to guilt, that she could take delight in reflecting upon it: this is a state of depravity, which human nature hardly ever attains, and seems peculiar to Calista. She now grows very humble, and concludes in a style well suited to her humility—'Lucilla shall conduct you, if you are kind enough to let me see you; it shall be the last trouble you shall meet with from —the lost Calista.'

It was very ill done of Horatio's curiosity to read this letter, and I must ever regret that he has so unhandsomely exposed a lady's private correspondence to the world.

***

## NUMBER LXXIX.

THOUGH the part which Horatio takes in the business of the drama, is exactly that which falls to the share of Romont in the *Fatal Dowry*, yet their characters are of a very different cast; for as Rowe had bestowed the fire and impetuosity of Romont upon his Lothario, it was a very judicious opposition to contrast it with the cool deliberate courage of the sententious Horatio, the friend and brother-in-law of Altamont.

When Horatio has read Calista's letter, which Lothario had dropped (an accident which more frequently happens to gentlemen in comedies than in tragedies), he falls into a very long meditation, and closes it with putting this question to himself:

What if I give this paper to her father?
It follows that his justice dooms her dead,
And breaks his heart with sorrow; hard return
For all the good his hand has heap'd on us!
Hold, let me take a moment's thought—

At this moment he is interrupted in his reflections by
the presence of Lavinia, whose tender solicitude
fills up the remaining part of the dialogue, and concludes the act without any decisive resolution on the
part of Horatio; an incident well contrived, and
introduced with much dramatic skill and effect:
though pressed by his wife to disclose the cause of
his uneasiness, he does not impart to her the fatal
discovery he has made; this also is well in character. Upon his next entrance he has withdrawn
himself from the company, and being alone, resumes
his meditation—

> What, if, while all are here intent on revelling,
> I privately went forth and sought Lothario?
> This letter may be forg'd; perhaps the wantonness
> Of his vain youth to stain a lady's fame;
> Perhaps his malice to disturb my friend.
> Oh! no, my heart forebodes it must be true.
> Methought e'en now I mark'd the starts of guilt
> That shook her soul, tho' damn'd dissimulation
> Screen'd her dark thoughts, and set to public view
> A specious face of innocence and beauty.

This soliloquy is succeeded by the much-admired
and striking scene between him and Lothario; rigid
criticism might wish to abridge some of the sententious declamatory speeches of Horatio, and shorten
the dialogue to quicken the effect; but the moral
sentiment and harmonious versification are much too
charming to be treated as intruders, and the author
has also struck upon a natural expedient for prolonging the dialogue, without any violence to probability, by the interposition of Rossano, who acts
as a mediator between the hostile parties. This
interposition is farther necessary to prevent a decisive rencounter, for which the fable is not ripe;
neither would it be proper for Horatio to anticipate
the revenge, which is reserved for Altamont: the

altercation, therefore, closes with a challenge from Lothario—

> West of the town a mile, amongst the rocks,
> Two hours ere noon to-morrow I expect thee;
> Thy single hand to mine.

The place of meeting is not well ascertained, and the time is too long deferred for strict probability; there are, however, certain things in all dramas, which must not be too rigidly insisted upon, and, provided no extraordinary violence is done to reason and common sense, the candid critic ought to let them pass: this I take to be a case in point; and though Horatio's cool courage and ready presence of mind are not just the qualities to reconcile us to such an oversight, yet I see no reason to be severe upon the incident, which is followed by his immediate recollection—

> Two hours ere noon to-morrow! Hah! Ere that
> He sees Calista.—Oh! unthinking fool!
> What if I urg'd her with the crime and danger?
> If any spark from Heav'n remain unquench'd
> Within her breast, my breath perhaps may wake it.
> Could I but prosper there, I would not doubt
> My combat with that loud vain-glorious boaster.

Whether this be a measure altogether in character with a man of Horatio's good sense and discretion, I must own is matter of doubt with me. I think he appears fully satisfied of her actual criminality; and in that case it would be more natural for him to lay his measures for intercepting Lothario, and preventing the assignation, than to try his rhetoric in the present crisis upon the agitated mind of Calista. As it has justly occurred to him, that he has been overreached by Lothario in the postponement of the duel, the measure I suggest would naturally tend to hasten that rencounter. Now, though the business of the drama may require an explanation between

Horatio and Calista, whereupon to ground an occasion for his interesting quarrel with Altamont, yet I
do not see any necessity to make that a premedi-
tated explanation, nor to sacrifice character by a measure that is inconsistent with the better judgment of
Horatio.    The poet, however, has decreed it otherwise, and a deliberate interview with Calista and Horatio accordingly takes place. This, although introduced with a solemn invocation on his part, is very
clumsily conducted—

> Teach me, some Power! that happy art of speech
> To dress my purpose up in gracious words,
> Such as may softly steal upon her soul,
> And never waken the tempestuous passions.

Who can expect, after this preparation, to hear
Horatio thus break his secret to Calista?

> Lothario and Calista!—Thus they join
> Two names which Heav'n decreed should never meet.
> Hence have the talkers of this populous city
> A shameful tale to tell for public sport,
> Of an unhappy beauty, a false fair-one,
> Who plighted to a noble youth her faith,
> When she had giv'n her honour to a wretch.

This I hold to be totally out of nature; first, because
it is a palpable departure from his resolution to use
*gracious words*; next, because it has a certain tendency to produce rage and not repentance; and
thirdly, because it is founded in exaggeration and
falsehood; for how is he warranted to say that the
story is the public talk and sport of the city? If it
were so, what can this interference avail? why seek
this interview?

> Why come to tell her how she might be happy?
> To soothe the secret anguish of her soul?
> To comfort that fair mourner, that forlorn one,
> And teach her steps to know the paths of peace?

No judge of nature will think he takes the means to
lead her into the *paths of peace*, by hurrying her to

the very brink of desperation. I need not enlarge upon this observation, and shall therefore only remark, that the scene breaks up, as might be expected, with the following proof of her penitence, and his success in persuasion—

> Henceforth, thou officious fool,
> Meddle no more, nor dare, e'en on thy life,
> To breathe an accent that may touch my virtue :
> I am myself the guardian of my honour,
> And will not bear so insolent a monitor.

Let us now inquire how Romont (the Horatio of Massinger) conducts this incident, a character from whom less discretion is to be expected than from his philosophical successor. Romont himself discovers Beaumelle and Novall engaged in the most wanton familiarities, and, with a warmth suitable to his zeal, breaks up the amorous conference by driving Novall off the scene with ineffable contempt: he then applies himself to the lady, and with a very natural and manly spirit says,

> ———— I respect you
> Not for yourself, but in remembrance of
> Who is your father, and whose wife you now are.

She replies to him with contempt and ridicule: he resumes the same characteristic strain he set out with, and proceeds—

> My intents,
> Madam, deserve not this ; nor do I stay
> To be the whetstone of your wit : preserve it
> To spend on such as know how to admire
> Such colour'd stuff. In me there is now speaks to you
> As true a friend and servant to your honour,
> And one that will with as much hazard guard it,
> As ever man did goodness. But then, lady,
> You must endeavour, not alone to be,
> But to appear worthy such love and service.

We have just now heard Horatio reproach Calista with the reports that were circulated against her re-

putation; let us compare it with what Romont says
upon the same subject—

> But yet be careful
> Detraction's a bold monster, and fears not
> To wound the fame of princes, if it find
> But any blemish in their lives to work on.
> But I'll be plainer with you: had the people
> Been learnt to speak but what even now I saw,
> Their malice out of that would raise an engine
> To overthrow your honour.   In my sight,
> With yonder painted fool I frighted from you,
> You us'd familiarity beyond
> A modest entertainment: you embrac'd him
> With too much ardour for a stranger, and
> Met him with kisses neither chaste nor comely:
> But learn you to forget him, as I will
> Your bounties to him; you will find it safer
> Rather to be uncourtly than immodest.

What avails it to attempt drawing a comparison between this conduct and that of Horatio's, where no
comparison is to be made? I leave it to the reader,
and decline a task at once so unnecessary and ungrateful.

When Romont finds no impression is to be made
upon Beaumelle, he meets her father, and immediately falls into the same reflection that Horatio
had struck upon—

> Her father!—Hah!
> How if I break this to him?  Sure it cannot
> Meet with an ill construction.  His wisdom,
> Made powerful by the authority of a father,
> Will warrant and give privilege to his counsels.
> It shall be so.

If this step needs excuse, the reader will consider
that it is a step of prevention.  The experiment,
however, fails, and he is rebuffed with some asperity
by Rochfort; this draws on a scene between him
and Charalois, which, as it is too long to transcribe,
so it is throughout too excellent to extract any part
from it.  I can only express my surprise that the

author of *The Fair Penitent*, with this scene before him, could conduct his interview between Altamont and Horatio upon a plan so widely different and so much inferior: I must suppose he thought it a strong incident to make Altamont give a blow to his friend, else he might have seen an interview carried on with infinitely more spirit, both of language and character, between Charalois and Romont, in circumstances exactly similar, where no such violence was committed, or even meditated. Was it because Pierre had given a blow to Jaffier, that Altamont was to repeat the like indignity to Horatio, for a woman, of whose aversion he had proofs not to be mistaken? Charalois is a character at least as high and irritable as Altamont, and Romont is out of all comparison more rough and plain-spoken than Horatio: Charalois might be deceived into an opinion of Beaumelle's affection for him; Altamont could not deceive himself into such a notion, and the lady had testified her dislike of him in the strongest terms, accompanied with symptoms which he himself had described as indicating some rooted and concealed affliction: could any solution be more natural than what Horatio gives? Novall was a rival so contemptible, that Charalois could not, with any degree of probability, consider him as an object of his jealousy; it would have been a degradation of his character, had he yielded to such a suspicion: Lothario, on the contrary, was of all men living the most to be apprehended by a husband, let his confidence or vanity be ever so great. Rowe, in his attempt to *surprise*, has sacrificed nature and the truth of character for stage effect; Massinger, by preserving both nature and character, has conducted his friends through an angry altercation with infinitely more spirit, more pathos, and more dramatic effect, and yet dismissed them with the following

animated and affecting speech from Charalois to his
friend :

> Thou'rt not my friend ;
> Or being so, thou'rt mad.    I must not buy
> Thy friendship at this rate.    Had I just cause
> Thou know'st I durst pursue such injury
> Thro' fire, air, water, earth, nay, were they all
> Shuffled again to chaos ; but there's none.
> Thy skill, Romont, consists in camps, not courts.
> Farewell, uncivil man ! let's meet no more :
> Here our long web of friendship I untwist.
> Shall I go whine, walk pale, and lock my wife
> For nothing from her birth's free liberty,
> That open'd mine to me ?    Yes ; if I do,
> The name of cuckold then dog me with scorn :
> I am a Frenchman, no Italian born.
>                                                    [Exit.

It is plain that Altamont at least was an exception
to this remark upon Italian husbands.    I shall pursue this comparison no farther, nor offer any other
remark upon the incident of the blow given by Altamont, except with regard to Horatio's conduct upon
receiving it ; he draws his sword, and immediately
suspends resentment upon the following motive :

> Yet hold ! By heav'n, his father's in his face !
> Spite of my wrongs, my heart runs o'er with tenderness,
> And I could rather die myself than hurt him.

We must suppose it was the martial attitude that
Altamont had put himself into, which brought the
resemblance of his father so strongly to the observation of Horatio, otherwise it was a very unnatural
moment to recollect it in, when he had just received
the deepest insult one man can give to another ; it
is however worth a remark, that this father of Altamont should act on both sides, and yet miscarry in
his mediation ; for it is but a few passages before
that Altamont says to Horatio,

> Thou wert my father's friend ; he lov'd thee well ;
> A venerable mark of him
> Hangs round thee, and protects thee from my vengeance.
> I cannot, dare not, lift my sword against thee.

What this *mark* was is left to conjecture; but it is plain it was as seasonable for Horatio's rescue at this moment, as it was for Altamont a few moments after, who had certainly overlooked it when he struck the very friend against whom he could not, dared not *lift his sword.*

When Lavinia's entrance had parted Altamont and Horatio, her husband complains to her of the ingratitude with which he has been treated, and says—

> He who was all to me, child, brother, friend,
> With barbarous, bloody malice, sought my life.

These are very extraordinary terms for a man like Horatio to use, and seem to convey a charge very unfit for him to make, and of a very different nature from the hasty insult he had received; in fact it appears as if the blow had totally reversed his character, for the resolution he takes in consequence of this personal affront, is just such a one as would be only taken by the man who dared not to resent it—

> From Genoa, from falsehood and inconstancy,
> To some more honest distant clime we'll go;
> Nor will I be beholden to my country
> For aught but thee, the partner of my flight.

That Horatio's heroism did not consist in the ready forgiveness of injuries, is evident from the obstinate sullenness with which he rejects the penitent apologies of Altamont in the farther progress of the play; I am at a loss therefore to know what colour the poet meant to give his character by disposing him to quit his country with this insult unatoned for, and the additional stigma upon him of running away from his appointment with Lothario for the next morning *amongst the rocks.* Had he meant to bring him off upon the repugnance he felt of resenting any injury against the son of a father, whose image was so visible *in his face,* that his 'heart ran o'er with fondness

in spite of his wrongs, and he could rather die than
hurt him;' surely that image would have interceded
no less powerfully for him, when, penetrated with
remorse, he intercedes for pity and forgiveness, and
even faints at his feet with agony at his unrelenting
obduracy: it would be unfair to suppose he was more
like his father when he had dealt him an insulting
blow, than when he was atoning for an injury by the
most ample satisfaction and submission.

This is the light in which the conduct of Horatio
strikes me; if I am wrong, I owe an atonement to
the manes of an elegant poet, which, upon conviction of my error, I will study to pay in the fullest
manner I am able.

It now remains only to say a few words upon the
catastrophe, in which the author varies from his
original, by making Calista destroy herself with a
dagger, put into her hand for that purpose by her
father. If I am to moralize upon this proceeding of
Sciolto, I know full well the incident cannot bear up
against it: a Roman father would stand the discussion better than a Christian one; and I also know
that the most natural expedient is unluckily a most
undramatic one; yet the poet did not totally overlook it, for he makes Sciolto's first thought turn
upon a convent, if I rightly understand the following
passage—

> Hence from my sight! thy father cannot bear thee:
> Fly with thy infamy to some dark cell,
> Where, on the confines of eternal night,
> Mourning, misfortunes, cares, and anguish, dwell;
> Where ugly Shame hides her opprobrious head,
> And Death and Hell detested rule maintain;
> There howl out the remainder of thy life,
> And wish thy name may be no more remember'd.

Whilst I am transcribing these lines a doubt strikes
me that I have misinterpreted them, and yet Calista's answer seems to point to the meaning I had

suggested; perhaps, however, they are mere ravings in fine numbers without any determinate idea; whatever they may be, it is clear they do not go to the length of death: he tells Altamont, as soon as she is departed—

> I wo' not kill her;
> Yet by the ruin she has brought upon us,
> The common infamy that brands us both,
> She sha' not 'scape.

He seems in this moment to have formed the resolution, which he afterward puts into execution; he prompts her to self-murder, and arms her for the act: this may save the spectators a sight too shocking to behold, but does it convey less horror to the heart, than if he had put her to death with his own hand? A father killing his child for incontinence with the man whom he had not permitted to marry her, when he solicited his consent, is an act too monstrous to reflect upon: is that father less a monster, who, deliberately and after full reflection, puts a dagger into her hand and bids her commit self-murder? I should humbly conceive the latter act a degree in guilt beyond the former; especially when I hear that father coolly demanding of his victim, if she has reflected upon what may happen after death—

> Hast thou consider'd what may happen after it?
> How thy account may stand, and what to answer?

A parent surely would turn that question upon his own heart, before he precipitated his unprepared child to so awful and uncertain an account: rage and instant revenge may find some plea: sudden passion may transport even a father to lift his hand against his own offspring; but this act of Sciolto has no shelter but in heathen authority—

> 'Tis justly thought, and worthy of that spirit,
> That dwelt in ancient Latian breasts, when Rome
> Was mistress of the world.

Did ever poetry beguile a man into such an allusion?
And to what does that piece of information tend,
*that Rome was mistress of the world?* If this is human nature, it would almost tempt one to reply in
Sciolto's own words—

> I could curse nature.

But it is no more like nature, than the following sentiments of Calista are like the sentiments of a *Penitent* or a *Christian:*

> That I must die it is my only comfort:
> Death is the privilege of human nature,
> And life without it were not worth our taking.

And again,

> Yet Heav'n, who knows our weak imperfect natures,
> How blind with passions, and how prone to evil,
> Makes not too strict inquiry for offences,
> But is aton'd by penitence and prayer.
> Cheap recompense! here 'twould not be receiv'd;
> Nothing but blood can make the expiation.

Such is the catastrophe of Rowe's *Fair Penitent,* such
is the representation he gives us of human nature,
and such the moral of his tragedy.

I shall conclude with an extract or two from the
catastrophe of *The Fatal Dowry;* and first, for the
*penitence* of Beaumelle, I shall select only the following speech, addressed to her husband:

> I dare not move you
> To hear me speak. I know my fault is far
> Beyond qualification or excuse;
> That 'tis not fit for me to hope, or you
> To think of mercy, only I presume
> To entreat you would be pleas'd to look upon
> My sorrow for it, and believe these tears
> Are the true children of my grief, and not
> A woman's cunning.

I need not point out the contrast between this and
the quotations from Calista. It will require a longer
extract to bring the conduct of Rochfort into com-

parison with that of Sciolto : the reader will observe
that Novall's dead body is now on the scene, Charalois, Beaumelle, and Rochfort her father, are present.
The charge of adultery is urged by Charalois, and
appeal is made to the justice of Rochfort in the case.

> *Rochfort.* What answer makes the prisoner?
> *Beaumelle.* I confess
> The fact I'm charg'd with, and yield myself
> Most miserably guilty.
> *Rochfort.* Heaven take mercy
> Upon your soul then! It must leave your body—
> —Since that the politic law provides that servants,
> To whose care we commit our goods shall die
> If they abuse our trust; what can we look for,
> To whose charge this most hopeful Lord gave up
> All he received from his brave ancestors,
> All he could leave to his posterity?
> His honour—Wicked woman, in whose safety
> All his life's joys and comforts were lock'd up,
> Which thy lust, a thief, hath now stolen from him!
> And therefore——
> *Charalois.* Stay, just Judge—May not what's lost
> By her one fault (for I am charitable
> And charge her not with many) be forgotten
> In her fair life hereafter.
> *Rochfort.* Never, Sir!
> The wrong that's done to the chaste married bed,
> Repentant tears can never expiate:
> And be assur'd to pardon such a sin,
> Is an offence as great as to commit it.

In consequence of this the husband strikes her dead
before her father's eyes; the act indeed is horrid;
even tragedy shrinks from it, and Nature with a father's voice instantly cries out—*Is she dead then?—
And you have kill'd her?*—Chalarois avows it, and
pleads his sentence for the deed; the revolting, ago-
nzied parent breaks forth into one of the most pathetic, natural, and expressive lamentations that the
English drama can produce—

> ————But I pronounc'd it
> As a judge only, and a friend to justice,

And, zealous in defence of your wrong'd honour,
Broke all the ties of nature, and cast off
The love and soft affection of a father:
I in your cause put on a scarlet robe
Of red-dy'd cruelty ; but in return
You have advanc'd for me no flag of mercy ;
I look'd on you as a wrong'd husband, but
You clos'd your eyes against me as a father.
Oh, Beaumelle ! Oh, my daughter !—
   *Charalois.* This is madness.
   *Rochfort.* Keep from me!—Could not one good thought rise up
To tell you that she was my age's comfort,
Begot by a weak man, and born a woman,
And could not therefore but partake of frailty ?
Or wherefore did not thankfulness step forth
To urge my many merits, which I may
Object to you, since you prove ungrateful ?
Flinty-hearted Charalois !
   *Charalois.* Nature does prevail above your virtue.

What conclusions can I draw from these comparative examples, which every reader would not anticipate? Is there a man, who has any feeling for real nature, dramatic character, moral sentiment, tragic pathos, or nervous diction, who can hesitate, even for a moment, where to bestow the palm?

## NUMBER LXXX.

I was some nights ago much entertained with an excellent representation of Mr. Congreve's comedy of *The Double Dealer*. When I reflected upon the youth of the author, and the merit of the play, I acknowledged the truth of what the late Dr. Samuel Johnson says, in his life of this poet, that, 'amongst all the efforts of early genius, which literary history records, I doubt whether any one can be produced, that more surpasses the common limits of nature than the plays of Congreve.'

The author of this comedy, in his dedication, informs us, that he ' designed the moral first, and to that moral invented the fable;' *and does not know* that he has borrowed one hint of it any where.— ' I made the plot,' says he, ' as strong as I could; because it was single; and I made it single, because I would avoid confusion, and was resolved to preserve the three unities of the drama.' As it is impossible not to give full credit to this assertion, I must consider the resemblance which many circumstances in *The Double Dealer* bear to those in a comedy of Beaumont and Fletcher, entitled *Cupid's Revenge*, as a casual coincidence; and I think the learned biographer, above quoted, has good reason to pronounce of Congreve, ' that he is an original writer, who borrowed neither the models of his plot, nor the manner of his dialogue.'

Mellafont, the nephew and heir of Lord Touchwood, being engaged to Cynthia, daughter of Sir Paul Pliant, the traversing this match forms the object of the plot, on which this comedy of *The Double Dealer* is constructed; the intrigue consists in the various artifices employed by Lady Touchwood and her agents for that purpose.

That the object is (as the author himself states it to be) *singly* this, will appear upon considering, that although the ruin of Mellafont's fortune is for a time effected by these contrivances, that are employed for traversing his marriage, yet it is rather a measure of necessity and self-defence in Lady Touchwood, than of original design; it springs from the artifice of incident, and belongs more properly to the intrigue, than to the object of the plot.

The making, or obstructing marriages, is the

common hinge on which most comic fables are contrived to turn; but in this match of Mellafont's, which the author has taken for the ground-work of his plot, I must observe, that it would have been better to have given more interest to an event, which he has made the main object of the play: he has taken little pains to recommend the parties to his spectators, or to paint their mutual attachment with any warmth of colouring. Who will feel any concern whether Mellafont marries Cynthia or not, if they themselves appear indifferent on the occasion, and, upon the eve of their nuptials, converse in the following strain?

*Mel.* You seem thoughtful, Cynthia.

*Cyn.* I am thinking, though marriage makes man and wife one flesh, it leaves them still two fools, and they become more conspicuous by setting off one another.

*Mel.* That's only when two fools meet, and their follies are opposed.

*Cyn.* Nay, I have known two wits meet, and by the opposition of their wit, render themselves as ridiculous as fools. 'Tis an old game we are going to play at; what think you of drawing stakes, and giving over in time?

*Mel.* No, hang it, that's not endeavouring to win, because it is possible we may lose—&c. &c.

This scene, which proceeds throughout in the same strain, seems to confirm Dr. Johnson's remark that ' Congreve formed a peculiar idea of comic excellence, which he supposed to consist in gay remarks and unexpected answers—*that* his scenes exhibit not much of humour, imagery, or passion; his personages are a kind of intellectual gladiators; every sentence is to ward or strike; the contest of smartness is never intermitted; and his wit is a meteor, playing to and fro with alternate coruscations.'

There is but one more interview between Cynthia and Mellafont, which is the opening of the fourth act, and this is of so flat and insipid a sort, as to be with reason omitted in the representation; I think therefore it may be justly observed, that this match, for the prevention of which artifices of so virulent and diabolical a nature are practised by Lady Touchwood and the Double Dealer, is not pressed upon the feelings of the spectators in so interesting a manner, as it should and might have been.

Having remarked upon the object of the plot, I shall next consider the intrigue; and, for this purpose, we must methodically trace the conduct of Lady Touchwood, who is the poet's chief engine, and that of her under-agent Maskwell.

The scene lies in Lord Touchwood's house, but, whether in town or country, does not appear. Sir Paul Pliant, his lady and daughter, are naturally brought thither, upon the day preceding Cynthia's marriage, to adjust the settlement: Lord and Lady Froth, Careless, and Brisk, are visitors on the occasion; Mellafont and Maskwell are inmates; this disposition is as happy as can be devised. The incident, related by Mellafont to Careless, of the attempt upon him, made by Lady Touchwood, artfully prepares us to expect every thing that revenge and passion can suggest for frustrating his happiness; and it is judicious to represent Mellafont incredulous as to the criminality of Maskwell's intercourse with Lady Touchwood; for, if he had believed it upon Careless's suggestion, it would have made his blindness to the character of Maskwell not only weak (which in fact it is), but unnatural, and even guilty.

Maskwell, in the first act, makes general promises to Lady Touchwood, that he will defeat Mellafont's match—' You shall possess, and ruin him too.'—The lady presses him to explain particulars; he opens no other resource but that of possessing Lady Pliant with an idea that Mellafont is fond of her—' She must be thoroughly persuaded that Mellafont loves her.'

—So shallow a contrivance as this cannot escape the lady's penetration, and she naturally answers—'I don't see what you can propose from so trifling a design; for her first conversing with Mellafont will convince her of the contrary.' In fact, the author's good sense was well aware how weak this expedient is, and it seems applied to no other purpose than as an incident to help on the underplot, by bringing forward the comic effect of Lady Pliant's character, and that of Sir Paul: Maskwell himself is so fairly gravelled by the observation, that he confesses he 'does not depend upon it;' but he observes, that 'it will prepare something else, and gain him leisure to lay a stronger plot: if I gain a little time,' says he, 'I shall not want contrivance.'

In the second act this design upon Lady Pliant is played off, and Maskwell in an interview with Mellafont avows the plot, and says—'to tell you the truth, I encouraged it for your diversion.' He proceeds to say, that in order to gain the confidence of Lady Touchwood, 'he had pretended to have been long secretly in love with Cynthia;' that thereby he had drawn forth ' the secrets of her heart,' and that 'if he accomplished her designs, she had engaged to put Cynthia with all her fortune into his power;' he then discloses by soliloquy that his motive for *double dealing* was founded in his passion for Cynthia, and observes that ' the name of rival cuts all ties asunder, and is a general acquittance.' This proceeding is in nature, and is good comedy.

The third act opens with a scene between Lord and Lady Touchwood, which is admirably conceived and executed with great spirit; I question if there is any thing of the author superior to this dialogue. The design of alarming the jealousy and resentment of Lord Touchwood now appears to have originated with the lady, although Maskwell was privy to it, and 'ready for a cue to come in and confirm all,' had there been occasion;' he proposes to her to say that he was 'privy to Mellafont's design, but that he used his utmost endeavours to dissuade him from it;' and on the credit he thinks to establish by this proof of his honour and honesty, he grounds another plot, which he keeps as his ultimate and most secret re-source, that 'of cheating her (Lady Touchwood) *as* well as the rest.' He now reveals to Mellafont a criminal assignation with Lady Touchwood in her chamber at eight, and proposes to him to come and surprise them together, 'and then,' says he, 'it will be hard if you cannot bring her to any conditions.'

This appears to me to be a very dangerous experi-ment, and scarce within the bounds of nature and probability. If Maskwell, under cover of the pro-posal, had in view nothing more than the introduction of Mellafont into Lady Touchwood's bedchamber, there to put them together, and then to bring Lord Touchwood secretly upon them in the moment of their interview, his contrivance could not have been better laid for the purpose of confirming the impres-sion, which that lord had received against his ne-phew; in which Maskwell had nothing more to do than to apprise the lady of his design, and she of course could have managed the interview to the pur-poses of the plot, and effectually have completed the ruin of Mellafont: this, it should seem, would have answered his object completely, for he would have risen upon the ruin of Mellafont, possessed himself of Lord Touchwood's favour, bound Lady Touch-wood to concealment of his villany, and been as able to lay his train for the possession of Cynthia, as by any other mode he could choose for obtaining her; but if he put it to the issue of a surprise upon Lady Touchwood, when she was not prepared for the ma-nagement of that surprise, what was he to expect from the introduction of Lord Touchwood, but discovery and defeat? Was it not natural to suppose Mellafont would seize the opportunity of reproaching her with her criminality with Maskwell? It was for that very purpose he brings him thither: he tells him, ' it will be hard if he cannot then bring her to any conditions ;'—and if this was to pass under the terror of his reproaches, how could Maskwell set Lord Touchwood upon listening to their conversation, and not apprehend for a consequence apparently so unavoidable? He puts every thing to risk by proposing to Mellafont to conceal himself in Lady Touchwood's bedchamber, whilst she is in the closet; he then meets Lord Touchwood, appoints him to come to the lobby by the bedchamber in a quarter of an hour's time : he keeps his assignation with the lady, Mellafont starts from his hiding-place, and Maskwell escapes, but soon returns, secretly introducing Lord Touchwood to listen to the dialogue between his lady and nephew: she accidentally discovers him without his being seen by Mellafont, and turns that accidental discovery against Mellafont. What a combination of improbabilities is here fortuitously thrown together to produce this lucky incident ! Could Maskwell reasonably presume upon a chance so beyond expectation? Every thing is made to turn upon the precarious point of a minute: if Lord Touchwood, who was appointed for a quarter of an hour, had anticipated that appointment, if Lady Touchwood had been less punctual to her assignation, if Mellafont had happened to have dropped one word in his uncle's hearing, charging her with his discovery, as had been agreed, or if either she had happened not to have seen Lord Touchwood, or Mellafont had seen him; in short, if any one thing had turned up, which ought not to have come to pass, or otherwise than it was made to come to pass by the greatest violence to probability, Maskwell was inevitably undone: it must be owned he laid a train for his own destruction, but stage incident rescued him; and this, with the lady's adroitness, effaces the improbability, when it passes in representation, and keeps nature out of sight. Had Mellafont told the plain story to his uncle, after Lady Touchwood had so unexpectedly turned it against him, it would at least have put the plot to risk, and of this the author seems so conscious, that he does not suffer him to attempt a single word in his defence: to save his villain, he is compelled to sacrifice his hero.

It is not sufficient to say that a poet has his characters in his power, and can fashion incidents according to his own discretion; he must do no violence to nature and probability for the purposes of his plot.

Maskwell having in this manner escaped with success, begins next to put in execution his plot for obtaining Cynthia, and this constitutes the intrigue and catastrophe of the fifth act: his plan is as follows——Having imparted to Lord Touchwood his love for Cynthia by the vehicle of a soliloquy, which is to be overheard by his lordship, he proposes to himself to carry off Cynthia to St. Alban's with the chaplain in the coach, there to be married; this she is to be trepanned into by persuading her that the chaplain is Mellafont, and Mellafont is brought to co-operate, by a promise that he shall elope with Cynthia under that disguise, and that the chaplain shall be made to follow on the day after and then marry him to Cynthia; with this view Mellafont is appointed to meet Maskwell in one chamber, and Cynthia in another; the real chaplain is to be passed upon the lady for Mellafont, and Mellafont is to be left in the lurch; this plot upon Cynthia, Maskwell confides to Lord Touchwood, telling him there is no other way to possess himself of her but by surprise.

Though the author undoubtedly meant his villain should in the end outwit himself, yet he did not mean him to attempt impossibilities, and the absurdities of this contrivance are so many, that I know not which to mention first. How was Maskwell to possess himself of Cynthia by this scheme? By what force or fraud is he to accomplish the object of marrying her? We must conclude he was not quite so desperate as to sacrifice all his hopes from Lord Touchwood by any violence upon her person; there is nothing in his character to warrant the conjecture. It is no less unaccountable how Mellafont could be caught by this project, and induced to equip himself in the chaplain's gown to run off with a lady, who had pledged herself to him never to marry any other man: there was no want of consent on her part; a reconciliation with Lord Touchwood was the only object he had to look to, and how was that to be effected by this elopement with Cynthia?

The jealousy of Lady Touchwood was another rock on which Maskwell was sure to split: it would have been natural for him to have provided against this danger by binding my lord to secrecy, and the lady's pride of family was a ready plea for that purpose; when he was talking to himself for the purpose of being overheard by Lord Touchwood, he had nothing to do but to throw in this observation amongst the rest to bar that point against discovery.

The reader will not suppose I would suggest a plan of operation for *The Double Dealer*, to secure him against discovery; I am only for adding probability and common precaution to his projects: I allow that it is in character for him to grow wanton with success; there is a moral in a villain outwitting himself; but the catastrophe would in my opinion have been far more brilliant, if his schemes had broke up with more force of contrivance : laid as they are, they melt away and dissolve by their own weakness and inconsistency ; Lord and Lady Touchwood, Careless and Cynthia, all join in the discovery; every one but Mellafont sees through the plot, and he is blindness itself.

Mr. Congreve, in his dedication above-mentioned, defends himself against the objection to soliloquies ; but I conceive he is more open to criticism for the frequent use he makes of listening ; Lord Touchwood three times has recourse to this expedient.

Of the characters in this comedy Lady Touchwood, though of an unfavourable cast, seems to have been the chief care of the poet, and is well preserved throughout ; her elevation of tone, nearly approaching to the tragic, affords a strong relief to the lighter sketches of the episodical persons, Sir Paul and Lady Pliant, Lord and Lady Froth, who are highly entertaining, but much more loose than the stage in its present state of reformation would endure : nothing more can be said of Careless and Brisk, than that they are the young men of the theatre, at the time when they were in representation. Of Maskwell enough has been said in these remarks, nor need any thing be added to what has been already observed upon Mellafont and Cynthia. As for the moral of the play, which the author says he designed in the first place, and then applied the fable to it, it should seem to have been his principal object in the formation of the comedy, and yet it is not made to reach several characters of very libertine principles, who are left to reform themselves at leisure ; and the plot, though subordinate to the moral, seems to have drawn him off from executing his good intentions so completely, as those professions may be understood to engage for.

# NUMBER LXXXI.

Citò scribendo non fit ut benè scribatur ; benè scribendo fit ut citò.
                                                          QUINTIL. lib. x.

THE celebrated author of the Rambler in his con-
cluding paper says, ' I have laboured to refine our
language to grammatical purity, and to clear it from
colloquial barbarisms, licentious idioms, and irregular
combinations : something perhaps I have added to
the elegance of its construction, and something to
the harmony of its cadence.'  I hope our language
hath gained all the profit, which the labours of this
meritorious writer were exerted to produce ; in style
of a certain description he undoubtedly excels ; but
though I think there is much in his essays for a
reader to admire, I should not recommend them as
a model for a disciple to copy.

Simplicity, ease, and perspicuity, should be the
first objects of a young writer : Addison, and other
authors of his class, will furnish him with examples,
and assist him in the attainment of these excellences ;
but after all, the style, in which a man shall write,
will not be formed by imitation only ; it will be the
style of his mind : it will assimilate itself to his
mode of thinking, and take its colour from the complexion of his ordinary discourse, and the company
he consorts with.  As for that distinguishing characteristic, which the ingenious essayists terms very
properly *the harmony of its cadence*, that I take to be
incommunicable, and immediately dependant upon
the ear of him who models it.  This *harmony of cadence* is so strong a mark of discrimination between
authors of note in the world of letters, that we can

depose to a style, whose modulation we are familiar with, almost as confidently as to the hand-writing of a correspondent. But though I think there will be found in the periods of every established writer a certain peculiar tune (whether harmonious or otherwise) which will depend rather upon the natural ear than upon the imitative powers, yet I would not be understood to say that the study of good models can fail to be of use in the first formation of it. When a subject presents itself to the mind, and thoughts arise, which are to be committed to writing, it is then for a man to choose whether he will express himself in simple or in elaborate diction, whether he will compress his matter or dilate it, ornament it with epithets and robe it in metaphor, or whether he will deliver it plainly and naturally in such language as a well-bred person and scholar would use, who affects no parade of speech, nor aims at any flights of fancy. Let him decide as he will, in all these cases he hath models in plenty to choose from, which may be said to court his imitation.

For instance; if his ambition is to glitter and surprise with the figurative and metaphorical brilliancy of his period, let him tune his ear to some such passages as the following, where Doctor Johnson in the character of critic and biographer is pronouncing upon the poet Congreve. 'His scenes exhibit not much of humour, imagery, or passion : his personages are a kind of intellectual gladiators; every sentence is to ward or strike; the contest of smartness is never intermitted; his wit is a meteor playing to and fro, with alternate coruscations.' If he can learn to embroider with as much splendour, taste, and address, as this and many other samples exhibited from the same master, he cannot study in a better school.

On the contrary, if simplicity be his object, and

a certain serenity of style which seems in unison
with the soul he may open the Spectator, and take
from the first paper of Mr. Addison the first paragraph that meets his eye—the following, for instance
—'There is nothing that makes its way more directly
to the soul than *beauty*, which immediately diffuses
a secret satisfaction and complacency through the
imagination, and gives a finishing to any thing that
is great or uncommon: the very discovery of it
strikes the mind with an inward joy, and spreads a
cheerfulness and delight through all its faculties.'
Or again, in the same essay : ' We no where meet
with a more glorious or pleasing show in nature,
than what appears in the heavens at the rising and
setting of the sun, which is wholly made up of those
different stains of light that shew themselves in
clouds of a different situation.' A florid writer would
hardly have resisted the opportunities which here
court the imagination to indulge its flights, whereas
few writers of any sort would have been tempted on
a topic merely critical, to have employed such figurative and splendid diction, as that of Doctor Johnson : these little samples, therefore, though selected
with little or no care, but taken as they came to
hand, may serve to exemplify my meaning, and in
some degree characterize the different styles of the
respective writers.

Now as every student, who is capable of copying
either of these styles, or even of comparing them,
must discern on which side the greater danger of
miscarrying lies, as well as the greater disgrace in
case of such miscarriage, prudence will direct him
in his outset not to hazard the attempt at a florid
diction.  If his ear hath not been vitiated by vulgar
habitudes, he will only have to guard against mean
expressions, while he is studying to be simple and
perspicuous ; he will put his thoughts into language

naturally as they present themselves, giving them for the present little more than mere grammatical correction; afterward, upon a closer review, he will polish those parts that seem rude, harmonize them where they are unequal, compress what is too diffusive, raise what is low, and attune the whole to that general cadence, which seems most grateful to his ear.

But if our student hath been smitten with the turbulent oratory of the senate, the acrimonious declamation of the bar, or the pompous eloquence of the pulpit, and shall take the lofty speakers in these several orders for his models, rather than such as address the ear in humbler tones, his passions will in that case hurry him into the florid and figurative style, to a sublime and swelling period ; and if in this he excels, it must be owned he accomplishes a great and arduous task, and he will gain a liberal share of applause from the world, which in general is apt to be captivated with those high and towering images, that strike and surprise the senses. In this style the Hebrew prophets write, ' whose discourse (to use the words of the learned Doctor Bentley) after the genius of the Eastern nations, is thick set with metaphor and allegory ; the same bold comparisons and dithyrambic liberty of style every where occurring—For when " *the Spirit of God came upon them*," and breathed a new warmth and vigour through all the powers of the body and soul: when, by the influx of divine light the whole scene of Christ's heavenly kingdom was represented to their view, so that their hearts were ravished with joy, and their imaginations turgid and pregnant with the glorious ideas ; then surely, if ever, their style would be strong and lofty, full of allusions to all that is great and magnificent in the kingdoms of this world.' (*Commencement Sermon*).—And these flights of imagination, these effusions of rapture and sublimity, will occasionally be found in the pulpit eloquence of some of our most correct and temperate writers; witness that brilliant apostrophe at the conclusion of the ninth discourse of Bishop Sherlock, than whom few or none have written with more didactic brevity and simplicity—' Go, (says he to the deists) go to your natural religion: lay before her Mahomet and his disciples arrayed in armour and in blood, riding in triumph over the spoils of thousands, and tens of thousands, who fell by his victorious sword: shew her the cities which he set in flames, the countries which he ravaged and destroyed, and the miserable distress of all the inhabitants of the earth. When she has viewed him in this scene, carry her into his retirements; shew her the prophet's chamber, his concubines and wives; let her see his adultery, and hear him allege revelation and his divine commission to justify his lust and oppression. When she is tired with this prospect, then shew her the blessed Jesus, humble and meek, doing good to all the sons of men, patiently instructing both the ignorant and perverse; let her see him in his most retired privacies; let her follow him to the mount, and hear his devotions and supplications to God; carry her to his table to view his poor fare, and hear his heavenly discourse: let her see him injured but not provoked; let her attend him to the tribunal, and consider the patience with which he endured the scoffs and reproaches of his enemies: lead her to his cross, and let her view him in the agony of death, and his last prayer for his persecutors—' Father, forgive them, for they know not what they do.'

This is a lofty passage in the high imperative tone of declamation; it is richly coloured, boldly contrasted, and replete with imagery, and is amongst the strongest of those instances, where the orator addresses himself to the senses and passions of his hearers : but let the disciple tread this path with caution ; let him wait the call, and be sure he has an occasion worthy of his efforts before he makes them.

Allegory, personification, and metaphor, will press upon his imagination at certain times, but let him soberly consult his judgment in those moments, and weigh their fitness before he admits them into his style. As for allegory, it is at best but a kind of fairy form ; it is hard to naturalize it, and it will rarely fill a graceful part in any manly composition. With respect to personification, as I am speaking of prose only, it is but an exotic ornament, and may be considered rather as the loan of the muses than as the property of prose ; let our student therefore beware how he borrows the feathers of the jay, lest his unnatural finery should only serve to make him pointed at and despised. Metaphor, on the other hand, is common property, and he may take his share of it, provided he has discretion not to abuse his privilege, and neither surfeits the appetite with repletion, nor confounds the palate with too much variety : let his metaphor be apposite, single, and unconfused, and it will serve him as a kind of rhetorical lever to lift and elevate his style above the pitch of ordinary discourse ; let him also so apply this machine, as to make it touch in as many points as possible ; otherwise it can never so poise the weight above it, as to keep it firm and steady on its proper centre.

To give an example of the right use and application of this figure, I again apply to a learned author already quoted—' Our first parents having fallen from their native state of innocence, the tincture of evil, like an hereditary disease, infected all their posterity ; and the leaven of sin having once corrupted the whole mass of mankind, all the species ever

after would be soured and tainted with it : the vicious
ferment perpetually diffusing and propagating itself
through all generations.'—(*Bentley Comm. Sermon.*)

There will be found also in certain writers a pro-
fusion of words, ramifying indeed from the same
root, yet rising into climax by their power and importance, which seems to burst forth from the overflow and impetuosity of the imagination : resembling
at first sight what Quintilian characterizes as the
' *Abundantia Juvenilis,*' but which, when tempered by
the hand of a master, will upon closer examination
be found to bear the stamp of judgment under the
appearance of precipitancy. I need only turn to the
famous ' *Commencement Sermon !*' before quoted, and
my meaning will be fully illustrated—' Let them tell
us then what is the chain, the cement, the magnetism,
what they will call it, the invisible tie of that union,
whereby matter and incorporeal mind, things that
have no similitude or alliance to each other, can so
sympathise by a mutual league of motion and sensation. No : they will not pretend to that, for they
can frame no conceptions of it : they are sure there
is such a union from the operations and effects, but
the cause and the manner of it are too subtle and
secret to be discovered by the eye of reason : tis
mystery, tis divine magic, tis natural miracle.

---

# NUMBER LXXXII.

*Defunctus jam sum, nihil est quod dicat mihi.*—TERENT.

IN all ages of the world men have been in habits of
praising the time past at the expense of the time
present. This was done even in the Augustan era,

and in that witty and celebrated period the *laudator temporis acti* must have been either a very splenetic, or a very silly character.

Our present grumblers may perhaps be better warranted; but, though there may not be the same injustice in their cavilling complaints, there is more than equal impolicy in them: for if by discouraging their contemporaries they mean to mend them, they take a very certain method of counteracting their own designs: and if they have any other meaning, it must be something worse than impolitic, and they have more to answer for than a mere mistake.

Who but the meanest of mankind would wish to damp the spirit and degrade the genius of the country he belongs to? Is any man lowered by the dignity of his own nation, by the talents of his contemporaries? Who would not prefer to live in an enlightened and a rising age, rather than in a dark and declining one? It is natural to take a pride in the excellence of our free constitution, in the virtues of our soveriegn; is it not as natural to sympathise in the prosperity of our arts and sciences, in the reputation of our countrymen? But these splenetic *dampers* are for ever sighing over the decline of wit, the decline of genius, the decline of literature, when if there is any one thing that has declined rather than another, it is the wretched state of criticism, so far as they have to do with it.

As I was passing from the city the other day, I turned into a coffee-house, and took my seat at a table, next to which some gentlemen had assembled and were conversing over their coffee. A dispute was carried on between a little prattling volatile fellow and an old gentleman of a sullen, morose aspect, who in a dictatorial tone of voice was declaiming against the times, and treating them and their puisny advocate with more contempt than either one or the

other seemed to deserve: still the little fellow, who
had abundance of zeal and no want of words, kept
battling with might and main for the world as it
goes against the world, as it had gone by, and I
could perceive he had an interest with the junior
part of his hearers, whilst the sullen orator was no
less popular amongst the elders of the party: the
little fellow, who seemed to think it no good reason
why any work should be descried only because the
author of it was living, had been descanting upon the
merit of a recent publication, and had now shifted
his ground from the sciences to the fine arts, where
he seemed to have taken a strong post and stood resolutely to it; his opponent, who was not a man to
be tickled out of his spleen by a few fine dashes of
arts merely elegant, did not relish this kind of
skirmishing argument, and tauntingly cried out—
‘ What tell you me of a parcel of gew-gaw artists,
fit only to pick the pockets of a dissipated, trifling
age? You talk of your painters and portrait-mongers,
what use are they of? Where are the philosophers
and the poets, whose countenances might interest
posterity to sit to them? Will they paint me a Bacon,
a Newton, or a Locke? I defy them; there are not
three heads upon living shoulders in the kingdom,
worth the oil that would be wasted upon them. Will
they or you find me a Shakspeare, a Milton, a Dryden, a Pope, an Addison? You cannot find a limb,
a feature, or even the shadow of the least of them:
these were men worthy to be recorded; poets, who
reached the very topmost summits of Parnassus; our
moderns are but pismires crawling at its lowest
root.’—This lofty defiance brought our little advocate to a nonplus; the moment was embarrassing,
the champion of time past was echoed by his party
with a cry of—‘ No, no! there are no such men as
these now living.’—‘ I believe not,’ he replied, ‘ I

believe not: I could give you a score of names more, but these are enough: honest Tom Durfey would be more than a match for any poetaster now breathing!'

In this style he went on crowing and clapping his wings over a beaten cock, for our poor little champion seemed dead upon the pit: he muttered something between his teeth, as if struggling to pronounce some name that stuck in his throat; but either there was in fact no contemporary, whom he thought it safe to oppose to these Goliahs in the lists, or none were present to his mind at this moment.

Alas! thought I, your cause, my beloved contemporaries, is desperate: *Væ Victis!* You are but dust in the scale, while this *Brennus* directs the beam. All that I have admired and applauded in my zeal for those with whom I have lived and still live; all that has hitherto made my heart expand with pride and reverence for the age and nation I belong to, will be immolated to the manes of these departed worthies, whom though I revere, I cannot love and cherish with that sympathy of soul, which I feel towards you, my dear but degenerate contemporaries!

There was a young man, sitting at the elbow of the little crest-fallen fellow, with a round clerical curl, which tokened him to be a son of the church. Having silently awaited the full time for a rally, if any spirit of resurrection had been left in the fallen hero, and none such appearing, he addressed himself to the challenger with an air so modest, but withal so impressive, that it was impossible not to be prejudiced in his favour, before he opened his cause.

'I cannot wonder,' said he, 'if the gentleman who has challenged us to produce a parallel to any one of the great names he has enumerated, finds us unprepared with any living rival to those illustrious characters: their fame, though the age in which they

lived did not always appreciate it as it ought, hath
yet been rising day by day in the esteem of posterity,
till time hath stamped a kind of sacredness upon it,
which it would now be a literary impiety to blas-
pheme.   There are some amongst those whom their
advocate hath named, I cannot speak or think of but
with a reverence only short of idolatry.   Not this
nation only but all Europe hath been enlightened by
their labours : the great principle of nature, the very
law upon which the whole system of the universe
moves and gravitates, hath been developed and de-
monstrated by the penetrating, I had almost said
the preternatural, powers of our immortal Newton.
The present race of philosophers can only be considered as his disciples ; but they are disciples who
do honour to their master : if the principle of gravi-
tation be the grand *desideratum* of philosophy, the
discovery is with him, the application, inferences,
and advantages of that discovery, are with those who
succeed him ; and can we accuse the present age of
being idle, or unable to avail themselves of the
ground he gave them ?   Let me remind you that our
present solar system is furnished with more planets
than Newton knew ; that our late observations upon
the transit of the planet Venus were decisive for the
proof and confirmation of his system : that we have
circumnavigated the globe again and again ; that we
can boast the researches and discoveries of a Captain Cook, who, though he did not invent the compass, employed it as no man ever did, and left a map
behind him, compared to which Sir Isaac Newton's
was a sheet of nakedness and error : it is with gra-
vitation, therefore, as with the loadstone ; their
powers have been discovered by our predecessors,
but we have put them to their noblest uses.

   ' The venerable names of Bacon and Locke were,
if I mistake not, mentioned in the same class with

Newton, and though the learned gentleman could no doubt have made his selection more numerous, I doubt if he could have made it stronger, or more to the purpose of his own assertions.

'I have always regarded Bacon as the father of philosophy in this country; yet it is no breach of candour to observe, that the darkness of the age which he enlightened, affords a favourable contrast to set off the splendour of his talents: but do we, who applaud him, read him? Yet if such is our veneration for times long since gone by, why do we not? The fact is, intermediate writers have disseminated the original matter through more pleasing vehicles, and we concur, whether commendably or not, to put his volumes upon the superannuated list, allowing him however an inalienable compensation upon our praise, and reserving to ourselves a right of taking him from the shelf, whenever we are disposed to sink the merit of a more recent author by a comparison with him. I will not therefore disturb his venerable dust, but turn without farther delay to the author of the Essay upon the Human Understanding.

'This essay, which professes to define every thing, as it arises or passes in the mind, must ultimately be compiled from observations of its author upon himself and within himself: before I compare the merit of this work therefore with the merit of any other man's work of our own immediate times, I must compare what it advances in general to mankind, with what I perceive within my particular self: and upon this reference, speaking only for an humble individual, I must own to my shame, that my understanding and the author's do by no means coincide either in definitions or ideas. I may have reason to lament the inaccuracy or the sluggishness of my own senses and perceptions, but I cannot submit to any man's doctrine against their conviction:

I will only say that Mr. Locke's metaphysics are not
my metaphysics, and, as it would be an ill compliment to any one of our contemporaries to compare
him with a writer, who is to me unintelligible, so will
I hope it can never be considered as a reflection
upon so great a name as Mr. Locke's not to be understood by so insignificant a man as myself.'

'Well, Sir,' cried the sullen gentleman with a
sneer, 'I think you have contrived to dispatch our
philosophers; you have now only a few obscure
poets to dismiss in like manner, and you will have a
clear field for yourself and your friends.'

## NUMBER LXXXIII.

Ingeniis non ille favet plauditque sepultis,
Nostra sed impugnat, nos nostraque lividus odit.—HORAT.

THE sarcastic speech of the old snarler, with which
we concluded the last paper, being undeserved on
the part of the person to whom it was applied, was
very properly disregarded; and the clergyman proceeded as follows :—

'The poets you have named will never be mentioned by me, but with a degree of enthusiasm,
which I should rather expect to be accused of carrying to excess, than of erring in the opposite extreme,
had you not put me on my guard against partiality,
by charging me with it beforehand. I shall, therefore, without farther apology or preface, begin with
Shakspeare, first named by you, the first in fame,
as well as time: it would be madness in me to think
of bringing any poet, now living, into competition
with Shakspeare; but I hope it will not be thought

madness, or any thing resembling to it, to observe
to you, that it is not in the nature of things possible
for any poet to appear in an age so polished as this
of ours, who can be brought into any critical comparison with that extraordinary and eccentric genius.

'For, let us consider the two great striking features
of his drama, sublimity and character. Now, sublimity involves sentiment and expression; the first of
these is the soul of the poet; it is that portion of
inspiration, which we personify, when we call it the
Muse: so far I am free to acknowledge there is no
immediate reason to be given, why her visits should
be confined to any age, nation, or person; she may
fire the heart of the poet on the shores of Ionia three
thousand years ago, or on the banks of the Cam or
Isis at the present moment; but, so far as language
is concerned, I may venture to say, that modern
diction will never strike modern ears with that awful
kind of magic, which antiquity gives to words and
phrases, no longer in familiar use: in this respect,
our great dramatic poet hath an advantage over his
distant descendants, which he owes to time, and
which of course is one more than he is indebted for
to his own pre-eminent genius. As for character,
which I suggested as one of the two most striking
features in Shakspeare's drama (or, in other words,
the true and perfect delineation of nature), in this
our poet is indeed a master unrivalled; yet who will
not allow the happy coincidence of time for this
perfection in a writer of the drama? The different
orders of men, which Shakspeare saw and copied,
are in many instances extinct, and such must have
the charms of novelty, at least, in our eyes: and has
the modern dramatist the same rich and various
field of character? The level manners of a polished
age furnish little choice to an author, who now
enters on the task, in which such numbers have

gone before him, and so exhausted the materials,
that it is justly to be wondered at, when any thing
like variety can be struck out. Dramatic characters
are portraits drawn from nature, and, if all the
sisters have a family-likeness, the artist must either
depart from the truth, or preserve the resemblance;
in like manner, the poet must either invent characters,
of which there is no counterpart in existence, or
expose himself to the danger of an insipid and
tiresome repetition: to add to his difficulties, it so
happens, that the present age, whilst it furnishes
less variety to his choice, requires more than ever
for its own amusement; the dignity of the stage
must of course be prostituted to the unnatural
resources of a wild imagination, and its propriety
disturbed; music will supply those resources for
a time, and accordingly, we find the French and
English theatres in the dearth of character, feeding
upon the airy diet of sound; but this, with all the
support that spectacle can give, is but a flimsy substitute, whilst the public, whose taste in the mean
time becomes vitiated—

————media inter carmina poscunt
Aut ursum aut pugiles————

the latter of which monstrous prostitutions we have
lately seen our national stage most shamefully exposed to.

'By comparing the different ages of poetry in our
own country with those of Greece, we shall find
the effects agree in each; for, as the refinement of
manners took place, the language of poetry became
also more refined, and with greater correctness
had less energy and force: the style of the poet,
like the characters of the people, takes a brighter
polish, which, whilst it smooths away its former
asperities and protuberances, weakens the staple of
its fabric, and, what it gives to the elegance and

delicacy of its complexion, takes away from the strength and sturdiness of its constitution. Whoever will compare Æschylus with Euripides, and Aristophanes with Menander, will need no other illustration of this remark.

' Consider only the inequalities of Shakspeare's dramas: examine not only one with another, but compare even scene with scene in the same play. Did ever the imagination of man run riot into such wild and opposite extremes? Could this be done, or, being done, would it be suffered in the present age? How many of these plays, if acted as they were originally written, would now be permitted to pass? Can we have a stronger proof of the barbarous state of those times, in which *Titus Andronicus* first appeared, than the favour which that horrid spectacle was received with? Yet of this we are assured by Ben Jonson. If this play was Shakspeare's, it was his first production, and some of his best commentators are of opinion it was actually written by him, whilst he resided at Stratford-upon-Avon. Had this production been followed by the three parts of *Henry the Sixth*, by *Love's Labour Lost*, the *Two Gentlemen of Verona*, the *Comedy of Errors*, or some few others, which our stage does not attempt to reform, that critic must have had a very singular degree of intuition, who had discovered in those dramas a genius capable of producing the *Macbeth*. How would a young author be received, in the present time, who was to make his first essay before the public with such a piece as *Titus Andronicus?* Now, if we are warranted in saying there are several of Shakspeare's dramas, which could not live upon our present stage at any rate, and few, if any, that would pass without just censure in many parts, were they represented in their original state, we must acknowledge it is with reason that our living authors, standing in awe of their audiences, dare not aim at those bold and irregular flights of imagination, which carried our bard to such a height of fame; and therefore it was that I ventured awhile ago to say, there can be no poet in a polished and critical age like this, who can be brought into any fair comparison with so bold and eccentric a genius as Shakspeare, of whom we may say with Horace—

> Tentavit quoque rem, si dignè vertere posset,
> Et placuit sibi, naturà sublimis et acer:
> Nam spirat tragicum satis, et feliciter audet:
> Sed turpem putat in scriptis metuitque lituram.

When I bring to my recollection the several periods of our English drama, since the age of Shakspeare, I could name many dates, when it has been in hands far inferior to the present; and, were it my purpose to enter into particulars, I should not scruple to appeal to several dramatic productions within the compass of our own times; but, as the task of separating and selecting one from another amongst our own contemporaries can never be a pleasant task, nor one I would willingly engage in, I will content myself with referring to our stock of modern acting plays; many of which, having passed the ordeal of critics (who speak the same language with what I have just now heard, and are continually crying down those they live with), may perhaps take their turn with posterity, and be hereafter as partially overrated, upon a comparison with the productions of the age to come, as they are now undervalued, when compared with those of the ages past.

'With regard to Milton, if we could not name any one epic poet of our nation since his time, it would be saying no more of us than may be said of the world in general, from the era of Homer to that of Virgil. Greece had one standard epic poet; Rome had no more: England has her Milton. If

Dryden pronounced, that "the force of nature could no farther go," he was at once a good authority and a strong example of the truth of the assertion: if his genius shrunk from the undertaking, can we wonder that so few have taken it up? Yet we will not forget Leonidas; nor speak slightly of its merit; and, as death has removed the worthy author where he cannot hear our praises, the world may now, as in the case of Milton heretofore, be so much the more forward to bestow them. If the Samson Agonistes is nearer to the simplicity of its Grecian original than either our own Elfrida or Caractacus, those dramas have a tender interest, a pathetic delicacy, which in that are wanting; and, though Comus has every charm of language, it has a vein of allegory that impoverishes the mine.

'The variety of Dryden's genius was such as to preclude comparison; were I disposed to attempt it. Of his dramatic productions he himself declares, "that he never wrote any thing in that way to please himself but his *All for Love*." For ever under arms, he lived in a continual state of poetic warfare with his contemporaries, galling and galled by turns: he subsisted also by expedients, and necessity, which forced his genius into quicker growth than was natural to it, made a rich harvest but slovenly husbandry; it drove him also into a duplicity of character that is painful to reflect upon; it put him ill at ease within himself, and verified the fable of the nightingale, singing with a thorn at its breast.

'Pope's versification gave the last and finishing polish to our English poetry: his lyre more sweet than Dryden's was less sonorous; his touch more correct, but not so bold; his strain more musical in its tones, but not so striking in its effect: review him as a critic, and review him throughout, you will pronounce him the most perfect poet in our language;

read him as an enthusiast and examine him in detail, you cannot refuse him your approbation, but your rapture you will reserve for Dryden.

‘ But you will tell me this does not apply to the question in dispute, and that instead of settling precedency between your poets, it is time for me to produce my own : for this I shall beg your excuse ; my zeal for my contemporaries shall not hurry them into comparisons, which their own modesty would revolt from : it hath prompted me to intrude upon your patience, whilst I submit a few mitigating considerations in their behalf ; not as an answer to your challenge, but as an effort to soften your contempt. I confess to you I have sometimes flattered myself I have found the strength of Dryden in our late Churchill, and the sweetness of Pope in our lamented Goldsmith : enraptured as I am with the lyre of Timotheus in the Feast of Alexander, I contemplate with awful delight Gray’s enthusiastic bard—

> On a rock, whose haughty brow
> Frowns o’er old Conway’s foaming flood,
> Rob’d in the sable garb of woe,
> With haggard eyes the poet stood ;
> (Loose his beard and hoary hair
> Stream’d like a meteor to the troubled air)
> And with a master’s hand and prophet’s fire
> Struck the deep sorrows of his lyre.

Let the living muses speak for themselves ; I have all the warmth of a friend, but not the presumption of a champion : the poets you now so loudly praise when dead, found the world as loud in defamation when living ; you are now paying the debts of your predecessors, and atoning for their injustice ; posterity will in like manner atone for yours.

‘ You mentioned the name of Addison in your list, not altogether as a poet I presume, but rather as the man of morals, the reformer of manners, and the friend of religion; with affection I subscribe my tribute to his literary fame, to his amiable character; in sweetness and simplicity of style, in purity and perspicuity of sentiment, he is a model to all essayists. At the same time I feel the honest pride of a contemporary in recalling to your memory the name of Samuel Johnson, who as a moral and religious essayist, as an acute and penetrating critic, as a nervous and elaborate poet, an excellent grammarian, and a general scholar, ranks with the first names in literature.

'Not having named an historian in your list of illustrious men, you have precluded me from adverting to the histories of Hume, Robertson, Lyttleton, Henry, Gibbon, and others, who are a host of writers, which all antiquity cannot equal.'

Here the clergyman concluded: the conversation now grew desultory and uninteresting, and I returned home.

---

## NUMBER LXXXIV.

Est genus hominum, qui esse primos se omnium rerum volunt,
Nec sunt.—Terent. Eun.

WHAT a delightful thing it is to find one's self in a company, where tempers harmonize, and hearts are open; where wit flows without any checks but what decency and good nature impose, and humour indulges itself in those harmless freaks and caprices, that raise a laugh by which no man's feelings are offended.

This can only happen to us in a land of freedom: it is in vain to hope for it in those arbitrary countries, where men must lock the doors against spies and informers, and must intrust their lives, whilst they impart their sentiments to each other. In such circumstances, a mind enlightened by education is no longer a blessing; what is the advantage of discernment, and how is a man profited by his capacity of separating truth from error, if he dare not exercise that faculty? It were safer to be the blind dupe of superstition, than the intuitive philosopher, if born within the jurisdiction of an inquisitorial tribunal. Can a man felicitate himself in the glow of genius and the gaiety of wit, when breathing the air of a country, where so dire an instrument is in force as a *letter de cachet*? But experience hath shewn us, that if arbitrary monarchs cannot keep their people in ignorance, they cannot retain them in slavery; if men read they will meditate; if they travel they will compare, and their minds must be as dark as the dungeons which imprison their persons, if they do not rise with indignation against such monstrous maxims, as imprisonment at pleasure for undefined offences, self-accusations extorted by torments and secret trials, where the prisoner hath neither voice nor advocate. Let those princes, whose government is so administered, ' make darkness their pavilion,' and draw their very mountains down upon them to shut out the light, or expect the period of their despotism: illuminated minds will not be kept in slavery.

With a nation so free, so highly enlightened, and so eminent in letters as the English, we may well expect to find the social qualities in their best state; and it is but justice to the age we live in, to confess those expectations may be fully gratified. There are some, perhaps, who will not subscribe to this assertion, but probably those very people make the disappointments they complain of: if a man takes no pains to please his company, he is little likely to be pleased by his company. Liberty, though essential to good society, may in some of its effects operate against it, for as it makes men independent, independence will occasionally be found to make them arrogant, and none such can be good companions; yet, let me say for the contemporaries I am living with, that within the period of my own acquaintance with the world, the reform in its social manners and habits has been gradual and increasing. The feudal haughtiness of our nobility has totally disappeared, and, in place of a proud distant reserve, a pleasing suavity and companionable ease have almost universally obtained amongst the higher orders : the pedantry of office is gone, and even the animosity of party is so far in the wane, that it serves rather to whet our wits than our swords against each other : the agitation of political opinions is no longer a subject fatal to the peace of the table, but takes its turn with other topics, without any breach of good manners or good fellowship.

It were too much to say that there are no general causes still subsisting, which annoy our social comforts, and disgrace our tempers; they are still too many, and it is amongst the duties of an Observer to set a mark upon them, though by so doing I may run into repetition, for I am not conscious of having any thing to say upon the subject which I have not said before : but if a beggar who asks charity, because of his importunity, shall at length be relieved, an author, perhaps, who enforces his advice, shall in the end be listened to.

I must, therefore, again and again insist upon it, that there are two sides to every argument, and that it is the natural and unalienable right of man to be heard in support of his opinion, he having first lent a patient ear to the speaker, who maintains sentiments which oppose that opinion : I do humbly apprehend that an overbearing voice, and noisy volubility of tongue, are proofs of a very underbred fellow, and it is with regret I see society too frequently disturbed in its most delectable enjoyments, by this odious character : I do not see that any man hath a right, by obligation or otherwise, to lay me under a necessity of thinking exactly as he thinks : though I admit, that 'from the fulness of the heart the tongue speaketh,' I do not admit any superior pretensions it hath to be Sir Oracle from the fulness of the pocket. In the name of freedom, what claim hath any man to be the tyrant of the table ? As well he may avail himself of the greater force of his fists as of his lungs. Doth sense consist in sound, or is truth only to be measured by the noise it makes ? Can it be a disgrace to be convinced, or doth any one lose by the exchange, who resigns his own opinion for a better ? When I reflect upon the advantages of our public schools, where puerile tempers are corrected by collision ; upon the mathematical studies, and scholastic exercises of our universities, I am no less grieved than astonished to discover so few proficients in well-mannered controversy, so very few who seem to make truth the object of their investigation, or will spare a few patient moments, from the eternal repetition of their own deafening jargon, to the temperate reply of men, probably better qualified to speak than themselves.

There is another grievance not unfrequent, though inferior to this above-mentioned, which proceeds jointly from the mixed nature of society, and the ebullitions of freedom in this happy country, I mean that roar of mirth, and uncontrolled flow of spirits, which hath more vulgarity in it than ease, more noise than gaiety : the stream of elegant festivity will never overflow its banks : the delicacy of sex, the dignity of rank, and the decorum of certain professions should never be so overlooked, as to alarm the feelings of any person present, interested for their preservation. When the softer sex intrust themselves to our society, we should never forget the tender respect due to them even in our gayest hours. When the higher orders by descending, and the lower by ascending out of their sphere, meet upon the level of good fellowship, let not our superiors be revolted by a rusticity, however jovial, nor driven back into their fastnesses, by overstepping the partition line, and making saucy inroads into their proper quarters. Who questions a minister about news or politics? Who talks ribaldry before a bishop? once in seven years is often enough for the levelling familiarity of electioneering manners.

There is another remark which I cannot excuse myself from making, if it were only for the sake of those luckless beings, who being born with duller faculties, or stampt by the hand of nature with oddities either of humour or of person, seem to be set up in society as butts for the arrows of raillery and ridicule: if the object thus made the victim of the company, feels the shaft, who but must suffer with him? If he feels it not, we blush for human nature, whose dignity is sacrificed in his person; and as for the profest buffoon, I take him to have as little pretensions to true humour, as a punster has to true wit. There is scope enough for all the eccentricities of character without turning cruelty into sport; let satire take its share, but let vice only shrink before it; let it silence the tongue that wantonly violates truth, or defames reputation; let it batter the insulting towers of pride, but let the air-built castles of vanity, much more the humble roof of the indigent and infirm, never provoke its spleen.

It happened to me not long ago to fall into company with some very respectable persons, chiefly of the mercantile order, where a country gentleman, who was a stranger to most of the party, took upon him to entertain the company with a tedious string of stories, of no sort of importance to any soul present, and all tending to display his own consequence, fortune, and independence. Such conversation was ill calculated for the company present, the majority of whom had I dare say been the founders of their own fortunes, and I should doubt if there was any quarter of the globe accessible to commerce, which had not been resorted to by some one or other then sitting at the table. This uninteresting egotist, therefore, was the more unpardonable, as he shut out every topic of curious and amusing information, which could no where meet a happier opportunity for discussion.

He was endured for a considerable time with that patience which is natural to men of good manners, and experience in the world. This encouragement only rendered him more insupportable; when at last an elderly gentleman seized the opportunity of a short pause in his discourse, to address the following reproof to this eternal talker.

'We have listened to you, Sir, a long time with attention, and it does not appear that any body present is disposed to question, either your independence, or the comforts that are annexed to it; we rejoice that you possess them in so full a degree, and we wish every landed gentleman in the kingdom was in the same happy predicament with yourself; but we are traders, Sir, and are beholden to our industry and fair dealing, for what you inherit from your ancestors, and yourself never toiled for. Might it not be altogether as amusing to you to be told of our adventures in foreign climes and countries; of our dangers, difficulties, and escapes; our remarks upon the manners and customs of other nations, as to enclose the whole conversation within the hedge of your own estate, and shut up intelligence, wide as the world itself, within the narrow limits of your parish pound? Believe me, Sir, we are glad to hear you, and we respect your order in the state, but we are willing to hear each other also in our turns; for, let me observe to you in the style of the counting-house, that conversation, like trade, abhors a monopoly, and that a man can derive no benefit from society, unless he hears others talk as well as himself.'

## NUMBER LXXXV.

I was in company the other day with a young gentleman, who had newly succeeded to a considerable estate, and was a good deal struck with the conversation of an elderly person present, who was very deliberately casting up the several demands that the community at large had upon his property.———— ' Are you aware,' says he, ' how small a portion of your revenue will properly remain to yourself, when you have satisfied all the claims which you must pay to society and your country, for living amongst us, and supporting the character of what is called a landed gentleman? Part of your income will be stopt for the maintenance of them who have none, under the denomination of poor-rates; this may be called a fine upon the partiality of fortune, levied by the law of society, which will not trust its poor members to the precarious charity of the rich: another part must go to the debts and necessities of the government, which protects you in war and peace, and is also a fine which you must be content to pay for the

honour of being an Englishman, and the advantage
of living in a land of liberty and security. The
learned professions will also have their share: the
church for taking care of your soul, the physician
for looking after your body, and the lawyer must
have part of your property for superintending the
rest. The merchant, tradesman, and artisan will
have their profit upon all the multiplied wants, comforts, and indulgences of civilized life: these are not
to be enumerated, for they depend on the humours
and habits of men; they have grown up with the refinements and elegances of the age, and they will
farther increase, as these shall advance: they are
the conductors, which, like the blood-vessels in the
human frame, circulate your wealth, and every other
man's wealth, through every limb and even fibre of
the national body: the hand of industry creates that
wealth, and to the hand of industry it finally returns,
as blood does to the heart.'

If we trace the situation of man from a mere state
of nature to the highest state of civilization, we shall
find these artificial wants and dependences increase
with every stage and degree of his improvements;
so that if we consider each nation apart as one great
machine, the several parts and springs, which give
it motion, naturally become more and more complicated and multifarious, as the uses to which it is
applied are more and more diversified. Again, if
we compare two nations in an equal state of civilization, we may remark, that where the greater freedom
obtains, there the greater variety of artificial wants
will obtain also, and of course property will circulate
through more channels: this I take to be the case
upon a comparison between France and England,
arising from the different constitutions of them and
us with respect to civil liberty.

The natural wants of men are pretty much the

same in most states, but the humours of men will take different directions in different countries, and are governed in a great degree by the laws and constitution of the realm in which they are found : there are numbers of people in England, who get their living by arts and occupations, which would not be tolerated in a despotic government. Men's manners are simplified in proportion to the restraint and circumscription under which they are kept. The country sports of English gentlemen furnish maintenance and employment to vast numbers of our people, whereas in France and other arbitrary states, men of the first rank and fortune reside in the capital, and keep no establishments of this sort. What a train of grooms, jockeys, and stable-boys, follow the heels of our horses and hounds in tight boots and leather breeches! each of which carries the clothes of six men upon his back, cased in one skin of flannel under another, like the coats of an onion. The locomotive mania of an Englishman circulates his person, and of course his cash, into every quarter of the kingdom; a Frenchman takes a journey only when he cannot help it, an Englishman has no other reason but because he likes it; he moves with every shift of the weather, and follows the changes of the most variable climate in the world; a frosty morning puts him from his hunting, and he is in London before night; a thaw meets him in town, and again he scampers into the country: he has a horse to run at Epsom, another at Salisbury, and a third at York, and he must be on the spot to back every one of them; he has a stud at Newmarket, a mistress in London, a shooting-box in Norfolk, and a pack of fox-hounds in the New Forest: for one wheel that real business puts in motion, pleasure, whim, *ennui*, turn one hundred : sickness, which confines all the rest of the world, sends him upon his travels; one doctor plunges him

into the sea at Brighthelmstone, a second steeps him
in warm water at Buxton; and a third sends him to
Bath; for the gentlemen of the learned faculty,
whether they help us into life, or help us out of it,
make us pay toll at each gate; and if at any time
their art keeps us alive, the fine we must pay to their
ingenuity makes the renewal in some cases too hard
a bargain for a poor man to profit by. In all other
countries upon earth a man is contented to be well
and pay nothing for being so, but in England even
health is an expensive article, as we are for ever con-
triving how to be a little better, and physicians are
too conscientious to take a fee and do nothing for
it. If there is any thing like ridicule in this, it is
against the patient and not against the physician I
would wish to point it: it is in England that the
profession is truly dignified, and if it is here accompanied with greater emoluments, it is proportion-
ably practised with superior learning; if life is more
valuable in a land of freedom than in a land of slavery, why should it not be paid for according to its
value? In despotic states, where men's lives are in
fact the property of the prince, all subjects should
in justice be cured or killed at his proper charge;
but where a man's house is his castle, his health is
his own concern.

As to the other learned profession of the law, to
its honour be it spoken, there is that charming per-
plexity about it, that we can ruin one another and
ourselves with the greatest certainty and facility. It
is so superior to all other sciences, that it can turn
demonstration into doubt, truth into contradiction,
make improbability put matter of fact out of countenance, and hang up a point for twenty years which
common sense would decide in as many minutes. It
is the glorious privilege of the freemen of England
to make their own laws, and they have made so

many that they can neither count them up nor comprehend them. The parliament of England is without comparison the most voluminous author in the world; and there is such a happy ambiguity in its works, that its students have as much to say on the wrong side of every question as upon the right: in all cases of discussion it is one man's business to puzzle, and another's to explain, and though victory be ever so certain, it is agreed between the parties to make a long battle: there must be an extraordinary faculty of expression in the law, when the only parts clearly understood are those which it has not committed to writing.

I shall say very little in this place upon the sacred profession of divinity; it is to be lamented that the church of England is not provided with a proper competency for all who are engaged in performing its functions; but I cannot close with their opinion, who are for stripping its dignities, and equalizing those splendid benefices, which are at once the glory and the support of its establishment. Levellers and reformers will always have the popular cry on their side, and I have good reason to know with what inveteracy a man is persecuted for an opinion which opposes it; and yet it is hard to give credit to the sincerity and disinterestedness of him who courts popularity, and deny it to the man who sacrifices his repose, and stands the brunt of abuse in defence of what he believes to be the truth.

And now having fallen upon the mention of Popularity, I shall take leave to address that divinity with a few lines picked up from an obscure author, which, though below poetry, are not quite prose, and on that account pretty nearly suited to the level of their subject.

O Popularity, thou giddy thing!
What grace or profit dost thou bring?

Thou art not honesty, thou art not fame;
I cannot call thee by a worthy name:
To say I hate thee were not true ;
Contempt is properly thy due;
I cannot love thee and despise thee too.

Thou art no patriot, but the veriest cheat
That ever traffick'd in deceit;
A state empiric, bellowing loud
Freedom and frenzy to the mobbing crowd ;
And what car'st thou, if thou canst raise
Illuminations and huzzas,
Tho' half the city sunk in one bright blaze?

A patriot ! no ; for thou dost hold in hate
The very peace and welfare of the state;
When anarchy assaults the sovereign's throne,
Then is the day, the night, thine own ;
Then is thy triumph, when the foe
Levels some dark insidious blow,
Or strong rebellion lays thy country low.

Thou canst affect humility to hide
Some deep device of monstrous pride ;
Conscience and charity pretend
For compassing some private end ;
And in a canting conventicle note
Long Scripture passages canst quote,
When persecution rankles in thy throat.

Thou hast no sense of nature at thy heart,
No ear for science, and no eye for art,
Yet confidently dost decide at once
This man a wit, and that a dunce;
And (strange to tell !) howe'er unjust,
We take thy dictates upon trust,
For if the world will be deceiv'd, it must.

In truth and justice thou hast no delight,
Virtue thou dost not know by sight ;
But, as the chymist by his skill
From dross and dregs a spirit can distil;
So from the prisons, or the stews,
Bullies, blasphemers, cheats, or Jews,
Shall turn to heroes, if they serve thy views.

Thou dost but make a ladder of the mob,
Whereby to climb into some courtly job;

> There safe reposing, warm and snug,
> Thou answer'st with a patient shrug,
> ' Miscreants, begone! who cares for you,
> Ye base-born, brawling, clamorous crew,
> You've serv'd my turn, and, vagabonds, adieu!'

## NUMBER LXXXVI.

BEING now arrived at the conclusion of my third volume,* and having hitherto given my readers very little interruption in my own person, I hope I may be permitted to make one short valedictory address to these departing adventurers, in whose success I am naturally so much interested.

I have employed much time and care in rearing up these Essays to what I conceived maturity, and qualifying them, as far as I was able, to shift for themselves, in a world where they are to inherit no popularity from their author, nor to look for any favour but what they can earn for themselves. To any, who shall question them who they are, and whence they come, they may truly answer—*We are all one man's sons*—we are indeed *Observers* but no *Spies*. If this shall not suffice, and they must needs give a farther account of themselves, they will have to say, that he who sent them into the world, sent them as an offering of his good-will to mankind; that he trusts they have been so trained as not to hurt the feelings or offend the principles of any man who shall admit them into his company; and that for their errors (which he cannot doubt are many) he hopes they will be found errors of the understanding, not of the

* This alludes to the original form of publishing these volumes.—C.

heart: they are the first-fruits of his leisure and retirement; and as the mind of a man in that situation
will naturally bring the past scenes of active life
under its examination and review, it will surely be
considered as a pardonable zeal for being yet serviceable to mankind, if he gives his experience and
observations to the world, when he has no farther
expectations from it on the score of fame or fortune.
These are the real motives for the publication of
these papers, and this the author's true state of mind:
to serve the cause of morality and religion is his
first ambition; to point out some useful lessons for
amending the education and manners of young people of either sex, and to mark the evil habits and
unsocial humours of men, with a view to their reformation, are the general objects of his undertaking.
He has formed his mind to be contented with the
consciousness of these honest endeavours, and with
a very moderate share of success. He has ample
reason notwithstanding to be more than satisfied with
the reception these papers have already had in their
probationary excursion; and it is not from any disgust, taken up in a vain conceit of his own merits,
that he has more than once observed upon the frauds
and follies of popularity, or that he now repeats his
opinion, that it is the worst guide a public man can
follow, who wishes not to go out of the track of honesty: for at the same time that he has seen men
force their way in the world by effrontery, and heard
others applauded for their talents, whose only recommendation has been their ingenuity in wickedness, he can recollect very few indeed who have
succeeded, either in fame or fortune, under the disadvantages of modesty and merit.

To such readers, as shall have taken up these Essays with a candid disposition to be pleased, he will
not scruple to express a hope that they have not been

altogether disappointed; for though he has been unassisted in composing them, he has endeavoured to
open a variety of resources, sensible that he had
many different palates to provide for. The subject
of politics, however, will never be one of these resources; a subject which he has neither the will nor
the capacity to meddle with. There is yet another
topic, which he has been no less studious to avoid,
which is personality; and though he professes to
give occasional delineations of living manners, and
not to make men in his closet (as some Essayists
have done), he does not mean to point at individuals;
for as this is a practice which he has ever rigidly ab-
stained from, when he mixed in the world, he should
hold himself without the excuse even of temptation,
if he was now to take it up, when he has withdrawn
himself from the world.

In the Essays (which he has presumed to call *Literary*, because he cannot strike upon any apposite
title of an humbler sort) he has studied to render
himself intelligible to readers of all descriptions,
and the deep-read scholar will not fastidiously pronounce them shallow, only because he can fathom
them with ease; for that would be to wrong both
himself and their author, who, if there is any vanity
in a pedantic margin of references, certainly resisted
that vanity, and as certainly had it at his choice to
have loaded his page with as great a parade of authorities as any of his brother writers upon classical
subjects have ostentatiously displayed. But if any
learned critic, now or hereafter, shall find occasion
to charge these Essays on the score of false authority or actual error, their author will most thankfully meet the investigation; and the fair reviewer
shall find that he has either candour to adopt correction, or materials enough in reserve to maintain
every warrantable assertion.

The Moralist and the Divine, it is hoped, will here find nothing to except against; it is not likely such an offence should be committed by one, who has rested all his hope in that revelation, on which his faith is founded; whom nothing could ever divert from his aim of turning even the gayest subjects to moral purposes, and who reprobates the jest, which provokes a laugh at the expense of a blush.

The Essays of a critical sort are no less addressed to the moral objects of composition, than to those which they have more professedly in view: they are not undertaken for the invidious purpose of developing errors, and stripping the laurels of departed poets, but simply for the uses of the living. The specimens already given, and those which are intended to follow in the farther prosecution of the work, are proposed as disquisitions of instruction rather than of subtilty; and if they shall be found more particularly to apply to dramatic composition, it is because their author looks up to the stage, as the great arbiter of more important delights, than those only which concern the taste and talents of the nation: it is because he sees with serious regret the buffoonery and low abuse of humour to which it is sinking, and apprehends for the consequences such an influx of folly may lead to. It will be readily granted there are but two modes of combating this abasement of the drama with any probability of success: one of these modes is, by an exposition of some one or other of the productions in question, which are supposed to contribute to its degradation; the other is, by inviting the attention of the public to an examination of better models, in which the standard works of our early dramatists abound. If the latter mode therefore should be adopted in these Essays, and the former altogether omitted, none of their readers will regret the preference that has been given upon such an alternative.

If the ladies of wit and talents do not take offence at some of these Essays, it will be a test of the truth of their pretensions, when they discern that the raillery, pointed only at affectation and false character, has no concern with them. There is nothing in which this nation has more right to pride itself, than the genius of its women; they have only to add a little more attention to their domestic virtues, and their fame will fly over the face of the globe. If I had ever known a good match broken off on the part of the man, because a young lady had too much modesty and discretion, or was too strictly educated in the duties of a good wife, I hope I understand myself too well to obtrude my old-fashioned maxims upon them. They might be as witty as they pleased, if I thought it was for their good; but if a racer, that has too great a share of heels, must lie by because it cannot be matched, so must every young spinster if her wits are too nimble. If I could once discover that men choose their wives, as they do their friends, for their manly achievements and convivial talents, for their being jolly fellows over a bottle, or topping a five-barred gate in a fox-chase, I should then be able to account for the many Amazonian figures I encounter in slouched hats, great coats, and half-boots, and I would not presume to set my face against the fashion; or if my experience of the fair sex could produce a single instance in the sect of Sentimentalists, which could make me doubt of the pernicious influence of a Musidorus and a Lady Thimble, I would not so earnestly have pressed the examples of a Sappho, a Calliope, or a Melissa.

The first Numbers of the present collection, to the amount of forty, have already been published; but being worked off at a country press, I find myself under the painful necessity of discontinuing the edition. I have availed myself of this opportunity, not

only by correcting the imperfections of the first publication, but by rendering this as unexceptionable
(in the external at least) as I possibly could. I should
have been wanting to the public and myself, if the
flattering encouragement I have already received had
not prompted me to proceed with the work; and if
my alacrity in the farther prosecution of it shall meet
any check, it must arise only from those causes,
which no human diligence can control.

> Vos tamen O nostri, ne festinate, libelli!
> Si post fata venit gloria, non propere.

## NUMBER LXXXVII.

*Jam te premet nox.*—Horat.

I am sitting down to begin the task of adding a new
volume to these Essays, when the last day of the
year 1789 is within a few hours of its conclusion, and
I shall bid farewell to this eventful period with a
grateful mind for its having passed lightly over my
head without any extraordinary perturbation or misfortune on my part suffered, gently leading me towards that destined and not far distant hour, when
I, like it, shall be no more.

I have accompanied it through all those changes
and successions of seasons, which in our climate are
so strongly discriminated; have shared in the pleasures and productions of each, and if any little idle
jars or bickerings may occasionally have started up
betwixt us, as will sometimes happen to the best of
friends, I willingly consign them to oblivion, and keep
in mind only those kind and good offices, which will

please on reflection, and serve to endear the memory of the deceased.

All days in twelve months will not be days of sunshine; but I will say this for *my friend in his last moments*, that I cannot put my finger upon one in the same century, that hath given birth to more interesting events, been a warmer advocate for the liberties and rights of mankind in general, or a kinder patron to this country in particular: I could name a day (if there was any need to point out what is so strongly impressed on our hearts) a day of gratulation and thanksgiving which will ever stand forth amongst the whitest in our calendar.

> Hic dies verè mihi festus atras
> Eximet curas: ego nec tumultum,
> Nec mori per vim metuam, tenente
>     Cæsare terras.—HORAT.
>
> This is indeed a festal day,
> A day that heals my cares and pains,
> Drives death and danger far away,
> And tells me Cæsar lives and reigns.

Though *my friend in his last moments* hath in this and other instances been so considerate of our happiness, I am afraid he is not likely to leave our morals much better than he found them: I cannot say that in the course of my duty as an Observer any very striking instance of amendment hath come under my notice; and though I have all the disposition in life to speak as favourably in my friend's behalf as truth will let me, I am bound to confess he was not apt to think so seriously of his latter end as I could have wished; there was a levity in his conduct, which he took no pains to conceal; he did not seem to reflect upon the lapse of time, how speedily his *spring, summer,* and *autumn* would pass away, and the winter of his days come upon him; like Wolsey he was not aware how soon the *frost, the killing frost*

*would nip his root;* he was, however, a gay convivial fellow, loved his bottle and his friend,
passed his time peaceably amongst us, and certainly merits the good word of every loyal subject in
this kingdom.

As for his proceedings in other countries, it is not
here the reader must look for an account of them;
politics have no place in these volumes; but it cannot be denied that he has made many widows and
orphans in Europe, been an active agent for the
court of death, and dipped his hands deep in Christian and Mahometan blood. By the friends of freedom he will be celebrated to the latest time. He
has begun a business, which if followed up by his
successor with equal zeal, less ferocity, and more discretion, may lead to wonderful revolutions: there
are indeed some instances of cruelty, which bear
hard upon his character; if separately viewed, they
admit of no palliation; in a general light allowances
may be made for that frenzy, which seizes the
mind, when impelled to great and arduous under-
takings; when the wound is gangrened the incision
must be deep, and if that is to be done by coarse
instruments and unskilful hands, who can wonder
if the gash more resembles the stab of an assassin,
than the operation of a surgeon. An era is now open,
awful, interesting, and so involved in mystery, that
the acutest speculation cannot penetrate to the issue
of it: in short, *my friend in his last moments* hath
put a vast machine in motion, and left a task to
futurity, that will demand the strongest hands and
ablest heads to complete: in the mean time I shall
hope that my countrymen, who have all those blessings by inheritance, which less-favoured nations are
now struggling to obtain by force, will so use their
liberty, that the rest of the world, who are not so
happy, may think it an object worth contending for,

and quote our peace and our prosperity as the best proofs existing of its real value.

Whilst my thoughts have been thus employed in reflecting upon the last day of an ever-memorable year, I have composed a few elegiac lines to be thrown into the grave which time is now opening to receive his reliques.

> The year's gay verdure, all its charms are gone,
> And now comes old December chill and drear,
> Dragging a darkling length of evening on,
> Whilst all things droop, as Nature's death were near.
>
> Time flies amain with broad expanded wings,
> Whence never yet a single feather fell,
> But holds his speed, and through the welkin rings
> Of all that breathe th' inexorable knell.
>
> Oh ! for a moment stop—a moment's space
> For recollection mercy might concede,
> A little pause for man's unthinking race
> To ponder on that world, to which they speed.
>
> But 'tis in vain ; old Time disdains to rest,
> And moment after moment flits along,
> Each with a sting to pierce the idler's breast,
> And vindicate its predecessor's wrong.
>
> Though the new dawning year in its advance
> With hope's gay promise may entrap the mind,
> Let memory give one retrospective glance
> Through the bright period which it leaves behind.
>
> Era of mercies ! my wrapt bosom springs
> To meet the transport recollection gives :
> Heaven's angel comes with healing on his wings ;
> He shakes his plumes, my country's father lives.
>
> The joyful tidings o'er the distant round
> Of Britain's empire the four winds proclaim,
> Her sun-burnt islands swell the exulting sound,
> And farthest Ganges echoes George's name.
>
> Period of bliss ! can any British muse
> Bid thee farewell without a parting tear ?
> Shall the historian's gratitude refuse
> His brightest page to this recorded year ?
> Thou Freedom's nursing-mother shall be styl'd,
> The glories of its birth are all thine own,

Upon thy breasts hung the Herculean child,
    And tyrants trembled at its baby frown.

A sanguine mantle the dread infant wore,
    Before it roll'd a stream of human blood:
Smiling it stood, and, pointing to the shore,
    Beckon'd the nations from across the flood.

Then at that awful sight, as with a spell,
    The everlasting doors of Death gave way,
Prone to the dust Oppression's fortress fell,
    And rescu'd captives hail'd the light of day.

Meanwhile Ambition chas'd its fairy prize
    With moonstruck madness down the Danube's stream,
The Turkish crescent glittering in its eyes,
    And lost an empire to pursue a dream.

The trampled serpent (Superstition) wreath'd
    Her fest'ring scales with anguish to and fro,
Torpid she lay, then darting forward sheath'd
    Her deadly fangs in the unguarded foe.

Oh Austria! why so prompt to venture forth,
    When fate now hurries thee to life's last goal?
Thee too, thou crowned eagle of the north,
    Death's dart arrests, though tow'ring to the pole.

Down then, Ambition; drop into the grave!
    And by thy follies be this maxim shewn—
'Tis not the monarch's glory to enslave
    His neighbour's empire, but to bless his own.

Come then, sweet Peace! in Britain fix thy reign,
    Bid Plenty smile, and Commerce crowd her coast:
And may this ever-blessed year remain
    Her king's, her people's, and her muse's boast!

---

# NUMBER LXXXVIII.

NICOLAS PEDROSA, a busy little being, who followed
the trades of shaver, surgeon, and man-midwife in
the town of Madrid, mounted his mule at the door
of his shop in the Plazuela de los Affligidos, and

pushed through the gate of San Bernardino, being called to a patient in the neighbouring village of Foncarral, upon a pressing occasion. Every body knows that the ladies in Spain in certain cases do not give long warning to practitioners of a certain description, and nobody knew it better than Nicolas, who was resolved not to lose an inch of his way, nor of his mule's best speed by the way, if cudgelling could beat it out of her. It was plain to Nicolas's conviction, as plain could be, that his road laid straight forward to the little convent in front; the mule was of opinion, that the turning on the left down the hill towards the Prado was the road of all roads most familiar and agreeable to herself, and accordingly began to dispute the point of topography with Nicolas by fixing her four feet resolutely in the ground, dipping her head at the same time between them, and launching heels and crupper furiously into the air in the way of argument. Little Pedrosa, who was armed at heel with one massy silver spur of stout, though ancient, workmanship, resolutely applied the rusty rowel to the shoulder of his beast, driving it with all the good will in the world to the very butt, and at the same time adroitly tucking his blue cloth capa under his right arm, and flinging the skirt over the left shoulder *en cavalier*, began to lay about him with a stout ashen sapling upon the ears, poll, and cheeks of the recreant mule. The fire now flashed from a pair of Andalusian eyes, as black as charcoal and not less inflammable, and taking the segara from his mouth, with which he had vainly hoped to have regaled his nostrils in a sharp winter's evening by the way, raised such a thundering troop of angels, saints, and martyrs, from St. Michael downwards, not forgetting his own namesake Saint Nicolas de Tolentino by the way, that if curses could have made the mule to go, the dispute would have

been soon ended, but not a saint could make her
stir any other ways than upwards and downwards at
a stand. A small troop of mendicant friars were at
this moment conducting the host of a dying man.—
'Nicolas Pedrosa,' says an old friar, 'be patient
with your beast, and spare your blasphemies; remember Balaam.'—'Ah father,' replied Pedrosa,
'Balaam cudgelled his beast till she spoke, so will
I mine till she roars.'—'Fie, fie, profane fellow,'
cries another of the fraternity. 'Go about your
work friend,' quoth Nicolas, 'and let me go about
mine; I warrant it is the more pressing of the two;
your patient is going out of the world, mine is coming into it.'—'Hear him,' cries a third, 'hear the
vile wretch, how he blasphemes the body of God.'—
And then the troop past slowly on to the tinkling of
the bell.

A man must know nothing of a mule's ears who
does not know what a passion they have for the
tinkling of a bell, and no sooner had the jingling
cords vibrated in the sympathetic organs of Pedrosa's
beast, than boulting forward with a sudden spring
she ran roaring into the throng of friars, trampling
on some and shouldering others at a most profane
rate; when Nicolas availing himself of the impetus,
and perhaps not able to control it, broke away, and
was out of sight in a moment. 'All the devils in
hell blow fire into thy tail, thou beast of Babylon,'
muttered Nicolas to himself as he scampered along,
never once looking behind him or stopping to apologize for the mischief he had done to the bare feet
and shirtless ribs of the holy brotherhood.

Whether Nicolas saved his distance, as likewise,
if he did, whether it was a male or female Castilian
he ushered into the world, we will not just now inquire, contented to wait his return in the first of the
morning next day, when he had no sooner dismounted

at his shop and delivered his mule to a sturdy Arragonese wench, than Don Ignacio de Santos Aparicio, alguazil mayor of the supreme and general inquisition, put an order into his hand, signed and sealed by the inquisidor-general, for the conveying his body to the Casa, whose formidable door presents itself in the street adjoining the square in which Nicolas's brazen basin hung forth the emblem of his trade.

The poor little fellow, trembling in every joint, and with a face as yellow as saffron, dropped a knee to the altar, which fronts the entrance, and crossed himself most devoutly; as soon as he had ascended the first flight of stairs, a porter habited in black opened the tremendous barricade, and Nicolas with horror heard the grating of the heavy bolts that shut him in. He was led through passages and vaults and melancholy cells till he was delivered into the dungeon, where he was finally left to his solitary meditations. Hapless being! what a scene of horror. Nicolas felt all the terrors of his condition, but being an Andalusian, and like his countrymen of a lively imagination, he began to turn over all the resources of his invention for some happy fetch, if any such might occur, for helping him out of the dismal limbo he was in : he was not long to seek for the cause of his misfortune : his adventure with the barefooted friars was a ready solution of all difficulties of that nature, had there been any : there was however another thing, which might have troubled a stouter heart than Nicolas's—He was a Jew.—This of a certain would have been a staggering item in a poor devil's confession, but then it was a secret to all the world but Nicolas, and Nicolas's conscience did not just then urge him to reveal it; he now began to overhaul the inventory of his personals about him, and with some satisfaction counted three little medals of the Blessed Virgin, two Agnus Deis, a Saint Nico-

las de Tolentino, and a formidable string of beads
all pendant from his neck and within his shirt; in
his pockets he had a paper of dried figs, a small
bundle of segars, a case of lancets, squirt, and forceps, and too old razors in a leathern envelop;
these he had delivered one by one to the alguazil,
who first arrested him,—' and let him make the most
of them,' said he to himself, ' they can never prove
me an Israelite by a case of razors.'—Upon a closer
rummage however he discovered in a secret pocket
a letter, which the alguazil had overlooked, and
which his patient Donna Leonora de Casafonda had
given him in charge to deliver as directed—' Well,
well,' cried he, ' let it pass; there can be no mystery
in this harmless scrawl; a letter of advice to some
friend or relation, I'll not break the seal; let the
fathers read it if they like, 'twill prove the truth of
my deposition, and help out my excuse for the hurry
of my errand, and the unfortunate adventure of my
damned refractory mule.'—And now no sooner had
the recollection of the wayward mule crossed the
brain of poor Nicolas Pedrosa, than he began to
blast her at a furious rate,—' The scratches and the
scab to boot confound thy scurvy hide,' quoth he,
' thou ass-begotten bastard whom Noah never let
into his ark!  The vengeance take thee for an un-
created barren beast of promiscuous generation!
What devil's crotchet got into thy capricious noddle,
that thou shouldst fall in love with that Nazaritish
bell, and run bellowing like Lucifer into the midst
of those barefooted vermin, who are more malicious
and more greedy than the locusts of Egypt? Oh!
that I had the art of Simon Magus to conjure thee
into this dungeon in my stead; but I warrant thou
art chewing thy barley straw without any pity for
thy wretched master, whom thy jade's tricks have
delivered bodily to the tormentors, to be the sport

of these uncircumcised sons of Dagon.' And now
the cell door opened, when a savage figure entered
carrying a huge parcel of clanking fetters, with a
collar of iron, which he put round the neck of poor
Pedrosa, telling him with a truly diabolic grin, whilst
he was rivetting it on, that it was a proper cravat for
the throat of a blasphemer.—'Jesu-Maria,' quoth
Pedrosa, ' is all this fallen upon me for only cudgelling a restive mule ?'—'Aye,' cried the demon, 'and
this is only a taste of what is to come,' at the same
time slipping his pincers from the screw he was
forcing to the head, he caught a piece of flesh in the
forceps, and wrenched it out of his cheek, laughing
at poor Nicolas, whilst he roared aloud with the
pain, telling him it was a just reward for the torture
he had put him to awhile ago, when he tugged at a
tooth till he broke it in his jaw. ' Ah, for the love
of Heaven,' cried Pedrosa, ' have more pity on me
for the sake of Saint Nicolas de Tolentino, my holy
patron be not so unmerciful to a poor barber-sur-
geon, and I will shave your worship's beard for nothing as long as I have life.' One of the messengers
of the auditory now came in, and bade the fellow
strike off the prisoner's fetters, for that the holy fathers were in council, and demanded him for examination. ' This is something extraordinary,' quoth
the tormentor : ' I should not have expected it this
twelvemonth to come.' Pedrosa's fetters were struck
off; some brandy was applied to staunch the bleed-
ing of his cheeks : his hands and face were washed,
and a short jacket of coarse ticking thrown over
him, and the messenger with an assistant taking
him each under an arm, led him into a spacious
chamber, where at the head of a long table sate his
excellency the inquisidor-general, with six of his
assessors, three on each side the chair of state : the
alguazil mayor, a secretary, and two notaries, with

other officers of the holy council, were attending in
their places.

The prisoner was placed behind a bar at the foot
of the table between the messengers who brought
him in, and having made his obeisance to the awful
presence in the most supplicating manner, he was
called upon according to the usual form of questions
by one of the junior judges to declare his name,
parentage, profession, age, place of abode, and to
answer various interrogatories of the like trifling
nature: his excellency the inquisidor-general now
opened his reverend lips, and in a solemn tone of
voice, that penetrated to the heart of the poor trembling prisoner, interrogated him as follows—

'Nicolas Pedrosa, we have listened to the account
you give of yourself, your business and connexions,
now tell us for what offence, or offences, you are
here standing a prisoner before us: examine your
own heart, and speak the truth from your conscience
without prevarication or disguise.'—'May it please
your excellency,' replied Pedrosa, 'with all due submission to your holiness and this reverend assembly,
my most equitable judges, I conceive I stand here
before you for no worse a crime, than that of cudgelling a refractory mule; an animal so restive in
its nature (under correction of your holiness be it
spoken), that although I were blest with the forbearance of holy Job (for like him too I am married, and
my patience hath been exercised by a wife), yet
could I not forbear to smite my beast for her obstinacy, and the rather because I was summoned in the
way of my profession, as I have already made known
to your most merciful ears, upon a certain crying
occasion, which would not admit of a moment's
delay.'

'Recollect yourself, Nicolas,' said his excellency
he inquisidor-general, 'was there nothing else you
did, save smiting your beast?'

'I take Saint Nicolas de Tolentino to witness,' replied he, 'that I know of no other crime, for which I can be responsible at this righteous tribunal, save smiting my unruly beast.'

'Take notice, brethren,' exclaimed the inquisidor, 'this unholy wretch holds trampling over friars to be no crime.'

'Pardon me, holy father,' replied Nicolas, 'I hold it for the worst of crimes, and therefore willingly surrender my refractory mule to be dealt with as you see fit, and if you impale her alive it will not be more than she deserves.'

'Your wits are too nimble, Nicolas,' cried the judge; 'have a care they do not run away with your discretion: recollect the blasphemies you uttered in the hearing of those pious people.'

'I humbly pray your excellency,' answered the prisoner, 'to recollect that anger is a short madness, and I hope allowances will be made by your holy council for words spoken in haste to a rebellious mule: the prophet Balaam was thrown off his guard with a simple ass, and what is an ass compared to a mule: if your excellency had seen the lovely creature that was screaming in an agony till I came to her relief, and how fine a boy I ushered into the world, which would have been lost but for my assistance, I am sure I should not be condemned for a few hasty words spoke in passion.'

'Sirrah!' cried one of the puisne judges, 'respect the decency of the court.'

'Produce the contents of this fellow's pockets before the court,' said the president: 'lay them on the table.'

'Monster,' resumed the aforesaid puisne judge, taking up the forceps, 'what is the use of this diabolical machine?'

'Please your reverence,' replied Pedrosa, '*aptum*

*est ad extrahendos fœtus.'*—'Unnatural wretch,' again
exclaimed the judge, ' you have murdered the mother.'

'The mother of God forbid!' exclaimed Pedrosa,
'I believe I have a proof in my pocket that will acquit me of that charge;' and so saying, he tendered
the letter we have before made mention of: the secretary took it, and by command of the court read
as follows:

'SENOR DON MANUEL DE HERRERA;

' When this letter, which I send by Nicolas Pedrosa, shall reach your hands, you shall know that I
am safely delivered of a lovely boy after a dangerous
labour, in consideration of which I pray you to pay
to the said Nicolas Pedrosa the sum of twenty gold
pistoles, which sum his excellency'—

' Hold!' cried the inquisidor-general, starting
hastily from his seat, and snatching away the letter,
' there is more in this than meets the eye : break up
the court; I must take an examination of this prisoner in private.'

---

## NUMBER LXXXIX.

As soon as the room was cleared the inquisidor-general beckoning to the prisoner to follow him, retired
into a private closet, where throwing himself care-
lessly into an arm-chair, he turned a gracious countenance upon the poor affrighted accoucheur, and bidding him sit down upon a low stool by his side, thus
accosted him :—' Take heart, Senor Pedrosa, your
imprisonment is not likely to be very tedious, for I
have a commission you must execute without loss of

time : you have too much consideration for yourself
to betray a trust, the violation of which must involve
you in inevitable ruin, and can in no degree attaint
my character, which is far enough beyond the reach
of malice : be attentive therefore to my orders ; execute them punctually, and keep my secret as you
tender your own life : dost thou know the name and
condition of the lady whom thou hast delivered?'
Nicolas assured him he did not, and his excellency
proceeded as follows :—' Then I tell thee, Nicolas,
it is the illustrious Donna Leonora de Casafonda :
her husband is the president of Quito, and daily expected with the next arrivals from the South Seas ;
now, though measures have been taken for detaining
him at the port, wherever he shall land, till he shall
receive farther orders, yet you must be sensible
Donna Leonora's situation is somewhat delicate : it
will be your business to take the speediest measures
for her recovery, but as it seems she has had a dangerous and painful labour, this may be a work of
more time than could be wished, unless some medicines more efficacious than common are administered : art thou acquainted with any such, friend Nicolas ?'—' So please your excellency,' quoth Nicolas,
' my processes have been tolerably successful ; I
have bandages and cataplasms with oils and con-
serves, that I have no cause to complain of : they
will restore nature to its proper state in all decent
time'—' Thou talkest like a fool, friend Nicolas,'
interrupting him, said the inquisidor : ' What tellest
thou me of thy swathings and swaddlings? quick
work must be wrought by quick medicines : hast
thou none such in thy botica? I'll answer for it
thou hast not ; therefore look you, sirrah, here is a
little vial compounded by a famous chymist ; see
that you mix it in the next apozem you administer
to Donna Leonora ; it is the most capital sedative in

nature; give her the whole of it, and let her husband return when he will, depend upon it he will make no discoveries from her.'—' Humph!' quoth Nicolas within himself, ' Well said, inquisidor!' He took the vial with all possible respect, and was not wanting in professions of the most inviolable fidelity and secresy—' No more words, friend Nicolas,' quoth the inquisidor, ' upon that score; I do not believe thee one jot the more for all thy promises; my dependance is upon thy fears, and not thy faith; I fancy thou hast seen enough of this place not to be willing to return to it once for all.'—Having so said, he rang a bell, and ordered Nicolas to be forthwith liberated, bidding the messenger return his clothes instantly to him with all that belonged to him, and having slipped a purse into his hand well filled with doubloons, he bade him begone about his business, and not see his face again till he had executed his commands.

Nicolas boulted out of the porch without taking leave of the altar, and never checked his speed till he found himself fairly housed under shelter of his own beloved brass basin.—' Aha!' quoth Nicolas, ' my lord inquisidor, I see the king is not likely to gain a subject more by your intrigues: a pretty job you have set me about; and so, when I have put the poor lady to rest with your damned sedative, my tongue must be stopped next to prevent its blabbing: but I'll shew you I was not born in Andalusia for nothing.' Nicolas now opened a secret drawer and took out a few pieces of money, which in fact was his whole stock of cash in the world: he loaded and primed his pistols, and carefully lodged them in the housers of his saddle, he buckled to his side his trusty spada, and hastened to caparison his mule. ' Ah, thou imp of the old one,' quoth he as he entered the stable, ' art not ashamed to look me in the face?' But come, hussy, thou owest me a good turn methinks, stand by me this once, and be friends for ever! thou art in good case, and if thou wilt put thy best foot foremost, like a faithful beast thou shalt not want for barley by the way.' The bargain was soon struck between Nicolas and his mule, he mounted her in the happy moment, and pointing his course towards the bridge of Toledo, which proudly strides with half a dozen lofty arches over a stream scarce three feet wide, he found himself as completely in a desert in half a mile's riding, as if he had been dropped in the centre of Arabia Petræa. As Nicolas's journey was not a tour of curiosity, he did not amuse himself with a peep at Toledo, or Talavera, or even Merida by the way; for the same reason he took a *circumbendibus* round the frontier town of Badajoz, and crossing a little brook refreshed his mule with the last draught of Spanish water, and instantly congratulated himself upon entering the territory of Portugal. ' Brava!' quoth he patting the neck of his mule, thou shalt have a supper this night of the best sieve-meat that Estramadura can furnish: we are now in a country where the scattered flock of Israel fold thick and fare well.' He now began to chant the song of Solomon, and gently ambled on in the joy of his heart.

When Nicolas at length reached the city of Lisbon, he hugged himself in his good fortune: still he recollected that the inquisition has long arms, and he was yet in a place of no perfect security. Our adventurer had in early life acted as assistant-surgeon in a Spanish frigate bound to Buenos Ayres, and being captured by a British man of war, and carried into Jamaica, had very quietly passed some years in that place as journeyman apothecary, in which time he had acquired a tolerable acquaintance

with the English language: no sooner then did he
discover the British ensign flying on the poop of an
English frigate then lying in the Tagus, than he
eagerly caught the opportunity of paying a visit to
the surgeon, and finding he was in want of a mate,
offered himself, and was entered in that capacity for
a cruise against the French and Spaniards, with
whom Great Britain was then at war. In this secure
asylum Nicolas enjoyed the first happy moments he
had experienced for a long time past, and being a
lively good-humoured little fellow, and one that
touched the guitar and sung sequidillas with a tolerable grace, he soon recommended himself to his
shipmates, and grew in favour with every body on
board from the captain to the cook's mate.

When they were out upon their cruise hovering
on the Spanish coast, it occurred to Nicolas that the
inquisidor-general at Madrid had told him of the expected arrival of the president of Quito, and having
imparted this to one of the lieutenants, he reported
it to the captain, and as the intelligence seemed of
importance, he availed himself of it by hauling into
the track of the homeward-bound galleons, and
great was the joy, when at the break of the morning the man at the mast-head announced a square-
rigged vessel in view: the ardour of a chace now
set all hands at work, and a few hours brought them
near enough to discern that she was a Spanish frigate, and seemingly from a long voyage; little Pedrosa, as alert as the rest, stripped himself for his
work, and repaired to his post in the cock-pit, whilst
the thunder of the guns rolled incessantly over-head;
three cheers from the whole crew at length announced
the moment of victory, and a few more minutes ascertained the good news that the prize was a frigate
richly laden from the South Seas, with the governor
of Quito and his suite on board.

Pedrosa was now called upon deck, and sent on board the prize as interpreter to the first lieutenant, who was to take possession of her. He found every thing in confusion, a deck covered with the slain and the whole crew in consternation at an event they were in no degree prepared for, not having received any intimation of a war. He found the officers in general, and the passengers without exception, under the most horrid impressions of the English, and expecting to be plundered, and perhaps butchered without mercy. Don Manuel de Casafonda the governor, whose countenance bespoke a constitution far gone in a decline, had thrown himself on a sofa in the last state of despair, and given way to an effusion of tears: when the lieutenant entered the cabin he rose trembling from his couch, and with the most supplicating action presented to him his sword, and with it a casket which he carried in his other hand; as he tendered these spoils to his conqueror, whether through weakness or of his own will, he made a motion of bending his knee: the generous Briton, shocked at the unmanly overture, caught him suddenly with both hands, and turning to Pedrosa, said aloud—'Convince this gentleman he is fallen into the hands of an honourable enemy.'—'Is it possible!' cried Don Manuel, and lifting up his streaming eyes to the countenance of the British officer, saw humanity, valour, and generous pity so strongly charactered in his youthful features, that the conviction was irresistible. 'Will he not accept my sword?' cried the Spaniard. 'He desires you to wear it, till he has the honour of presenting you to his captain.'—'Ah then he has a captain,' exclaimed Don Manuel, 'his superior will be of another way of thinking; tell him this casket contains my jewels; they are valuable; let him present them as a lawful prize, which will enrich the captor; his superior will not hesitate to take them from me.'—'If they are your excellency's private property,' replied Pedrosa, 'I am ordered to assure you, that if your ship was loaded with jewels, no British officer, in the service of his king, will take them at your hands; the ship and effects of his Catholic Majesty are the only prize of the captors; the personals of the passengers are inviolate.'—'Generous nation!' exclaimed Don Manuel, 'how greatly have I wronged thee!'—The boats of the British frigate now came alongside, and part of the crew were shifted out of the prize, taking their clothes and trunks along with them, in which they were very cordially assisted by their conquerors. The barge soon after came aboard with an officer in the stern-sheets, and the crew in their white shirts and velvet caps, to escort the governor and the ship's captain on board the frigate, which lay with her sails to the mast awaiting their arrival; the accommodation ladder was slung over the side, and manned for the prisoners, who were received on the gang-way by the second lieutenant, whilst perfect silence and the strictest discipline reigned in the ship, where all were under the decks, and no inquisitive curious eyes were suffered to wound the feelings of the conquered even with a glance; in the door of his cabin stood the captain, who received them with that modest complaisance, which does not revolt the unfortunate by an overstrained politeness; he was a man of high birth and elegant manners, with a heart as benevolent as it was brave: such an address, set off with a person finely formed and perfectly engaging, could not fail to impress the prisoners with the most favourable ideas; and as Don Manuel spoke French fluently, he could converse with the British captain without the help of an interpreter: as he expressed an impatient desire of being admitted to his parole, that he might revisit friends and connexions, from which he had been long separated, he was overjoyed to hear that the English ship would cary her prize into Lisbon; and that he would be there set on shore, and permitted to make the best of his way from thence to Madrid; he talked of his wife with all the ardour of the most impassionate lover, and apologized for his tears, by imputing them to the agony of his mind, and the infirmity of his health, under the dread of being longer separated from an object so dear to his heart, and on whom he doted with the fondest affection. The generous captor indulged him in these conversations, and, being a husband himself, knew how to allow for all the tenderness of his sensations. 'Ah, Sir,' cried Don Manuel, 'would to Heaven it were in my power to have the honour of presenting my beloved Leonora to you on our landing at Lisbon.—Perhaps,' added he, turning to Pedrosa, who at that moment entered the cabin, 'this gentleman, whom I take to be a Spaniard, may have heard the name of Donna Leonora de Casafonda: if he has been at Madrid, it is possible he may have seen her; should that be the case, he can testify to her external charms; I alone can witness to the exquisite perfection of her mind.'—'Senor Don Manuel,' replied Pedrosa, 'I have seen Donna Leonora, and your excellency is warranted in all you can say in her praise; she is of incomparable beauty.' These words threw the uxorious Spaniard into raptures; his eyes sparkled with delight; the blood rushed into his emaciated cheeks, and every feature glowed with unutterable joy: he pressed Pedrosa with a variety of rapid inquiries, all which he evaded by pleading ignorance, saying, that he had only had a casual glance of her, as she passed along the Pardo. The embarrassment however which accompanied these answers, did not escape the English captain, who shortly after drawing Pedrosa aside into the surgeon's cabin, was by him made acquainted with the melancholy situation of that unfortunate lady, and every particular of the story as before related; nay the very vial was produced with its contents, as put into the hands of Pedrosa by the inquisidor.

# NUMBER XC.

'Can there be such villany in man!' cried the British captain, when Pedrosa had concluded his detail: 'Alas! my heart bleeds for this unhappy husband: assuredly that monster has destroyed Leonora: as for thee, Pedrosa, whilst the British flag flies over thy head, neither Spain, nor Portugal, nor inquisitors, nor devils, shall annoy thee under its protection; but if thou ever venturest over the side of this ship, and rashly settest one foot upon Catholic soil, when we arrive at Lisbon, thou art a lost man.' —'I were worse than a madman,' replied Nicolas, 'should I attempt it.'—'Keep close in this asylum then,' resumed the captain, 'and fear nothing. Had it been our fate to have been captured by the Spaniard, what would have become of thee?'—'In the worst of extremities,' replied Nicolas, 'I should have applied to the inquisidor's vial; but I confess I had no fears of that sort; a ship so commanded and so manned is in little danger of being carried into a Spanish port.'—'I hope not,' said the captain, 'and I promise thee thou shalt take thy chance in her, as long as she is afloat under my command, and if we live to conduct her to England, thou shalt have thy proper share of prize-money, which if the galleon breaks up according to her entries, will be something towards enabling thee to shift, and if thou art as diligent in thy duty, as I am persuaded thou wilt be, whilst I live thou shalt never want a seaman's friend.' At these cheering words, little Nicolas threw himself at the feet of his generous preserver, and with streaming eyes, poured out his thanks from a heart animated with joy and gratitude.—The captain raising him by the hand, forbade him, as he prized his friendship, ever to address him in that posture any more : ' Thank me, if you will,' added he, ' but thank me as one man should another ; let no knees bend in this ship but to the name of God.—But now,' continued he, ' let us turn our thoughts to the situation of our unhappy Casafonda : we are now drawing near to Lisbon, where he will look to be liberated on his parole.'—' By no means let him venture into Spain,' said Pedrosa ; ' I am well assured there are orders to arrest him in every port or frontier town, where he may present himself.'—' I can well believe it,' replied the captain ; ' his piteous case will require farther deliberation ; in the mean time let nothing transpire on your part, and keep yourself out of his sight as carefully as you can.'—This said, the captain left the cabin, and both parties repaired to their several occupations.

As soon as the frigate and her prize cast anchor in the Tagus, Don Manuel de Casafonda impatiently reminded our captain of his promised parole. The painful moment was now come, when an explanation of some sort became unavoidable : the generous Englishman, with a countenance expressive of the tenderest pity, took the Spaniard's hand in his, and seating him on a couch beside him, ordered the sentinel to keep the cabin private, and delivered himself as follows :

' Senor Don Manuel, I must now impart to you

an anxiety which I labour under on your account; I have strong reason to suspect you have enemies in your own country, who are upon the watch to arrest you on your landing: when I have told you this, I expect you will repose such trust in my honour, and the sincerity of my regard for you, as not to demand a farther explanation of the particulars on which my intelligence is founded.'—' Heaven and earth!' cried the astonished Spaniard, ' who can be those enemies I have to fear, and what can I have done to deserve them?'—' So far I will open myself to you,' answered the captain, ' as to point out the principal to you, the inquisidor-general.'—' The best friend I have in Spain,' exclaimed the governor, ' my sworn protector, the patron of my fortune. He my enemy! impossible.'—' Well, Sir,' replied the captain, ' if my advice does not meet belief, I must so far exert my authority for your sake, as to make this ship your prison till I have waited on our minister at Lisbon, and made the inquiries necessary for your safety; suspend your judgment upon the seeming harshness of this measure till I return to you again?' and at the same time rising from his seat, he gave orders for the barge, and leaving strict injunctions with the first lieutenant not to allow of the governor's quitting the frigate, he put off for the shore, and left the melancholy Spaniard buried in profound and silent meditation.

The emissaries of the inquisition having at last traced Pedrosa to Lisbon, and there gained intelligence of his having entered on board the frigate, our captain had no sooner turned into the porch of the hotel at Buenos Ayres, than he was accosted by a messenger of state, with a requisition from the prime minister's office for the surrender of one Nicolas Pedrosa, a subject of Spain and a criminal, who had escaped out of the prison of the inquisition in Ma-

drid, where he stood charged with high crimes and
misdemeanours. As soon as this requisition was explained to our worthy captain, without condescend-
ing to a word in reply, he called for pen and ink,
and writing a short order to the officer commanding
on board, instantly dispatched the midshipman, who
attended him, to the barge, with directions, to make
the best of his way back to the frigate, and deliver
it to the lieutenant; then, turning to the messenger,
he said to him in a resolute tone—' That Spaniard
is now borne on my books, and before you shall take
him out of the service of my king, you must sink his
ship.'—Not waiting for a reply, he immediately proceeded without stop to the house of the British minister at the farther end of the city: here he found
Pedrosa's intelligence with regard to the governor
of Quito, expressly verified, for the order had come
down even to Lisbon, upon the chance of the Spanish
frigate's taking shelter in that port: to this minister
he related the horrid tale which Pedrosa had delivered to him, and with his concurrence it was determined to forward letters into Spain, which Don
Manuel should be advised to write to his lady and
friends at Madrid, and to wait their answer before
any farther discoveries were imparted to him respecting the blacker circumstances of the case. In
the mean time it was resolved to keep the prisoner
safe in his asylum.

The generous captain lost no time in returning to
his frigate, where he immediately imparted to Don
Manuel the intelligence he had obtained at the British minister's.—' This, indeed,' cried the afflicted
Spaniard, ' is a stroke I was in no respect prepared
for; I had fondly persuaded myself there was not in
the whole empire of Spain a more friendly heart than
that of the inquisidor's; to my beloved Leonora he
had ever shewn the tenderness of a paternal affection

from her very childhood; by him our hands were
joined; his lips pronounced the nuptial benediction,
and through his favour I was promoted to my government: grant, Heaven, no misfortune hath befallen my Leonora; surely she cannot have offended
him, and forfeited his favour.'—'As I know him
not,' replied the captain, 'I can form no judgment of
his motives; but this I know, that if a man's heart
is capable of cruelty, the fittest school to learn it in
must be the inquisition.' The proposal was now
suggested of sending letters into Spain, and the governor retired to his desk for the purpose of writing
them; in the afternoon of the same day the minister
paid a visit to the captain, and receiving a packet
from the hands of Don Manuel, promised to get it
forwarded by a safe conveyance according to direction.

In due course of time this fatal letter from Leonora, opened all the horrible transaction to the
wretched husband:—

'The guilty hand of an expiring wife, under the
agonizing operation of a mortal poison, traces these
few trembling lines to an injured wretched husband.
If thou hast any pity for my parting spirit, fly the
ruin that awaits thee, and avoid this scene of villany and horror. When I tell thee I have born a
child to the monster, whose poison runs in my veins,
thou wilt abhor thy faithless Leonora; had I strength
to relate to thee the subtle machinations, which betrayed me to disgrace, thou wouldst pity and perhaps
forgive me. Oh agony! can I write his name?
The inquisidor is my murderer—My pen falls from
my hand—Farewell for ever.'

Had a shot passed through the heart of Don Manuel, it could not more effectually have stopped its
motions than the perusal of this fatal writing: he
dropped lifeless on the couch, and but for the care

and assistance of the captain and Pedrosa, in that posture he had probably expired. Grief like his will not be described by words, for to words it gave no utterance: 'twas suffocating, silent woe.

Let us drop the curtain over this melancholy pause in our narration, and attend upon the mournful widower now landed upon English ground, and conveyed by his humane and generous preserver to the house of a noble Earl, the father of our amiable captain, and a man by his virtues still more conspicuous than by his rank. Here amidst the gentle solicitudes of a benevolent family, in one of the most enchanting spots on earth, in a climate most salubrious and restorative to a constitution exhausted by heat, and a heart nearly broken with sorrow, the reviving spirits of the unfortunate Don Manuel gave the first symptoms of a possible recovery. At the period of a few tranquillizing weeks here passed in the bosom of humanity, letters came to hand from the British minister at Lisbon, in answer to a memorial, that I should have stated to have been drawn up by the friendly captain before his departure from that port, with a detail of facts deposed and sworn to by Nicolas Pedrosa, which memorial, with the documents attached to it, was forwarded to the Spanish court by special express from the Portuguese premier. By these letters it appeared, that the high dignity of the person impeached by this statement of facts, had not been sufficient to screen him from a very serious and complete investigation: in the course of which facts had been so clearly brought home to him by the confession of his several agents, and the testimony of the deceased Leonora's attendants, together with her own written declarations, whilst the poison was in operation, that though no public sentence had been executed upon the criminal, it was generally understood he was either no longer

in existence, or in a situation never to be heard of
any more, till roused by the awakening trump he
shall be summoned to his tremendous last account.
As for the unhappy widower, it was fully signified to
him from authority, that his return to Spain, whether
upon exchange or parole, would be no longer opposed, nor had he any thing to apprehend on the
part of government when he should there arrive.
The same was signified in fewer words to the excul-
pated Pedrosa.

Whether Don Manuel de Casafonda will in time
to come avail himself of these overtures, time alone
can prove : as for little Nicolas, whose prize-money
has set him up in a comfortable little shop in Duke's-
place, where he breathes the veins, and cleanses the
bowels of his Israelitish brethren, in a land of freedom and toleration, his merry heart is at rest, save
only when, with fire in his eyes, and vengeance on
his tongue, he anathematizes the inquisition, and
struts into the synagogue every Sabbath with as bold
a step, and as erect a look, as if he was himself
High Priest of the Temple, going to perform sacrifice upon the reassembling of the scattered tribes.

## NUMBER XCI.

A GOOD man will live with the world as a wise man
lives with his wife : he will not let himself down to
be a dupe to its humours, a devotee to its pleasures,
or a flatterer of its faults ; he will make himself as
happy as he can in the connexion for his own sake,
reform where he is able, and complain only when
he cannot help it.   I am sick of that conversation

which spends itself in railing at the times we live in:
I am apt to think they are not made better by those
complaints, and I have oftentimes occasion to know
they are made worse by those very people who are
loudest to complain of them. If this be really one
of the habits of age, it is high time for every man,
who grows old, to guard against it: for there is no
occasion to invite more peevish companions for the
last hours of life, than time and decrepitude will
bring in their train: let us look back upon things past
with what content we can, salute time present with
the best grace we are able, and resign ourselves to
futurity with calmness and a patient mind. If we do
not wish to be banished from society before death
withdraws us from it, do not let us trust to the world's
respect only, let us strive also to conciliate its love.

But I do not wish to argue this point with the sect
of the Murmurers merely upon the ground of good
policy; I should be sorry for the world, if I could
give no better reason for keeping well with it than
in self-defence: I really think it a world very easy
to live with upon passable good terms; I am free to
confess it has mended me since I have lived with it,
and I am fully of opinion it has mended itself: I do
not deny but it has its failings; it still cuts out work
for the moralists, and I am in no fear of finding
subject matter for three more volumes of essays,
before I have exhausted the duty of an Observer.
However, though I have presumed upon taking up
this character late in life, yet I feel no provocation
from what I observe in others, or in myself, to turn
Murmurer; I can call the time past under my review,
as far back as my experience will go, and comfort
myself by the comparison of it with the time present; I can turn to the authors, who have delineated
the manners of ages antecedent to my own, without
being ashamed of my contemporaries, or entertain-

ing a superior respect for theirs. I cannot look back to any period of our own annals, of which I can conscientiously pronounce, according to such judgment as I am possessed of, that the happiness of society was better secured, and more completely provided for, than at the present moment.

This may appear so hardy an assertion, that if the Murmurers take the field against me, I suspect that I shall find myself, as I frequently have done, in a very decided minority; for let the reader take notice, I know the world too well to think of getting popularity by defending it: if ever I make that my object, I must run counter to my own principles, and abuse many, that all may read me: in the mean time I shall make a show of some of my defences, if it be only to convince the Murmurers, that I shall not capitulate upon the first summons; and I will keep some strong posts masked from their view, that if they repeat their assault, I may still have resources in my reach.

Society is cemented by laws, upheld by religion, endeared by manners, and adorned by arts.

Let us now inquire what is the present state of these great fundamentals of social happiness, and whether any better period can be pointed out, compared to which their present state may be justly pronounced a state of declension.

The constitution of England has undergone many changes: the monarch, the nobles, and the people, have each in their turn for a time destroyed that proper balance, in which its excellence consists. In feudal times the aristocratic power preponderated, and the kingdom was torn to pieces with civil distractions. From the accession of Henry the Seventh to the breaking out of the great rebellion, the power of the sovereign was all but absolute; the rapacity of that monarch, the brutality of his successor, the persecuting spirit of Mary, and the imperious prerogative of Elizabeth, left scarce a shadow of freedom in the people; and, in spite of all the boasted glories of Elizabeth's golden days, I must doubt if any nation can be happy, whose lives and properties were no better secured than those of her subjects actually were: in all this period, the most tranquil moments are to be found in the peaceful reign of James the First; yet even then the king's *jus divinum* was at its height, and totally overturned the scale and equipoise of the constitution. What followed in Charles's day I need not dwell upon; a revolution ensued; monarchy was shaken to its foundations, and in the general fermentation and concussion of affairs, the very dregs of the people were thrown up into power, and all was anarchy, slaughter, and oppression. From the Restoration to the Revolution we contemplate a period full of trouble, and, for the most part, stained with the deepest disgrace: a pensioned monarch, an abandoned court, and a licentious people. The abdication, or more properly, the expulsion of a royal bigot, set the constitution upon its bottom, but it left the minds of men in a ferment that could not speedily subside: ancient loyalty and high monarchical principles were not to be silenced at once by the peremptory fiat of an act of parliament; men still harboured them in their hearts, and popery, three times expelled, was still upon the watch, and secretly whetting her weapons for a fourth attempt. Was this a period of social happiness?—The succession of the House of Hanover still left a pretender to the throne; and though the character of the new sovereign had every requisite of temper and judgment for conciliating his government, yet the old leaven was not exhausted, fresh revolutions were attempted, and the nation felt a painful repetition of its former sorrows.

So far therefore as the happiness of society depends upon the secure establishment of the constitution, the just administration of the laws, the strict and correct ascertainment of the subjects' rights, and those sacred and inviolable privileges as to person and property, which every man amongst us can now define, and no man living dares to dispute, so far we must acknowledge that the times we live in are happier times than ever fell to the lot of our ancestors, and if we complain of them, it must be on account of something which has not yet come under our review; we will therefore proceed to the next point, and take the present state of religion into our consideration.

Religious feuds are so terrible in their consequences, and the peace of this kingdom has been so often destroyed by the furiousness of zealots and enthusiasts, struggling for church-establishment, and persecuting in their turns the fallen party without mercy, that the tranquillity we now enjoy (greater, as I believe, than in any time past, but certainly as great) is of itself sufficient to put the modern *murmurer* to silence. To substantiate my assertion, let me refer to the rising spirit of toleration; wherever that blessed spirit prevails, it prevails for the honour of man's nature, for the enlargement of his heart, and for the augmentation of his social happiness. Whilst we were contending for our own rights, self-defence compelled us to keep off the encroachments of others, that were hostile to those rights; but these being firmly established, we are no longer warranted to hang the sword of the law over the head of religion, and oppress our seceding fellow-subjects. Is there any just reason to complain of our established clergy in their collective character? If they do not stun us with controversies, it is because they understand the spirit of their religion better than to engage in

them.   The publications of the pulpit are still numerous, and if they have dropt their high inflammatory tone, it is to the honour of Christianity that
they have so done, and taken up a milder, meeker
language in its stead.   As for the practice of religion, it is not in my present argument to speak of
that; my business is only to appeal to it as an establishment, essential to the support and happiness of
society; and when we reflect how often in times past
it has been made an engine for subverting that tranquillity and good order in the state, which it now
peaceably upholds, I think it will be clear to every
candid man, that this cannot be one of the causes of
complaint and murmur against the present times.

The *manners* of the age we live in is the next
point I am to review: and if I am to bring this into
any decent compass, I must reject many things out
of the account, that would make for my argument,
and speak very briefly upon all others.

To compare the manners of one age with those
of another, we must begin by calling to remembrance
the changes that may have been made in our own
time (if we have lived long enough to be witnesses
of any), or we must take them upon tradition, or
guess at them by the writings of those who describe
them: the comic poets are in general good de-
scribers of the living manners, and of all dramatic
painters in this class, Ben Jonson is decidedly the
best.   In the mirror of the stage we have the reflection of the times through all their changes, from the
reign of Elizabeth to that of Anne, with an exception to the days of Oliver, of which interval, if there
was no other delineation of the reigning manners
than what we find in the annals of Whitelocke and
Clarendon, we should be at no loss to form our judgment of them.   I stop at the age of Queen Anne,
because it was then that Sir Richard Steele and Mr.

Addison began to spread their pallets, and when they had completed The Spectator, nobody will dispute their having given a very finished portrait of the age they lived in. Where they stop tradition may begin; so that I think an observing man, with all these aids, and no short experience of his own to help them out, may form a pretty close comparison in his own thoughts upon the subject.

Here I must remind the reader that I am speaking of manners as they respect society. Now we can readily refer to certain times past, when the manners of men in this country were insufferably boisterous and unpolished; we can point to the period, when they were as notoriously reserved, gloomy, dark, and fanatical; we know when profligacy threw off all appearances, and libertinism went naked as it were into all societies; we can tell when pedantry was in general fashion, when duelling was the rage, and the point of honour was to be defined by a chain of logic that would have puzzled Aristotle; we can turn to the time, when it was reputable to get drunk, and when the fine gentleman of the comedy entertains his mistress with his feats over the bottle, and recommends himself to her good graces, by swearing, blustering, and beating the watch. We know there are such words in the language as fop and beau, and some can remember them in daily use; many are yet living, who have had their full-bottomed wigs brought home in a chair, and many an old lady now crowds herself into a corner, who once hooped herself in a circle hardly less than Arthur's round table. Here I may be told that dress is not manners; but I must contend that the manners of a man in a full-bottomed wig must partake something of the stiffness of the barber's buckle; nor do I see how he can walk on foot at his ease, when his wig goes in a chair. How many of us can call to mind the day when it was a mark of good-breeding to cram a poor surfeited guest to the throat, and the most social hours of life were thrown away in a continual interchange of solicitations and apologies? What a stroke upon the nerves of a modest man was it then to make his first approaches, and perform his awkward reverences to a solemn circle, all rising on their legs at the awful moment of his entry! and what was his condition at departing, when, after having performed the same tremendous ceremonies, he saw his retreat cut off by a double row of guards in livery, to every one of whom he was to pay a toll for free passage! A man will now find his superiors more accessible, his equals more at their ease, and his inferiors more mannerly than in any time past. The effects of public education, travel, and a general intercourse with mankind, the great influx of foreigners, the variety of public amusements, where all ranks and degrees meet promiscuously, the constant resort to bathing and water-drinking places in the summer, and above all the company of the fair sex, who mix so much more in society than heretofore, have, with many other conspiring causes, altogether produced such an ease and suavity of manners throughout the nation, as have totally changed the face of society, and levelled all those bars and barriers, which made the approaches to what was called good company so troublesome, and obstructed the intercourse between man and man. Here then I shall conclude upon this topic, and pass to the arts, which I said were the ornaments of society.

As I am persuaded my argument will not be contested in this quarter, I need spend few words upon so clear a point. If ever this country saw an age of artists, it is the present: Italy, Spain, Flanders, and France, have had their turn, but they are now in no capacity to dispute the palm, and England stands

without a rival; her painters, sculptors, and en-
gravers, are now the only schools, properly so called,
in Europe; Rome will bear witness that the English
artists are as superior in talents, as they are in numbers, to those of all nations besides. I reserve the
mention of her architects as a separate class, that I
may for once break in upon my general rule, by indulging myself in a prediction (upon which I am
willing to stake all my credit with the reader), that
when the modest genius of a Harrison shall be
brought into fuller display, England will have to
boast of a native architect, which the brightest age
of Greece would glory to acknowledge.

## NUMBER XCII.

### Etiam mortuus loquitur.

'To the Observer.

'SIR,

' If I am rightly advised, the laws of England have
provided no remedy for an injury, which I have received from a certain gentleman, who sets me at defiance, and whom I am not conscious of having offended in the smallest article in life. My case is as
follows:—Some time ago I went into the south of
France for the recovery of my health, which (thank
God) I have so far effected, that I should think I
was at this very moment enjoying as good a stock
of spirits and strength, as I have enjoyed for many
years of my life past, if I was not outfaced by the
gentleman in question, who swears I am dead, and
has proceeded so far as to publish me dead to all

the world, with a whole volume of memoirs which I have no remembrance of, and of sayings which I never said.

'I think this is very hard upon me, and if there is no redress for such proceedings, but that a man must be printed dead, whenever any fanciful fellow chooses to write a book of memoirs, I must take the freedom to say this is no country to live in; and let my ingenious biographer take it how he will, I shall still maintain to his face that I am alive, and do not see why my word in such a case should not go as far as his.

'There is yet another thing I will venture to say, that I did never in the whole course of my life utter one-half or even one-tenth part of the smart repartees and bon-mots he is pleased to impute to me: I don't know what he means by laying such things at my door; I defy any one of my acquaintance to say I was a wit, which I always considered as another name for an ill-tempered fellow. I do acknowledge that I have lived upon terms of acquaintance with my biographer, and have passed some social hours in his company, but I never suspected he was minuting down every foolish thing that escaped my lips in the unguarded moments of convivial gaiety; if I had, I would have avoided him like the pestilence. It is hard upon a man, let me tell you, Sir, very hard indeed, to find his follies upon record, and I could almost wish his words were true, and that I were dead in earnest, rather than alive to read such nonsense, and find myself made the father of it.

'Judge of my surprise, when passing along Vigo-lane upon a friendly call, as I intended it to this very gentleman of whom I complain, I took up a volume from a stall in a whitey-brown paper binding, and opening it at the title-page met my own face, staring me out of countenance full in the front:

I started back with horror; nature never gave me any reason to be fond of my own features; I never survey my face but when I shave myself, and then I am ashamed of it; I trust it is no true type of my heart, for it is a sorry sample of nature's handy-work, to say no worse of it. What the devil tempted him to stick it there I cannot guess, any more than I can at his publishing a bundle of nonsensical sayings and doings, which I detest and disavow. As for his printing my last will and testament, and disposing of my poor personals at pleasure, I care little about it; if he had taken only my money and spared my life, I would not have complained.

'And now what is my redress? I apply myself to you in my distress, as an author whose book is in pretty general circulation, and one, as I perceive, who assaults no man's living fame and character: I desire, therefore, you will take mine into your protection, and if you can think of any thing to deter the world in future from such flippancies, you are welcome to make what use you please of this letter; for as I have always strove to do what little service I could to the living, when I was allowed to be one of their number, so now I am voted out of their company, I would gladly be of some use to the dead. Yours whilst I lived,          H. POSTHUMOUS.

'P. S. I am sorry I did not leave you something in my will, as I believe you deserve it as well, and want it more than some that are in it. If I live to die a second time, I will be sure to remember you.'

As I am not versed in the law of libels, I know not what advice to give in Posthumous's case, whom I would by no means wish to see entangled in farther difficulties; though I think he might fairly say to his biographer with a courtly poet of this century,

Oh! libel me with all things but thy praise!

The practice which some of our public news-writers are in, of treating their readers with a farrago of puerile anecdotes and scraps of characters, has probably led the way to a very foolish fashion, which is gaining ground amongst us: no sooner does a great man die, than the small wits creep into his coffin, like a swarm of bees in the carcass of Samson's lion, to make honey from his corpse. It is high time that the good sense of the nation should correct this impertinence.

I have availed myself of Posthumous's permission to publish his letter, and I shall without scruple subjoin to it one of a very different sort, which I have received from a correspondent, whose name I do not mean to expose; it is with some reluctance I introduce it into this work, because it brings a certain person on the stage, whom I have no desire to exhibit oftener than I can help; but as I think it will be a consolation to Posthumous to shew him others in the same hazard with himself, I hope my readers will let it pass with this apology.

'TO THE OBSERVER.

'SIR,

'I am a man, who says a good many good things myself, and hear many good things said by others; for I frequent clubs and coffee-rooms in all parts of the town, attend the pleadings in Westminster-hall, and am remarkably fond of the company of men of genius, and never miss a dinner at the Mansion-house upon my Lord Mayor's day.

'I am in the habit of committing to paper every thing of this sort, whether it is of my own saying, or any other person's, when I am convinced I myself should have said it, if he had not: these I call my conscientious witticisms, and give them a leaf in my common-place book to themselves.

'I have the pleasure to tell you, that my collection is now become not only considerable in bulk, but (that I may speak humbly of its merit) I will also say, that it is to the full as good, and far more creditable to any gentleman's character, than the books which have been published about a certain great wit lately deceased, whose memory has been so completely dissected by the operators in Stationers'-hall.

'Though I have as much respect for posterity as any man can entertain for persons he is not acquainted with, still I cannot understand how a post-obit of this sort can profit me in my life, unless I could make it over to some purchaser upon beneficial conditions. Now as there are people in the world, who have done many famous actions, without having once uttered a real good thing, as it is called, I should think my collection might be an acceptable purchase to a gentleman of this description, and such a one should have it a bargain, as I would be very glad to give a finishing to his character, which I can best compare to a coat of Adams's plaster on a well-built house.

'For my own part, being neither more nor less than a haberdasher of small wares, and having scarcely rambled beyond the boundaries of the bills of mortality, since I was out of my apprenticeship, I have not the presumption to think the anecdotes of my own life important enough for posthumous publication; neither do I suppose my writings (though pretty numerous, as my books will testify, and many great names standing amongst them, which it is probable I shall never cross out) will be thought so interesting to the public, as to come into competition with the lively memoirs of a Bellamy and a Baddeley, who furnish so many agreeable records of many noble families, and are the solace of more than half the toilets in town and country.

'But to come more closely to the chief purport of this letter—It was about a fortnight ago, that I crossed upon you in the Poultry near the shop-door of your worthy bookseller: I could not help giving a glance at your looks, and methought there was a morbid sallowness in your complexion, and a sickly languor in your eye, that indicated speedy dissolution: I watched you for some time, and as you turned into the shop remarked the total want of energy in your step. I know whom I am saying this to, and therefore am not afraid of starting you by my observations, but if you actually perceive those threatening symptoms, which I took notice of, it may probable be your wish to lay in some store for a journey you are soon to take. You have always been a friend and customer to me, and there is nobody I shall more readily serve than yourself: I have long noticed with regret the very little favour you receive from your contemporaries, and shall gladly contribute to your kinder reception from posterity; now I flatter myself, if you adopt my collection, you will at least be celebrated for your sayings, whatever may become of your writings.

'As for your private history, if I may guess from certain events which have been reported to me, you may, with a little allowable embellishment, make up a decent life of it. It was with great pleasure I heard t'other day, that you were stabbed by a monk in Portugal, broke your limbs in Spain, and was poisoned with a sallad at Paris; these, with your adventures at sea, your sufferings at Bayonne, and the treatment you received from your employers on your return, will be amusing anecdotes; and as it is generally supposed you have not amassed any very great fortune by the plunder of the public, your narrative will be read without raising any envy in the reader, which will be so much in your favour.

Still your chief dependance must rest upon the collection I shall supply you with; and when the world come to understand how many excellent things you said, and how much more wit you had than any of your contemporaries gave you credit for, they will begin to think you had not fair play whilst you were alive, and who knows but they may take it in mind to raise a monument to you by subscription amongst other merry fellows of your day? I am yours,

H. B.'

I desire my correspondent will accept this short but serious answer: If I am so near the end of life, as he supposes, it will behove me to wind it up in another manner from what he suggests: I therefore shall not treat with my friend the haberdasher for his small wares.

---

## NUMBER XCIII.

'Αληθόμυθον χρὴ εἶναι, οὐ πολύλογον.—DEMOCRATES.

Remember only that your words be true,
No matter then how many or how few.

'TO THE OBSERVER.

'I HAVE a habit of dealing in the marvellous, which I cannot overcome: some people, who seem to take a pleasure in magnifying the little flaws to be found in all characters, call this by a name which no gentleman ought to use, or likes to hear; the fact is, I have so much tender consideration for truth in her state of nakedness, that, till I have put her into decent clothing, I cannot think of bringing her into company; and if her appearance is sometimes so much altered by dress, that her best friends cannot find her out, am I to blame for that?

'There is a matter-of-fact man of my acquaintance, who haunts me in all places, and is the very torment of my life; he sticks to me as the thrasher does to the flail, and is the perfect night-mare of my imagination: this fellow never lets one of my stories pass without docking it like an attorney's bill before a master in chancery: he cut forty miles out of a journey of one hundred, which but for him I had performed in one day upon the same horse; in which I confess I had stretched a point for the pleasure of out-riding a fat fellow in company, who, by the malicious veracity of my aforesaid Damper, threw me at least ten miles distance behind him.

'This provoking animal cut up my success in so many intrigues and adventures, that I was determined to lay my plan out of his reach, in a spot which I had provided for an evil day, and accordingly I led him a dance into Corsica, where I was sure he could not follow me: here I had certainly been, and knew my ground well enough to prance over it at a very handsome rate: I noticed a kind of sly leer in some of the company, which was pointed towards a gentleman present, who was a stranger to me, and so far from joining in the titter, was very politely attentive to what I was relating. I was at this moment warm in the cause of freedom, and had performed such prodigies of valour in its defence, that, before my story was well ended, I had got upon such close terms with General Paoli, that, had my hearers been but half as credulous as they ought to have been, they might have set us down for sworn friends and inseparables: but here again, as ill luck would have it, my evil genius tapped me on the shoulder, and remarking that I principally addressed myself to the gentleman, whose politeness and attention

were so flattering, said to me with a smile, that had
the malice of the devil in it—" Give me leave to introduce you to General Paoli here present."—Death
and confusion, what I felt! a stroke of lightning
would have been charity compared to this.—My
persecutor had not done with me.—" I am afraid
you have forgot your old friend and familiar, who
no doubt will be overjoyed at recognising a brother
warrior, who has performed such noble services
jointly with himself in the glorious struggle for the
liberties of his beloved country."—Can I paint the
shame I suffered at this moment? It is impossible;
I can only say there is a generosity in true valour,
which scorns to triumph over the fallen.—" There
were so many brave men," said that gallant person,
in a tone I shall never lose the impression of, " of
whose services I shall ever preserve a grateful memory, but whose persons have slipped from my recollection, that I have only to entreat your pardon for
a forgetfulness, which I desire you to believe is not
my fault, but my infirmity:"—if a bottle had been
vollied at my head, I could not have been more in
need of a surgeon, than I was at this instant: I
could never have suspected Truth of playing me
such a jade's trick; I always considered her as a
good-natured simple creature without gall or bitterness, and was in the habit of treating her accordingly; but this was such a specimen of her malice, that I fled out of her company as hastily as I
could.

  ' The very next morning I took my passage in the
stage-coach for my native town in the north of England, heartily out of humour with my trip to Corsica: but even here I could not shake off old habits,
so far as to resist the temptation of getting into a
post-chaise for the last stage, by which manœuvre I
took the credit of having travelled like a gentleman,

and became entitled to rail against the post-tax and the expenses of the road.

' I was now voted into a club of the chief inhabitants of the place, and as I had no reason to believe the story of my late discomfiture had reached them, I soon recovered my spirits, and with them the amplifying powers of my invention. My stories for a considerable time were swallowed so glibly, and seemed to sit so easy on the stomachs of these natural unsophisticated people, that I was encouraged to increase the dose to such a degree as seemed at length to produce something like a nausea with those I administered it to : especially with a certain precise personage of the sect of Quakers, one Simon Stiff, a wealthy trader, and much respected for his probity and fair dealing. Simon had a way of asking me at the end of a story—*But is it true?*—which sometimes disconcerted me, and considerably lessened the applauses that the rest of the club had been accustomed to bestow upon my narratives.

' One evening, when I had been describing an enormous shark, by which I had been attacked in one of my West-India voyages, Simon Stiff, lifting up both his hands in an attitude of astonishment, cried out—" Verily, friend Cracker, thou drawest a long bow." With an angry look I demanded the meaning of that expression. " I mean," replied Simon, thou speakest the thing which is not."— " That is as much as to say I tell a lie."—" Even so, friend, thou hast hit it," said Simon, without altering his voice, or regarding the tone of rage I had thrown mine into : the steady serenity of his countenance put me down, and I suffered him to proceed without interruption.—" Thou hast told us many things, friend Cracker, that are perfectly incredible; were I to attempt imposing upon my customers in the way of traffic, as thou dost upon thy company in the way of talk, the world would justly set me down for a dishonest man. Believe me, thou mayest be a very good companion without swerving from the truth, nay, thou canst no otherwise be a good one than by adhering to it; for if thou art in the practice of uttering falsehoods, we shall be in the practice of disbelieving thee, even when thou speakest the truth, and so there will be an end of all confidence in society, and thy word will pass for nothing. I have observed it is thy vanity that betrays thee into falsehood; I should have hoped thou wouldst not have forgotten how thy falsehood betrayed thee into shame, and how we received and welcomed thee into our society, when thy friends in the metropolis had hooted thee out of theirs. Think not thou canst establish a credit with us by the fictions of imagination: plain truths suit men of plain understandings. Had thy shark been as big again as thou wouldst have us believe it was, what wouldst thou have gained by it? Nothing but the merit of having seen a monster; and what is that compared to the risk of being thought a monster-maker? If thou wast snatched from the jaws of the animal by the hand of God, give God the praise: if thine own courage and address contributed to save thee, give him still the praise, who inspired thee with those means of furthering his providence in thy rescue: where is the ground for boasting in all this? Sometimes thou wouldst persuade us thou art a man of consequence, in the favour of princes, and in the secrets of ministers: if we are to believe all this, thou dost but libel those ministers for letting such a babbler into their councils, and if thou thinkest to gain a consequence with us thereby, thou art grievously deceived, friend Cracker, for we do not want to know what thou oughtest not to tell, and we despise the servant who betrayeth his master's trust.

As for wonders, what signifieth telling us of them? The time is full of wonders; the revolution of empires, the fall of despotism, and the emancipation of mankind, are objects, whose superior magnitude makes thy shark shrink into an atom. Had the monster gorged thee at a mouthful, how many thousands, nay, tens of thousands, have the voracious jaws of death devoured in a succession of campaigns, which have made creation melt? Didst thou escape the monster? what then? how can we have leisure to reflect upon thy single deliverance, when we call to mind the numbers of despairing captives, who have been liberated from the dungeons of tyranny? In a word, friend Cracker, if it is through a love for the marvellous thou makest so free with the sacred name of truth, thou dost but abuse our patience and thine own time in hunting after sharks and monsters of the deep; and if thou hast any other motive for fiction than the above, it must be a motive less innocent than what I have supposed, and in that case we hold thee dangerous to society, and a disgrace to human nature."

'Here he concluded, and though the length and deliberate solemnity of his harangue had given me time enough, yet I had not so availed myself of it as to collect my thoughts, and prepare myself for any kind of defence: how to deal with this formal old fellow I knew not; to cudgel him was a service of more danger than I saw fit to engage in, for he was of athletic limbs and stature; to challenge him to a gentleman's satisfaction, being a Quaker, would have subjected me to universal ridicule: I rose from my chair, took my hat from the peg, and abruptly quitted the room: next morning I sent to cut my name out of the club, but behold! they had saved me that ceremony over night, and I had once more a new set of acquaintance to go in search of.

' In this solitary interim I strove to lighten the burden of time by starting a correspondence with one of our public prints, and so long as I supplied it with anecdotes from the country, I may say without vanity there was neither fire nor flood, murder, rape, nor robbery, wanting to embellish it: I broke two or three necks at a horse-race without any detriment to the community, and for the amusement of my readers drove over blind beggars, drowned drunken farmers, and tossed women with child by mad bullocks, without adding one item to the bills of mortality; I made matches without number which the register never recorded; I was at the same time a correspondent at Brussels, a resident in Spain, and a traveller at Constantinople, who gave secret information of all proceedings in those several places, and by the mysterious style in which I enveloped my dispatches, nobody could fix a falsehood on my intelligence, till I imprudently fought a battle on the banks of the Danube, after the armies were gone into winter-quarters, which did the Turk no mischief, and effectually blasted me with the compiler, and him with the public.

' I am now out of business, and, if you want any thing in my way to enliven your Observers (which give me leave to remark are sometimes rather of the dullest) I shall be proud to serve you, being

Your very humble servant at command,

KIT CRACKER.'

N. B. I do not want any thing in Kit Cracker's way; but though I decline the offer of his assistance, I willingly avail myself of the moral of his example.

# NUMBER XCIV.

*Λυποῦντα τὸν πλησίον, οὐ ῥάδιον αὐτὸν ἄλυπον εἶναι.*
DEMOPHILI SENTENTIA.

He, who another's peace annoys,
By the same act his own destroys.

### ' TO THE OBSERVER.

' As I have lived long enough to repent of a fatal propensity, that has led me to commit many offences, not the less irksome to my present feelings for the secresy with which I contrived to execute them, and as these can now be no otherwise atoned for than by a frank confession, I have resolved upon this mode of addressing myself to you. Few people choose to display their own characters to the world in such colours as I shall give to mine, but as I have mangled so many reputations in my time without mercy, I should be the meanest of mankind if I spared my own ; and being now about to speak of a person whom no man loves, I may give vent to an acrimony at which no man can take offence. If I have been troublesome to others, I am no less uncomfortable to myself, and amidst vexations without number, the greatest of all is, that there is not one which does not originate from myself.

' I entered upon life with many advantages natural and acquired ; I am indebted to my parents for a liberal education, and to nature for no contemptible share of talents : my propensities were not such as betrayed me into dissipation and extravagance : my mind was habitually of a studious cast ; I had a passion for books, and began to collect them at an early period of my life : to them I devoted the greatest

portion of my time, and had my vanity been of a
sort to be contented with the literary credit I had
now acquired, I had been happy; but I was ambitious of convincing the world I was not the idle
owner of weapons which I did not know the use of;
I seized every safe opportunity of making my pretensions respected by such dabblers in the belles
lettres who paid court to me, and as I was ever cautious of stepping an inch beyond my tether on these
occasions, I soon found myself credited for more
learning than my real stock amounted to. I received
all visitors in my library, affected a studious air, and
took care to furnish my table with volumes of a select sort: upon these I was prepared to descant, if
by chance a curious friend took up any one of them,
and as there is little fame to be got by trading in the
beaten track of popular opinion, I sometimes took
the liberty to be eccentric and paradoxical in my
criticisms and cavils, which gained me great respect
from the ignorant (for upon such only I took care to
practise this chicanery), so that in a short time I became a sovereign dictator within a certain set, who
looked up to me for second-hand opinions in all matters of literary taste, and saw myself inaugurated by
my flatterers censor of all new publications.

' My trumpeters had now made such a noise in the
world, that I began to be in great request, and men
of real literature laid out for my acquaintance; but
here I acted with a coldness, that was in me consti-
tutional as well as prudential: I was resolved not to
risk my laurels, and throw away the fruits of a
triumph so cheaply purchased: solicitations, that
would have flattered others, only alarmed me; such
was not the society I delighted in; against such attacks, I intrenched myself with the most jealous
caution: if however by accident I was drawn out of
my fastnesses, and trapped unawares into an am-

buscade of wicked wits, I armed myself to meet them with a triple tier of smiles; I primed my lips with such a ready charge of flattery, that when I had once engaged them in the pleasing contemplation of their own merits, they were seldom disposed to scrutinize into mine, and thus in general I contrived to escape undetected. Though it was no easy matter to extort an opinion from me in such companies, yet sometimes I was unavoidably entangled in conversation, and then I was forced to have recourse to all my address; happily my features were habituated to a smile of the most convertible sort, for it would answer the purposes of affected humility, as well as those of actual contempt, to which in truth it was more congenial: my opinion, therefore, upon any point of controversy flattered both parties and befriended neither; it was calculated to impress the company with an idea that I knew much more than I professed to know; it was in short so insinuating, so submitted, so hesitating, that a man must have had the heart of Nero to have prosecuted a being so absolutely inoffensive; but these sacrifices cost me dear, for they were foreign to my nature, and, as I hated my superiors, I avoided their society.

'Having sufficiently distinguished myself as a critic, I now began to meditate some secret attempts as an author: but in these the same caution attended me, and my performances did not rise above a little sonnet, or a parody, which I circulated through a few hands without a name, prepared to disavow it, if it was not applauded to my wishes: I also wrote occasional essays and paragraphs for the public prints, by way of trying my talents in various kinds of style; by these experiments I acquired a certain facility of imitating other people's manner, and disguising my own, and so far my point was gained; but as for the secret satisfaction I half promised my-

self in hearing my productions applauded, of that I
was altogether disappointed; for though I tried both
praise and dispraise for the purpose of bringing
them into notice, I never had the pleasure to be con-
tradicted by any man in the latter case, or seconded
by a living soul in the former: I had circulated a
little poem, which cost me some pains, and as I had
been flattered with the applause it gained from several of its readers, I put it one evening in my pocket,
and went to the house of a certain person, who was
much resorted to by men of genius: an opportunity
luckily offered for producing my manuscript, which
I was prepared to avow as soon as the company present had given sentence in its favour: it was put
into the hands of a dramatic author of some celebrity, who read it aloud, and in a manner as I
thought that clearly anticipated his disgust: as soon
therefore as he had finished it, and demanded of me
if I knew the author, I had no hesitation to declare
that I did not. Then, I presume, rejoined he, it is
no offence to say I think it the merest trash I ever
read—None in life, I replied, and from that moment
held him in everlasting hatred.

'Disgusted with the world, I now began to dip my
pen in gall, and as soon as I had singled out a proper
object for my spleen, I looked round him for his weak
side, where I could place a blow to best effect, and
wound him undiscovered: the author above mentioned had a full share of my attention: he was an
irritable man, and I have seen him agonized with the
pain, which my very shafts had given him, whilst I
was foremost to arraign the scurrility of the age,
and encourage him to disregard it: the practice I
had been in of masking my style facilitated my
attacks upon every body, who either moved my envy
or provoked my spleen.

'The meanest of all passions had now taken entire possession of my heart, and I surrendered myself to it without a struggle: still there was a consciousness about me, that sunk me in my own esteem, and when I met the eye of a man whom I had secretly defamed, I felt abashed; society became painful to me; and I shrunk into retirement, for my self-esteem was lost: though I had gratified my malice, I had destroyed my comfort; I now contemplated myself a solitary being, at the very moment when I had every requisite of fortune, health, and endowments, to have recommended me to the world, and to those tender ties and engagements which are natural to man, and constitute his best enjoyments.

' The solitude I resorted to, made me every day more morose, and supplied me with reflections that rendered me intolerable to myself, and unfit for society. I had reason to apprehend, in spite of all my caution, that I was now narrowly watched, and that strong suspicions were taken up against me; when I was feasting my jaundiced eye one morning with a certain newspaper, which I was in the habit of employing as the vehicle of my venom, I was startled at discovering myself conspicuously pointed out in an angry column as a cowardly defamer, and menaced with personal chastisement, as soon as ever proofs could be obtained against me; and this threatening denunciation evidently came from the very author, who had unknowingly given me such umbrage when he recited my poem.

' The sight of this resentful paragraph was like an arrow to my brain: habituated to skirmish only behind intrenchments, I was ill prepared to turn into the open field, and had never put the question to my heart, how it was provided for the emergency. In early life I had not any reason to suspect my courage, nay, it was rather forward to meet occasions in those days of innocence; but the meanness I had lately sunk into, had sapped every manly principle of my nature, and I now discovered to my sorrow, that, in taking up the lurking malice of an assassin, I had lost the gallant spirit of a gentleman.

'There was still an alleviation to my terrors: it so chanced that I was not the author of the particular libel which my accuser had imputed to me: and though I had been father of a thousand others, I felt myself supported by truth in almost the only charge against which I could have fairly appealed to it. It seemed to me therefore advisable to lose no time in disculpating myself from the accusation, yet to seek an interview with this irascible man, was a service of some danger: chance threw the opportunity in my way, which I had probably else wanted spirit to invite: I accosted him with all imaginable civility, and made the strongest asseverations of my innocence: whether I did this with a servility that might aggravate his suspicion, or that he had others impressed upon him besides those I was labouring to remove, so it was, that he treated all I said with the most contemptuous incredulity, and elevated his voice to a tone that petrified me with fear, bade me avoid his sight, threatening me both with words and actions in a manner too humiliating to relate.

'Alas! can words express my feelings? Is there a being more wretched than myself? to be friendless, an exile from society, and at enmity with myself, is a situation deplorable in the extreme: let what I have now written be made public; if I could believe my shame would be turned to others' profit, it might perhaps become less painful to myself; if men want other motives to divert them from defamation, than what their own hearts supply, let them turn to my example, and if they will not be reasoned, let them be frightened out of their propensity.

I am, Sir, &c.

WALTER WORMWOOD.'

The case of this correspondent is a melancholy one, and I have admitted his letter, because I do not doubt the present good motives of the writer; but I shall not easily yield a place in these essays to characters so disgusting, and representations so derogatory to human nature. The historians of the day, who profess to give us intelligence of what is passing in the world, ought not to be condemned, if they sometimes make a little free with our foibles and our follies: but downright libels are grown too dangerous, and scurrility is become too dull to find a market; the pillory is a great reformer. The detail of a court drawing-room, though not very edifying, is perfectly inoffensive; a lady cannot greatly complain of the liberty of the press, if it is contented with the humble task of celebrating the workmanship of her mantua-maker: as for such inveterate malice as my correspondent Wormwood describes, I flatter myself it is very rarely to be found: I can only say, that though I have often heard of it in conversation, and read of it in books, I do not meet in human nature originals so strongly featured as their paintings: among a small collection of sonnets in manuscript, descriptive of the human passions, which has fallen into my hands, the following lines upon Envy, as coinciding with my subject, shall conclude this paper.

ENVY.

Oh! never let me see that shape again,
  Exile me rather to some savage den,
    Far from the social haunts of men!
Horrible phantom, pale it was as death,
Consumption fed upon its meagre cheek,
And ever as the fiend essay'd to speak,
Dreadfully steam'd its pestilential breath.

Fang'd like the wolf it was, and all as gaunt,
And still it prowl'd around us and around,
  Rolling its squinting eyes askaunt,
  Wherever human happiness was found.

Furious threat, the self-tormenting sprite
Drew forth an asp, and (terrible to sight)
To its left pap the envenom'd reptile prest,
Which gnaw'd and worm'd into its tortur'd breast.

The desperate suicide with pain
Writh'd to and fro, and yell'd amain;
And then with hollow, dying cadence cries—
It is not of this asp that Envy dies;
'Tis not this reptile's tooth that gives the smart;
'Tis others' happiness that gnaws my heart.

## NUMBER XCV.

*Facilitas animæ ad partem stultitiæ rapit.*—P. Syrus.

'To the Observer.

'SIR,

'The ancient family of the Saplins, whereof your humble servant is the unworthy representative, has been for many generations distinguished for a certain pliability of temper, which with some people passes for good humour, and by others is called weakness; but however the world may differ in describing it, there seems a general agreement in the manner of making use of it.

'Our family estate, though far from contemptible, is considerably reduced from its ancient splendour, not only by an unlucky tumble that my grandfather Sir Paul got in the famous Mississippi scheme, but also various losses, bad debts, and incautious securities, which have fallen heavy upon the purses of my predecessors at different times; but as every man must pay for his good character, I dare say they did not repent of their purchase, and for my part it is a reflection that never gives me any disturbance. This aforesaid grandfather of mine, was supposed to have furnished Congreve with the hint for his character of Sir Paul Pliant, at least it hath been so whispered to me very frequently by my aunt Jemima, who was a great collector of family anecdotes; and to speak the truth, I am not totally without suspicion, that a certain ingenious author, lately deceased, had an eye towards my insignificant self in the dramatic portrait of his *Good-natured-Man*.

'Though I scorn the notion of setting myself off to the public and you by panegyrics of my own penning (as the manner of some is), yet I may truly say, without boasting, that I had the character at school of being the very best *fag* that ever came into it; and this I believe every gentleman, who was my contemporary at Westminster, will do me the justice to acknowledge. It was a reputation I confess that I did not earn for nothing; for whilst I worked the clothes off my back, and the skin off my bones in scouting upon every body's errands, I was pummeled to a mummy by the boys, *shewed up* by the ushers, flayed alive by the masters, and reported for an incorrigible dunce at my book; a report which, under correction, I must think had some degree of injustice in it, as it was impossible for me to learn a book I was never allowed to open. In this period of my education I took little food, and less sleep; so that whilst I shot up in stature after the manner of my progenitors, who were a tall race of men, I grew as gaunt as a grayhound: but having abundantly more spirit than strength, and being *voted* by the great boys to be what is called *true game*, I was singled out as a kind of trial cock, and pitted against every new comer to make proof of his bottom in fair fighting, though I may safely say I never turned out upon a quarrel of my own making in all my life. Notwithstanding all these honours, which I obtained from my colleagues,

I will not attempt to disguise from you that I left the school in disgrace, being expelled by the master, when head of my boarding house, for not supporting my authority over the petty boys belonging to it, who, I must confess, were just then not in the most orderly and correct state of discipline.

'My father, whose maxim it was never to let trifles vex him, received me with all the good humour in life, and admitted me of the University of Oxford: here I was overjoyed to find, that the affair of the expulsion was so far from having prejudiced my contemporaries against me, that I was resorted to by numbers whose time hung upon their hands, and my rooms became the rendezvous of all the loungers in the college: few or no schemes were set on foot without me, and if a loose guinea or two was wanted for the purpose, every body knew where to have it: I was allowed a horse for my health's sake, which was rather delicate, but I cannot say my health was much the better for him, as I never mounted his back above once or twice, whilst my friends kept him in exercise morning and evening, as long as he lasted, which indeed was only till the hunting season set in, when the currier had his hide, and his flesh went to the kennel. I must own I did not excel in any of my academical exercises, save that of circumambulating the colleges and public buildings with strangers, who came to gaze about them for curiosity's sake; in this branch of learning I gained such general reputation, as to be honoured with the title of *Keeper of the Lions:* neither will I disguise the frequent *jobations* I incurred for neglect of college duties, and particularly for non-attendance at chapel, but in this I should not perhaps have been thought so reprehensible, had it been known that my surplice never failed to be there, though I had rarely the credit of bearing it company.

'My mother died of a cold she caught by attending some young ladies on a water party before I had been a month in the world; and my father never married again, having promised her on her death-bed not to bring a step-dame into his family whilst I survived: I had the misfortune to lose him when I was in my twenty-second year; he got his death at a country canvas for Sir Harry Osier, a very obliging gentleman, and nearly related to our family: I attended my father's corpse to the grave, on which melancholy occasion, such were the lamentations and bewailings of all the servants in the house, that I thought it but a proper return for their affection to his memory, to prove myself as kind a master by continuing them in their several employs: this however was not altogether what they meant, as I was soon convinced every one amongst them had a remonstrance to make, and a new demand to prefer: the butler would have better perquisites, the footman wanted to be out of livery, the scullion demanded tea-money, and the cook murmured about kitchen-stuff.

'Though I was now a single being in the world, my friends and neighbours kindly took care I should not be a solitary one! I was young indeed, and of small experience in the world, but I had plenty of counsellors; some advised me to buy horses they wanted to sell, others to sell horses they wanted to buy; a lady of great taste fell in love with two or three of my best cows for their colour; they were upon her lawn the next day: a gentleman of extraordinary *vertue* discovered a picture or two in my collection that exactly fitted his pannels: an eminent improver, whom every body declared to be the first genius of the age for laying out grounds, had taken measures for transplanting my garden a mile out of my sight, and floating my richest meadow grounds with a lake of muddy water: as for my mansion and its append-

ages, I am persuaded I could never have kept them
in their places, had it not been that the several pro-
jectors, who all united in pulling them down, could
never rightly agree in what particular spot to build
them up again : one kind friend complimented me
with the first refusal of a mistress, whom for reasons
of economy he was obliged to part from ; and a
neighbouring gentlewoman, whose daughter had perhaps stuck on hand a little longer than was convenient, more than hinted to me that miss had every
requisite in life to make the married state perfectly
happy.

'In justice however to my own discretion, let me
say, that I was not hastily surprised into a serious
measure by this latter overture, nor did I ask the
young lady's hand in marriage, till I was verily persuaded, by her excessive fondness, that there were
no other means to save her life. Now whether it was
the violence of her passion before our marriage that
gave some shock to her intellects, or from what
other cause it might proceed, I know not; certain
however it is, that after marriage she became subject to very odd whims and caprices ; and though I
made it a point of humanity never to thwart her in
these humours, yet I was seldom fortunate enough
to please her ; so that had I not been sure to demonstration that love for me was the cause and origin of
them all, I might have been so deceived by appearances as to have imputed them to aversion. She was
in the habit of deciding upon almost every action in
her life by the interpretation of her dreams, in which
I cannot doubt her great skill, though I could not
always comprehend the principles on which she applied it ; she never failed as soon as winter set in, to
dream of going to London, and our journey as certainly succeeded. I remember upon our arrival there
the first year after our marriage, she dreamt of a new

coach, and at the same time put the servants in new liveries, the colours and patterns of which were circumstantially revealed to her in sleep: sometimes (dear creature!) she dreamt of winning large sums at cards, but I am apt to think those dreams were of the sort which should have been interpreted by their contraries: she was not a little fond of running after conjurers and deaf and dumb fortunetellers, who dealt in figures and cast nativities; and when we were in the country my barns and out-houses were haunted with gypsies and vagabonds, who made sad havoc with our pigs and poultry: of ghosts and evil spirits she had such terror, that I was fain to keep a chaplain in my house to exorcise the chambers, and when business called me from home, the good man condescended so far to her fears, as to sleep in a little closet within her call in case she was troubled in the night; and I must say this for my friend, that if there is any trust to be put in flesh and blood, he was a match for the best spirit that ever walked: she had all the sensibility in life towards omens and prognostics, and though I guarded every motion and action that might give any possible alarm to her, yet my unhappy awkwardnesses were always boding ill luck, and I had the grief of heart to hear her declare in her last moments, that a capital oversight I had been guilty of in handing to her a candle with an enormous winding-sheet appending to it, was the immediate occasion of her death and my irreparable misfortune.

‘ My second wife I married in mere charity and compassion, because a young fellow, whom she was engaged to, had played her a base trick by scandalously breaking off the match, when the wedding-clothes were bought, the day appointed for the wedding, and myself invited to it. Such transactions ever appeared shocking to me, and therefore to make

up her loss to her as well as I was able, I put myself
to extraordinary charges for providing her with every
thing handsome upon our marriage; she was a fine
woman, loved show, and was particularly fond of
displaying herself in public places, where she had
an opportunity of meeting and mortifying the young
man who had behaved so ill to her: she took this
revenge against him so often, that one day to my
great surprise I discovered that she had eloped from
me and fairly gone off with him. There was something so unhandsome, as I thought, in this proceeding, that I should probably have taken legal measures for redress, as in like cases other husbands
have done, had I not been diverted from my purpose
by a very civil note from the gentleman himself,
wherein he says—" That being a younger son of
little or no fortune, he hopes I am too much of a
gentleman to think of resorting to the vexatious
measures of the law for revenging myself upon him;
and as a proof of his readiness to make me all the
reparation in his power in an honourable way, he
begs leave to inform me, that he shall most respectfully attend upon me with either sword or pistols,
or with both, whenever I shall be pleased to lay my
commands upon him for a meeting, and appoint the
hour and place."

‘ After such atonement on the part of the offender,
I could no longer harbour any thoughts of a divorce,
especially as my younger brother the parson has
heirs to continue the family, and seems to think so
entirely with me in the business, that I have determined to drop it altogether, and give the parties no
farther molestation; for as my brother very properly
observes, it is the part of a Christian to forget and to
forgive; and in truth I see no reason why I should
disturb them in their enjoyments, or return evil for
good to an obliging gentleman, who has taken a

task of trouble off my hands, and set me at my ease
for the rest of my days; in which tranquil and contented state of mind, as becomes a man, whose inheritance is philanthropy, and whose mother's milk
hath been the milk of human kindness, I remain in
all brotherly charity and goodwill,

Yours and the world's friend,

Simon Sapling.'

## NUMBER XCVI.

Quis scit an adjiciant hodiernæ crastina summa<br>Tempora Dii Superi?—Horat.

To-morrow is the day, which procrastination always promises to employ and never overtakes: my
correspondent Tom Tortoise, whose letter I shall
now lay before the public, seems to have made these
promises, and broken them as often as most men.

' To the Observer.

' I have been resolving to write to thee every
morning for these two months, but something or
other has always come athwart my resolution to put
it by. In the first place I should have told thee that
aunt Gertrude was taken grievously sick, and had a
mighty desire to see thee upon affairs of consequence, but as I was in daily hopes she would mend
and be able to write to thee herself (for every body
you know understands their own business best), I
thought I would wait till she got well enough to tell
her own story; but, alas! she dwindled and dwindled away till she died; so, if she had any secrets

they are buried with her, and there's an end of that matter.

' Another thing I would fain have written to thee about was, to inquire into the character of a fellow, one John Jenkyns, who had served a friend of thine, Sir Theodore Thimble, as his house-steward, and offered himself to me in the same capacity: but this was only my own affair do you see, so I put it by from day to day, and in the mean time took the rascal upon his word without a character: but if he ever had one, he would have lost it in my service, for he plundered me without mercy, and at last made off with a pretty round sum of money, which I have never been able to get any wind of, probably because I never took the trouble to make any inquiry.

' I now sit down to let you know son Tom is come from Oxford, and a strapping fine fellow he is grown of his age: he has a mighty longing to set out upon his travels to foreign parts, which you must know seems to me a very foolish conceit in a young lad, who has only kept his first term and not completed his nineteenth year; so I opposed his whim manfully, which I think you will approve of, for I recollected the opinion you gave upon this subject when last here, and quoted it against him; to do him justice, he fairly offered to be ruled by your advice, and willed me to write to you on the matter; but one thing or other always stood in the way, and in the mean time came Lord Ramble in his way to Dover, and being a great crony of Tom's and very eager for his company, and no letter coming from you (which indeed I acquit you of, not having written to you on the subject), away the youngsters went together, and probably before this are upon French ground. Pray tell me what you think of this trip, which appears to me but a wild-goose kind of chase, and if I live till to-morrow I intend to write

Tom a piece of my mind to that purpose, and give him a few wholesome hints, which I had put together for our parting, but had not time just then to communicate to him.

'I intend very shortly to brush up your quarters in town, as my solicitor writes me word every thing is at a stand for the want of my appearance: what dilatory doings must we experience, who have to do with the law! putting off from month to month, and year to year: I wonder men of business are not ashamed of themselves: as for me, I should have been up and amongst them long enough ago, if it had not been for one thing or another that hampered me about my journey: horses are for ever falling lame, and farriers are such lazy rascals, that before one can be cured, another cries out; and now I am in daily expectation of my favourite brood mare dropping a foal, which I am in great hopes will prove a colt, and therefore I cannot be absent at the time, for a master's eye you know is every thing in those cases: besides I should be sorry to come up in this dripping season, and as the parson has begun praying for fair weather, I hope it will set in ere long in good earnest, and that it will please God to make it pleasant travelling.

'You will be pleased to hear that I mean soon to make a job of draining the marsh in front of my house: every body allows that as soon as there is a channel cut to the river, it will be as dry as a bowling-green, and as fine meadow land as any on my estate: it will also add considerably to the health as well as beauty of our situation, for at present 'tis a grievous eye-sore, and fills us with fogs and foul air at such a rate, that I have had my whole family down with the ague all this spring: here is a fellow ready to undertake the job at a very easy expense, and will complete it in a week, so that it will soon be done

when once begun; therefore you see I need not
hurry myself for setting about it, but wait till leisure
and opportunity suit.

'I am sorry I can send you no better news of your
old friend the vicar; he is sadly out of sorts; you
must know the incumbent of *Slow-in-the-Wilds* died
some time ago, and as the living lies so handy to my
own parish I had always intended it for our friend,
and had promised him again and again: when behold! time slipt away unperceived, and in came my
lord bishop of the diocess with a parson of his own,
ready cut and dried, and claimed it as a lapsed living, when it has been mine and my ancestors any
time these five hundred years for aught I know: if
these are not nimble doings I know not what are:
egad! a man need have all his eyes about him, that
has to do with these bishops. If I had been aware
of such a trick being played me, I would have hoisted
the honest vicar into the pulpit, before the old parson who is dead and gone had been nailed in his
coffin; for no man loves less to be taken napping
(as they call it) than I do: and as for the poor vicar
'tis surprising to see how he takes to heart the disappointment; whereas I tell him he has nothing for
it but to outlive the young fellow who has jumped
into his shoes, and then let us see if any bishop shall
jockey us with the like jade's trick for the future.

'I have now only to request you will send me
down a new almanack, for the year wears out apace,
and I am terribly puzzled for want of knowing how
it goes, and I love to be regular. If there is any
thing I can do for you in these parts, pray employ
me, for I flatter myself you believe no man living
would go farther, or more readily fly to do you service than yours, to command,

THOMAS TORTOISE.'

Alas! though the wise men in all ages have been

calling out as it were with one voice for us 'to know ourselves,' it is a voice that has not yet reached the ears or understanding of my correspondent Tom Tortoise. Somebody or other hath left us another good maxim, 'never to put off till to-morrow what we can do to-day.'——Whether he was indeed a wise man, who first broached this maxin, I'll not take on myself to pronounce, but I am apt to think he would be no fool who observed it.

If all the resolutions, promises and engagements of To-day, that lie over for To-morrow, were to be summed up and posted by items, what a cumbrous load of procrastinations would be transferred in the midnight crisis of a moment! Something perhaps like the following might be the outline of the deed, by which To-day might will and devise the foresaid contingences to its heir and successor.

'Conscious that my existence is drawing to its close, I hereby devise and make over to my natural heir and successor, all my right and title in those many vows, promises, and obligations, which have been so liberally made to me by sundry persons in my lifetime, but which still remained unfulfilled on their part, and stand out against them: but at the same time that I am heartily desirous all engagements, fair and lawful in their nature, may be punctually complied with, I do most willingly cancel all such as are of a contrary description; hereby releasing and discharging all manner of persons, who have bound themselves to me under rash and inconsiderate resolutions, from the performance of which evil might ensue to themselves, and wrong or violence be done society.

'In the first place I desire my said heir and successor will call in all those debts of conscience, which have been incurred by, and are due from, certain defaulters who stand pledged to repentance

and atonement, of all which immediate payment
ought in justice and discretion to be rigorously exacted from the several parties, forasmuch as every
hour, by which they outrun their debt, weakens their
security.

'It is my farther will and desire, that all those
free livers and profest voluptuaries, who have wasted
the hours of my existence in riot and debauchery,
may be made to pay down their lawful quota of sick
stomachs and aching heads, to be levied upon them
severally by poll at the discretion of my heir and
successor.

'Whereas I am apprized of many dark dealings
and malicious designs now in actual execution, to
the great annoyance of society and good fellowship,
I earnestly recommend the detection of all such evil-
minded persons with To-morrow's light, heartily
hoping they will meet their due shame, punishment,
and disappointment: and I sincerely wish that every
honest man, who hath this night gone to rest with a
good reputation, may not be deprived of To-morrow's
repose by any base efforts, which Slander, who works
in the dark, may conjure up to take it from him.

'It is with singular satisfaction I have been made
privy to sundry kind and charitable benevolences,
that have been privately bestowed upon the indigent
and distrest, without any ostentation or parade on
the part of the givers, and I do thereupon strictly
enjoin and require a fair and impartial account to be
taken of the same by my lawful heir and successor,
(be the amount what it may) that interest for the
same may be put into immediate course of payment;
whereby the parties so entitled may enjoy, as in justice they ought to do, all those comforts, blessings,
and rewards, which talents so employed are calculated to produce.

'All promises made by men of power to their dependants, and all verbal engagements to tradesmen on the score of bills, that lie over for To-morrow, I hereby cancel and acquit; well assured they were not meant by those who made them, nor expected by any who received them, then to be made good and fulfilled.

'To all gamesters, rakes, and revellers, who shall be found out of bed at my decease, I bequeath rotten constitutions, restless thoughts, and squalid complexions; but to all such regular and industrious people, who rise with the sun and carefully resume their honest occupations, I give the greatest of all human blessings—health of body, peace of mind, and length of days.

Given under my hand, &c. &c.

To-Day.'

## NUMBER XCVII.

'To the Observer.

'Sir,

'There is an old gentleman of my acquaintance who annoys me exceedingly with his predictions: I have reason to believe he bears me good will in the main, and does not know to what a degree he actually disturbs my peace of mind; I would therefore fain put up with his humour if I could; but when he is for ever ringing his knell in my ears, he sometimes provokes me to retort upon him, oftentimes to laugh at him, and never fails to put me out of patience or out of spirits.

'I have read your account of the Dampers with great fellow-feeling, and perceive that my old gentleman is very deep in that philosophy: but as I un-

fortunately have very little philosophy of any sort to
set against it, I find myself frequently at his mercy,
and without defence.

'I do not think this proceeds so much from any
radical vice in his nature, as from a foolish vanity to
seem wiser than his neighbours, and to put himself
off for a man who knows the world: the fact is, he
is an old bachelor, lives in absolute retirement, and
has scarcely stepped out of the precincts of his own
village three times in his life; yet he is ever telling
me of his experience and his observations: if I was
to put implicit faith in what he says, common honesty in mankind would be a miracle, and happiness
a disappointment; as for hope, that moonshine diet
as he calls it, which is so plentifully served up in the
fanciful repasts of the poets, and which is too often
the only standing dish at their tables, I should never
get a taste of it; and yet if ruining a merchant's
credit is tantamount to robbing him of his property,
I must think the Damper, who blasts my hope, is in
fact little better than a thief.

'I have a natural prejudice for certain people at
first sight, where a countenance impresses me in its
favour, for I am apt to fancy that honesty sets a mark
upon its owners; there is not a weakness incident
to human nature, for which he could hold my understanding in more sovereign contempt: if I was to be
advised by him, I should not trust my wife out of
my sight, for it is a maxim with him, that no love-
matches can be happy; mine was of that sort, and I
am happy; still I am out of credit with my Damper.
I was bound for a relation in public trust some years
ago; there I confess his augury sometimes staggered
me, and he urged me with proverbs out of holy writ,
which I was rather puzzled to parry; my friend however has done well in the world, discharged his obligation, and repaid it with grateful returns; still I

am out of credit with my Damper. I invested a small sum in a venture to the East Indies; he descanted upon the risk of the sea; I insured upon the ship, he denounced bankruptcy against the underwriter; the ship came home, and I doubled the capital of my investment; still I am out of credit with my Damper, and he shakes his head at my folly.

'I can plainly perceive that his predictions often-times are as troublesome to himself as to me; he loses many a fine morning's walk by foreseeing a change of weather; he never goes to church because he has had a suit with the parson; and part of his estate remains untenanted, because a farmer some time ago broke in his debt.

'Though I am no philosopher, I am not such a simpleton, as not to know how little we ought to depend upon worldly events in general; yet it appears to me that what a man has already enjoyed, he can no longer be said to depend upon: if therefore I have had real pleasure in any innocent and agreeable expectation, disappointment can at worst do no more than remove the meat after I have made my meal.

'Though I do not know how to define hope as a metaphysician, I am inclined to speak of it with respect, because I find it has been a good friend to me in my life; it has given me a thousand things, which malice and misfortune would have ravished from me, if I had not fairly worn them out before they could lay their fingers upon them: *spe pascit inani*—says the poet, and contradicts himself in the same breath: for my part, if it was not for the fear of appearing paradoxical, I should say upon experience, that hope, though called a shadow, is, together with that other phantom death, the sole reality beneath the sun: the unfaithfulness of friends, from whom I had the claim of gratitude, can never rob me of those pleasures I

enjoyed when I served them, loved them, and con-
fided in them; and in spite of all my friend the
Damper can say to the contrary, it is not on my own
account I am sorry to have thought better of mankind than they deserve.          I am, Sir, &c.

                                        BENEVOLUS.'

'TO THE OBSERVER.

'SIR,

'I have the honour to belong to a club of gentlemen of public spirit and talents, who make it a rule
to meet every Sunday evening in a house of entertainment behind St. Clement's, for the regulation of
literature in this metropolis. Our fraternity consists of two distinct orders, The Dampers and The
Puffers; and each of these are again classed into
certain inferior subdivisions. We take notice that
both these descriptions of persons have in turn been
the objects of your feeble raillery; but I must fairly
tell you, we neither think worse of ourselves nor any
better of you for those attempts. We consider the
republic of letters under obligations to us for its very
existence; for how could it be a republic, unless its
members were kept upon an equality with each other?
Now this is the very thing which our institution professes to do.

'We have an ingenious member of our society,
who has invented a machine for this purpose, which
answers to admiration: he calls it—*The Thermometer
of Merit*: this machine he has set in a frame, and
laid down a very accurate scale of gradations by the
side of it: one glance of the eye gives every author's
altitude to a minute. The middle degree on this
scale, and which answers to *temperate* on a common
thermometer, is that standard, or common level of
merit, to which all contemporaries in the same free
community ought to be confined; but as there will

always be some eccentric beings in nature, who will either start above standard height, or drop below it, it is our duty by the operation of the daily *press* either to screw them down, or to screw them up, as the case requires; and this brings me to explain the uses of the two grand departments of our fraternity: authors above par fall to the province of the Dampers, all below par appertain to the Puffers. The daily press being common to all men, and both the one class and the other having open access thereto, we can work either by *forcers* or *repellers*, as we see fit; and I can safely assure you our process seldom fails in either case, when we apply it timely, and especially to young poets in their *veal bones* as the saying is: with this view we are always upon terms with the conductors of the said press, who are fully sensible of the benefits of our institution, and live with us in the mutual interchange of friendly offices, like Shakspeare's Zephyrs————

Stealing and giving odours.——

'As we act upon none but principles of general justice, and hold it right that parts should be made subservient to the whole, our scheme of equalization requires, that accordingly as any individual rises on the scale, our depressing powers should counteract and balance his ascending powers: this process, as I said before, belongs to the Dampers' office, and is by them termed *pressing* an author, or more literally committing him to the *press*. This is laid on more or less forcibly, according to his degree of ascension; in most cases a few turns squeeze him down to his proper bearing, but this is always done with reasonable allowance for the natural reaction of elastic bodies, so that it is necessary to bring him some degrees below standard, lest he should mount above it when the *press* is taken off: if by chance his ascending powers run him up to *sultry* or *fever-*

*heat,* the Dampers must proportion their discipline accordingly. In like manner the Puffers have to blow an author up by mere strength of lungs, when he is heavy in ballast, and his sinking powers fall below the *freezing-point,* as sometimes happens even to our best friends : in that case the Puffers have *bursts of applause* and *peals of laughter* in petto, which, though they never reach vulgar ears, serve his purpose effectually.—But these are secrets, which we never reveal but to the *initiated,* and I shall conclude by assuring you I am yours as you deserve,

PRO BONO PUBLICO.'

---

## NUMBER XCVIII.

A WRITER of miscellaneous essays is open to the correspondence of persons of all descriptions, and though I think fit to admit the following letter into my collection, I hope my readers will not suppose I wish to introduce the writer of it into their company, or even into my own.

'TO THE OBSERVER.

'SIR,

' As we hear a great deal of the affluence of this flourishing country, and the vast quantity of *sleeping cash,* as it is called, locked up in vaults and strong boxes, we conceive it would be a good deed to waken some of it, and put it into use and circulation : we have therefore associated ourselves into a patriotic fraternity of circulators commonly called pickpockets : but with sorrow we let you know, that notwithstanding our best endeavours to put forward the purposes of our institution, and the great charges of providing ourselves with instruments and tools of all sorts for the better furtherance of our business, we have yet hooked up little except dirty handkerchiefs, leathern snuff-boxes, empty purses, and bath-metal watches from the pockets of the public; articles these, let me say, that would hardly be received at the depôt of the patriotic contributors at Paris. Are these the symptoms of a great and wealthy nation? we blush for our country, whilst we are compelled by truth and candour to reply—They are not.

'As we have a number of pretty articles on hand, which will not pass in our trade, nothing deters us from putting them up to public cant but the tax our unworthy parliament has laid upon auctions. I send you two or three papers, which a brother artist angled out of the pocket of a pennyless gentleman the other night at the playhouse door: the one a letter signed Urania, the other Gorgon: they can be of no use to us, as we have nothing to do with Urania's virtue, nor stand in need of Gorgon to paint scenes, which we can act better than he describes; neither do we want his effigy of a man under the gallows to remind us of what we must all come to. Yours,

CROOK-FINGERED JACK.'

The letter from Urania breathes the full spirit of that amiable ambition, which at present seems generally to inspire our heroines of the stage to accept of none but shining characters, and never to present themselves to the public but as illustrious models of purity and grace. If virtue be thus captivating by resemblance only, how beautiful must it be in the reality! I cannot, however, help pitying the unknown poet, whose hopes were dashed with the following rebuke:

'SIR,

'I have run my eye over your tragedy, and am

beyond measure surprised you could think of allotting a part to me, which is so totally unamiable. Sir, I neither can, nor will, appear in any public character, which is at variance with my private one ; and, though I have no objection to your scene of self-murder, and flatter myself I could do it justice, yet my mind revolts from spilling any blood but my own.

' I confess there are many fine passages and some very striking situations, that would fall to my lot in your drama, but permit me to tell you, Sir, that until you can clear up the legitimacy of the child, you have been pleased therein to lay at my door, and will find a father for it, whom I may not blush to own for a husband, you must never hope for the assistance of your humble servant,        URANIA.'

The other letter is addressed to the same unfortunate poet from an artist, who seems to have studied nature in her deformities only.

' DEAR DISMAL,

' I wait with impatience to hear of the success of your tragedy, and in the mean time have worked off a frontispiece for it, that you, who have a passion for the terrific, will be perfectly charmed with.

' I am scandalized when I hear people say that the fine arts are protected in this country; nothing can be farther from the truth, as I am one amongst many to witness. Painting I presume will not be disputed to be one of the fine arts, and I may say without vanity I have some pretensions to rank with the best of my brethren in that profession.

' My first studies were carried on in the capitol of a certain county where I was born; and being determined to choose a striking subject for my *debut* in the branch of portrait-painting, I persuaded my grandmother to sit to me, and I am bold to say there was great merit in my picture, considering it as a maiden production: particularly in the execution of a hair-mole upon her chin, and a wart under her eye, which I touched to such a nicety, as to make every body start who cast their eyes upon the canvas.

'There was a little dwarfish lad in the parish, who, besides the deformity of his person, had a remarkable hair-lip, which exposed to view a broken row of discoloured teeth, and was indeed a very brilliant subject for a painter of effect: I gave a full-length of him, that was executed so to the life, as to turn the stomach of every body, who looked upon it.

'At this time there came into our town a travelling showman, who amongst other curiosities of the savage kind brought with him a man-ape, or Ourang-Outang: and this person having seen and admired my portrait of the little hump-backed dwarf, employed me to take the figure of his celebrated savage for the purpose of displaying it on the outside of his booth. Such an occasion of introducing my art into notice spurred my genius to extraordinary exertions, and though I must premise that the savage was not the best sitter in the world, yet I flatter myself I acquitted myself to the satisfaction of his keeper, and did justice to the ferocity of my subject: I caught him in one of his most striking attitudes, standing erect with a huge club in his paw: I put every muscle into play, and threw such a terrific dignity into his features, as would not have disgraced the character of a Nero or a Caligula. I was happy to observe the general notice, which was taken of my performance by all the country folks, who resorted to the show, and I believe my employer had no cause to repent of having set me upon the work.

'The figure of this animal with the club in his paw suggested a hint to a publican in the place of treating his alehouse with a new sign; and as he had been in the service of a noble family, who from ancient times have borne the *Bear* and *Ragged Staff* for their crest, he gave me a commission to provide him with a sign to that effect. Though I spared no pains to get a real bear to sit to me for this portrait, my endeavours proved abortive, and I was forced to resort to such common prints of that animal as I could obtain, and trusted to my imagination for supplying what else might be wanted for the piece. As I worked upon this capital design in the room where my grandmother's portrait was before my eyes, it occurred to me to introduce the same hair mole into the whiskers of Bruin, which I had so successfully copied from her chin, and certainly the thought was a happy one, for it had a picturesque effect; but in doing this I was naturally enough, though undesignedly, betrayed into giving such a general resemblance to the good dame in the rest of Bruin's features, that when it came to be exhibited on the signpost all the people cried out upon the likeness, and a malicious rumour ran through the town, that I had painted my grandmother instead of the bear; which lost me the favour of that indulgent relation, though Heaven knows I was as innocent of the intention as the child unborn.

'The disgust my grandmother conceived against her likeness with the ragged staff, gave me incredible uneasiness; and as she was a good customer to the landlord, and much respected in the place, he was induced to return the bear upon my hands. I am now thinking to what use I can turn him; and as it occurs to me, that by throwing a little more authority into his features, and gilding his chain, he might very possibly hit the likeness of some lord mayor of London in his fur gown and gold chain, and make a respectable figure in some city hall, I am willing to dispose of him to any such at an easy price.

' As I have also preserved a sketch of my famous Ourang-Outang, a thought has struck me, that with a few finishing touches he might easily be converted into a Caliban for the Tempest, and, when that is done, I shall not totally despair of his obtaining a niche in the Shakspeare gallery.

' It has been common with the great masters, Rubens, Vandyke, Sir Joshua Reynolds, and others, when they paint a warrior, or other great personage, on horseback, to throw a dwarf, or some other contrasted figure, into the back ground: should any artist be in want of such a thing, I can very readily supply him with my hair-lipped boy; if otherwise, I am not totally without hopes that he may suit some Spanish grandee, when any such shall visit this country upon his travels, or in the character of ambassador from that illustrious court.

' Before I conclude I shall beg leave to observe, that I have a complete set of ready-made devils, that would do honour to Saint Anthony, or any other person, who may be in want of such accompaniments to set off the self-denying virtues of his character; I have also a fine parcel of murdered innocents, which I mean to have filled up with the story of Herod; but if any gentleman thinks fit to lay the scene in Ghent, and make a modern composition of it, I am bold to say my pretty babes will not disgrace the pathos of the subject, nor violate the *Costuma*. I took a notable sketch of a man hanging, and seized him just in the dying twitches, before the last stretch gave a stiffness and rigidity unfavourable to the human figure: this I would willingly accommodate to the wishes of any lady, who is desirous of preserving a portrait of her lover, friend, or husband, in that interesting attitude.

' These, *cum multis aliis*, are part of my stock on hand, and I hope, upon my arrival at my lodgings

in Blood-bowl-alley, to exhibit them with much credit to myself, and to the entire satisfaction of such
of my neighbours in that quarter, as may incline to
patronise the fine arts, and restore the credit of this
drooping country.          Yours,          GORGON.'

## NUMBER XCIX.

Cuncti adsint, meritæque expectent præmia palmæ!

A CURIOUS Greek fragment has been lately discovered by an ingenious traveller at Constantinople,
which is supposed to have been saved out of the famous Alexandrian library when set on fire by command of the Caliph.   There is nothing but conjecture to guide us to the author: some learned men,
who have examined it, give it to Pausanias, others
to Ælian : some contend for Suidas, others for Libanius : but most agree in ascribing it to some one of
the Greek sophists, so that it is not to be disguised
that just doubts are to be entertained of its veracity
in point of fact.   There may be much ingenuity in
these discussions, but we are not to expect conviction; therefore I shall pass to the subject matter,
and not concern myself with any previous argumen-
tation on a question that is never likely to be settled.

This fragment says, ' That some time after the
death of the great dramatic poet Æschylus, there was
a certain citizen of Athens named Philoteuchus, who
by his industry and fair character in trade had acquired a plentiful fortune, and came in time to be
actually chosen one of the Areopagites; this man
in an advanced period of his life engaged in a very
splendid undertaking for collecting a series of pic-

tures to be composed from scenes in the tragedies of the great poet above-mentioned, and to be executed by the Athenian artists, who were then both numerous and eminent.

' The old Areopagite, with a spirit that would have done honour to Pisistratus or Pericles, constructed a spacious lyceum for the reception of these pictures, which he laid open to the resort both of citizens and strangers, and the success of the work reflected equal credit upon the undertaker and the artists whom he employed.'

The chain of the narration is here broken by a loss of a part of the fragment, which however is fortunately resumed in that place, where the writer gives some account of the masters who painted for this collection, and of the scenes they made choice of for their several pictures.

' He tells us that Apelles was then living and in the vigour of his genius, though advanced in years; he describes the scene chosen for his composition minutely, and it appears to have been taken from that suit of dramas, which we know Æschylus composed from the story of the Atridæ, and of which we have still such valuable remains. He represents Ægisthus, after the murder of Agamemnon by the instigation of Clytemnestra, in the act of consulting certain Sybils, who by their magical spells and incantations have raised the ghost of Agamemnon, which is attended by a train of phantoms, emblematic of eight successive kings of Argos, his immediate descendants : the spectre is made *pointing* to his posterity, and at the same time looking on his murderer with a smile, in which Apelles contrived to give the several expressions of contempt, exultation, and revenge, with such a character of ghastly pain and horror, as to make the beholders shrink. Amongst these Sybils he introduces the person of

Cassandra the prophetess, whom Agamemnon brought captive from the destruction of Troy. The light, he says, only proceeds from a flaming cauldron, in which the Sybils have been making their libations to the infernal deities or furies, and he speaks of the reflected, ruddy tints, which by this management of the artist were cast upon the figures, as producing a wonderful effect, and giving an amazing horror and magnificence to the group. Upon the whole he states it as the most capital performance of the master, and that he got such universal honour thereby, that he was afterward employed to paint for the Persian monarch, and had a commission even from the queen of Scythia, a country then emerging from barbarity.

' Parrhasius, though born in the colony of Miletus on the coast of Asia, was an adopted citizen of Athens, and in great credit there for his celebrated picture on the death of Epaminondas: he contributed to this collection by a very capital composition taken from a tragedy, which was the third in a series of dramas, founded by Æschylus on the well-known story of Œdipus, all which are lost. The miserable monarch, whose misfortunes had overturned his reason, is here depicted taking shelter under a wretched hovel in the midst of a tremendous storm, where the elements seem conspiring against a helpless being in the last stage of human misery. The painter has thrown a very touching character of insanity into his features, which plainly indicates that his loss of reason has arisen from the tender rather than the inflammatory passions; for there is a majestic sensibility mixed with the wildness of his distraction, which still preserves the traces of the once benevolent monarch. In this desolate scene he has a few forlorn companions in his distress, which form a very peculiar group of personages; for they consist of a venerable old man in a very piteous condition, whose eyes have been torn from their sockets, together with a naked maniac who is starting from the hovel, where he had housed himself during the tempest: the effect of this figure is described with rapture, for he is drawn in the prime of youth, beautiful, and of a most noble air; his naked limbs display the finest proportions of the human figure, and the muscular exertion of the sudden action he is thrown into furnish ample scope to the anatomical science of the artist. The fable feigns him to be the son of the blind old man above described, and the fragment relates that his frenzy being not real but assumed, Parrhasius availed himself of that circumstance, and touched the character of his madness with so nice and delicate a discrimination from that of Œdipus, that an attentive observer might have discovered it to be counterfeited even without the clue of the story. There are two other attendant characters in the group; one of these is a rough, hardy veteran, who seems to brave the storm with a certain air of contemptuous petulance in his countenance that bespeaks a mind superior to fortune, and indignant under the visitation even of the gods themselves. The other is a character that seems to have been a kind of imaginary creature of the poet, and is a buffoon or jester upon the model of Homer's Thersites, and was employed by Æschylus in his drama upon the old burlesque system of the Satyrs, as an occasional chorus or parody upon the severer and more tragic characters of the piece.

'The next picture in our author's catalogue was by the hand of Timanthes: this modest painter, though residing in the capital of Attica, lived in such retirement from society, and was so absolutely devoted to his art, that even his person was scarce known to his competitors. Envy never drew a word from his lips to the disparagement of a contemporary, and emulation could hardly provoke his diffidence into a contest for fame, which so many bolder rivals were prepared to dispute.

' Æschylus, it is well known, wrote three plays on the fable of Prometheus: the second in this series is the " Prometheus chained," which happily survives ; the last was " Prometheus delivered," and from the opening scene of this drama Timanthes formed his picture. Prometheus is here discovered on the sea-shore upon an island inhabited only by himself and his daughter, a young virgin of exquisite beauty, who is supposed to have seen none other of the human species but her father, besides certain imaginary beings, whom Prometheus had either created by his stolen fire, or whom he employed in the capacity of familiars for the purposes of his enchantments, for the poet very justifiably supposes him endowed with supernatural powers, and by that vehicle brings to pass all the beautiful and surprising incidents of his drama. One of the aërial spirits had by his command conjured up a most dreadful tempest, in which a noble ship is represented as sinking in the midst of the breakers on this enchanted shore. The daughter of Prometheus is seen in a supplicating attitude imploring her father to *allay* the storm, and save the sinking mariners from destruction. In the back ground of the picture is a cavern, and at the entrance of it a misshapen savage being, whose evil nature is depicted in the deformity of his person and features, and who was employed by Prometheus in all servile offices, necessary for his accommodation in this solitude. The aërial spirit is in the clouds, which he is driving before him at the *behest* of his great master. In this composition, therefore, although not replete with characters, there is yet such diversity of style and sub-

ject, that we have all which the majesty and beauty
of real nature can furnish, with beings out of the
regions of nature, as strongly contrasted in form and
character, as fancy can devise: the scenery also is
of the sublimest cast, and whilst all Greece resounded with applauses upon the exhibition of this
picture, Timanthes alone was silent, and startled
at the very echo of his own fame, shrunk back
again to his retirement.'

As this fragment is now in the hands of an ingenious translator, I forbear for the present to intrude
upon his work by any farther anticipation of it, conscious withal as I am that the public curiosity will
shortly be gratified with a much more full and satisfactory delineation of this interesting narrative, than
I am able to give.

## NUMBER C.

*Magnum iter ad doctas proficisci cogor Athenas.* — PROPERT.

I WAS agreeably surprised the other day with an unexpected visit from a country friend who once made
a considerable figure in the fashionable world, and,
with an elegant taste for the fine arts, is possessed of
many valuable paintings and sculptures of his own
collecting in Italy: he told me, that after six years
absence from town, he had made a journey purposely to regale his curiosity for a few days with the
spectacles of this great capital, and desired I would
accompany him on his morning's tour to some of the
eminent artists, and afterward conduct him to the
theatre, where he had secured himself a seat for the
representation of Mr. Southern's tragedy of *The*

*Fatal Marriage.* Though I had just been honoured
with a card from Vanessa, purporting that she would
hold 'The Feast of Reason' that evening at her
house, where my company was expected, I did not
hesitate to accept the invitation of my country friend,
and excuse myself from that of Vanessa, though I
must confess my curiosity was somewhat roused by
the novelty of the entertainment to which I was
bidden. Our day passed so entirely to the satisfaction of my candid companion, that, when we
parted at night he shook me by the hand, and with
a smile of complacency, declared, that a day so spent
would not disgrace the diary of Pericles.

When I had returned to my apartment, this allusion of my friend to the age of Pericles, with the
recollection of what had passed in the day, threw
me into a reverie, in the course of which I fell
asleep, whilst my mind with more distinctness than
is usual in dreaming, pursued its waking train of
thought after the following manner :—

' I found myself in a stately portico, which being
on an eminence, gave me the prospect of a city en-
closing a prodigious circuit, with groves, gardens,
and fields, seemingly set apart for martial exercises
and sports: the houses were not clustered into streets
and alleys like our great trading towns, but were
placed apart and separated without any regular order, as if each man had therein consulted his own
particular taste and enjoyments. I thought I never
saw so delightful a place, nor a people who lived so
much at their ease : I felt a freshness and salubrity
in the climate, that seemed to clear the brain, and
give a spring to the spirits and whole animal frame:
the sun was bright and glowing, but the lightness of
the atmosphere and a refreshing breeze qualified the
heat in the most delicious manner. As I looked
about me with wonder and delight, I observed a

great many edifices of the purest architecture, that seemed calculated for public purposes; and wherever my eye went, it was encountered by a variety of statues in brass or marble; immediately at the foot of the steps leading to the portico, in which I stood, I observed a figure in brass of exquisite workmanship, which by its attributes I believed designed to represent the heathen deity Mercurius. In the centre of the city there was an edifice enclosed within walls, which I took to be the citadel: a rapid stream of clear water meandered about the place, and was trained through groves and gardens in the most picturesque and pleasing manner, while the prospect at distance was bounded by the sea.

'As I stood wrapt in contemplation of this new and brilliant scenery, methought I was accosted by a middle-aged man in a loose garment of fine purple, who wore his hair after the manner of our ladies, braided and coiled round upon the crown of his head, with great care and delicacy to a considerable height, and (which I thought remarkable) he had fastened the braids in several places with golden pins, on which were several figures of small grasshoppers of the same metal; behind him walked a servant youth or slave, carrying a light wicker chair for his master to repose in, a custom that seemed to me to argue great effeminacy; and looking about me I found it was pretty universal, many of the bettermost sort of citizens being seated in the streets, conversing at their ease, though there was certainly nothing in the climate, that made such an indulgence necessary.

'As I was eyeing this gentleman with a surprise, that I must own had some small tincture of contempt in it, he turned himself to me, and in the most complaisant manner imaginable accosted me in my own language, telling me, he perceived I was a stranger in Athens, and if I was curious to see what was remarkable in the place, he was ready to dedicate the day to my service. To this courteous address I returned the best answer I was able, adding that every thing was new to me, and many things appeared admirable. You will say so, replied he, before the day is past, and yet I cannot shew you in the space of a day the hundredth part of what this city contains worth a stranger's observation: of a certain, Arts and Sciences are now carried to their utmost pitch, and no future age, I think, will succeed, in which the glory of the Athenian commonwealth, and the genius of its citizens shall be found superior to their present lustre.

' The portico, in which you stand, continued the Athenian, is what we call *Pæcile*, or the *painted portico*: the brazen statue at the foot of the steps was raised by the nine Archons in honour of Mercurius Agoreus, or the Forensal: and dedicated by them to the tribes: that by its side is the statue of Solon, the other at some distance is the lawgiver Lycurgus. The gate before you, on which you see those warlike trophies, was so adorned in memory of the defeat of Plistarchus, who was brother of the famous Cassander, and commanded his cavalry and auxiliary troops in the action recorded. These paintings behind you, with which the portico is furnished, and from which it has its name, are all upon public subjects in commemoration of wise or valiant citizens: the pictures on your right hand are by the celebrated Polygnotus, these on your left by Micon, equal to his rival in art, but not in munificence; for Polygnotus would accept no other reward for his works, than the fame inseparable from such eminent performances; Micon on the contrary was paid by the state. There are several others by the hands of our great masters, particularly that incomparable piece, which represents the field of Marathon, a composition by the great Panænus, brother of the statuary Phidias; but this, as well as the others, will demand a more particular description.

'Examine this composition on your right; it is the work of Polygnotus: you see two armies drawn up front to front, and on the point of engaging: these are the Athenians, the adverse troops are the Lacedemonians; the scene is Œnoe; such is the contrivance of the artist, that you are sure victory is to declare for the Athenians, though the battle is not yet commenced.

'In the opposite piece you see the battle of Theseus with the Amazons; a capital composition by Micon; these warlike ladies are fighting on horseback; with what wonderful art has the master expressed the character of athletic beauty, without deviating into vulgarity and grossness! If you recollect the Lysistrata of Aristophanes you will meet an eulogium on this picture; it is thus the sister arts encourage and support each other.

'Now turn to Polygnotus's side, and look at that magnificent piece of art; the painter has chosen for the subject of his composition the council of the Grecian chiefs upon the violence done to Cassandra by Ajax after the capture of Troy; you see the brutal character of the man strongly expressed in the hero of the piece; amongst the group of Trojan captives, Cassandra is conspicuous: that figure which represents Laodice, is worth your notice, as being a portrait of Elpinice, a celebrated courtesan: scrupulous people have taken offence at it, but great painters will indulge themselves in these liberties, and are fond of painting after beautiful nature, of which I could give you innumerable examples.

'Now let us in the last place regale our eyes with this inestimable battle of Marathon by Panænus: What think you of it? Was it not a reward worthy

of the heroes, who preserved their country on that
glorious day? Which party is most honoured by the
work, the master who wrought it, or the valiant personages who are recorded by it? It is a question
difficult to decide. You will observe three different
groups in this superb composition, describing three
different periods of the action: here you see the
Athenians and their allies the Plateans just com-
mencing the action.—There, farther removed in per-
spective, the barbarians are defeated; the slaughter
is raging, and the Medes are plunging desperately
into the marshy lake to avoid their pursuers; examine the back ground, and you see the Phœnician
galleys; the barbarians are making a bold attack,
and the sea is covered with wrecks; all mouths are
open in applause of this picture, and it was but the
other day, that the great orator Demosthenes referred to it in a solemn harangue upon Neæra, as did
Eschines in his pleadings against Ctesiphon. All
our captains are taken from the life; that general
who is encouraging his troops is Miltiades; he is the
hero of the piece, and I can assure you the resemblance is in all points exact; this is the portrait of
Callimachus the Polemarch: there you see the hero
Echetlus, and this is the brave Epizelus: that Athenian who is valiantly fighting, is Cynœgirus himself,
who lost both his hands in the action: there goes an
extraordinary story with that dog which is by his side,
and has seized the dying barbarian by the throat;
the faithful creature would not forsake his master:
he was killed in the action, and is now deservedly
immortalized in company with the illustrious heroes,
who are the subject of the piece. Those splendid
warriors in the army of the Medes, who are standing in their chariots, and calling to their troops, are
the generals Datis and Artaphanes. They are drawn
in a proud and swelling style, and seem of a larger

size and proportion than our Athenian champions:
and the fact is, that this group was inserted by another master; they are by the hand of Micon, and
perhaps do not exactly harmonize with the rest; the
silly Athenians were piqued at their appearance, and
in a fit of jealousy punished Micon by a fine for having painted them too flatteringly; the painter suffered in his pocket, but the people in my opinion
were disgraced by the sentence: this circumstance
has given occasion for many on the part of Micon
to contest the honour of the painting with Panænus,
who in justice must be considered as principal author
of the work; and in course of time it may happen,
that posterity will be puzzled which master to ascribe
it to.

' There are many more pictures well deserving
your attentive notice, particularly that by Pamphi-
lus, which represents Alcmen with Heraclydæ asking aid of the Athenians against Eurystheus: and
this inspired old figure by Polygnotus with a lyre in
his hand, which is the portrait of no less a person
than the great Sophocles;—but come, let us be gone,
for we have much besides to see; and I perceive
Zeno coming this way with his scholars to hold his
lectures in this portico; and I, for one, must confess
I am no friend to the Stoics, or as we call them the
Zenonians.'

## NUMBER CI.

Ad vetustissimam et sapientissimam et Diis carissimam, in com-
munem amasiam, hominumque ac Deorum terram, Athenas
mittebaris.—LIBANIUS IN ORATIONE.

' FROM the painted portico, in which my last was
dated, my Athenian conductor took me to the Pto-

lemaic Gymnasium, in which I observed several statues of Mercury in marble, and others of brass, which he explained to me to be of Ptolemy the founder, Juba, and Chrysippus the philosopher. There was one of Berosus the astrologer with a tongue of pure gold, in commemoration of his divine predictions: on one hand of me stood the doric temple of Theseus, enriched with some inestimable paintings of Micon, particularly one upon the subject of the fight of the Lapithæ and Centaurs: on the other hand was the ancient temple of the Dioscuri, in which I was shewn many capital pictures by Polygnotus; it is here, says my conductor, we administer to the Athenian youth that solemn oath, which binds them not to desert their ranks in action, but to perish when necessity so requires, in defence of their country; the form is rather long, says he, but this is the substance of the oath. The Prytaneum, or Court-house, was now in view, where the magistracy of the city assemble for the dispatch of public business: here I saw the venerable laws of Solon in a chest of stone, the statues of Pax and Vesta, and (which were more interesting to me) the figures of Miltiades and Themistocles of exquisite workmanship in pure marble; in this place all those citizens, and the posterity of those who have deserved well of the state, receive their public doles or allowance of bread in cakes composed of meal, oil, and water; here also I saw the perpetual fire upon the altar of Vesta, and the celebrated image of the Bona Fortuna of the Athenians. In the adjoining temple of Lucina I was shewn the famous statues of that deity clothed in drapery to the feet: my guide now carried me to the great temple of Olympian Jupiter, founded by the tyrant Pisistratus, and perfected by his sons and successors. I observed to my conductor, that I had seen no temple in Athens, ex-

cept this, with interior columns; he informed me that
the great span of the roof made it necessary in this
instance, but that it was contrary to their rule of
architecture and obtained in no other: he farther
told me, that the city had expended ten thousand
talents in this edifice: the image of the god was cut
in ivory and gold; to every column was affixed a
brazen statue, representing the colonial cities of the
Athenian empire. The display of statuary exceeded
all description or belief, nor was the painter's art
wanting in its share of the decoration; for whatever
pictures could be disposed, and particularly about
the pedestal of the statue of Jupiter, the most capital paintings were to be seen.

' My sight was now so dazzled with the display
of brilliant images, and my mind so overpowered
with the miracles of art, which had passed in review,
that I beseeched my guide to carry me either to some
of those groves which were in my eye, where I could
meditate on what I had seen, or to spectacles of any
other sort according to his choice and discretion,
for otherwise, I should apprehend, from the variety
of objects, I should retain the memory of none. He
told me in reply, that this was his intention, observing that the proportion I had seen was very small
indeed to what the city contained; there was however one small statue, which he could not dispense
himself from shewing me, being a model of beauty
and perfection; and having so said, methought he
took me into a neighbouring garden, and in a grove
of cypress and myrtle presented to my view the most
exquisite piece of sculpture I had ever beheld.—
This, says he, is the Venus, called Celestial, the
workmanship of the immortal Alcamen.—After I had
contemplated this divine original with astonishment
and rapture, I was satisfied within myself, that we
are mistaken in supposing it has descended to us,

and I now acknowledge that our celestial Venus is a copy far inferior to its inimitable prototype. Having examined this statue for some time, I turned to my conductor and said, let us gratify our senses in some other way; I have seen enough of art.

'It is impossible to avoid it, replies he, in this city, and so saying led me into the Lyceum; this Gymnasium, says he, has been lately instituted by Pericles, and these plantations of plane-trees are of his making; so are these aqueducts; the Lyceum was originally dedicated to Pastoral Apollo; and owes its foundation and beauty in the first instance to the elegant Pisistratus, who from the surprising resemblance of their persons we now call the elder Pericles. The place is delightful, and before you leave it take notice of this statue of Apollo; the artist has described him in the attitude of resting after his daily course; you see he leans against a column; his right arm bent over his head, and in his left he holds his bow; it is a first-rate piece of sculpture. Leaving the Lyceum my conductor took me by the way of the Tripods; here he shewed me the inimitable satyr in brass, the boasted masterpiece of Praxiteles, and the Cupid and Bacchus of Thymilus; we were now close by the theatre, in the portico of which I was shewn the statue of Eschylus, and two pedestals for the statues of Sophocles and Euripides, then under the artist's hands, although both those poets were now living: the doors of the theatre were not yet opened, and the temple of Venus being near at hand, methought we entered, and I beheld the beautiful Cupid crowned with roses, painted by Zeuxis; from hence I could see the works that Pericles had been carrying on upon the citadel, but this we did not enter.

'Methought I was now carried into the theatre amidst a prodigious crowd of people; the comedy of the night was entitled *The Clouds*, and the famous Aristophanes was announced to be the author of it. It was expected that Socrates would be personally attacked, and a great party of that philosopher's enemies were assembled to support the poet. I was much surprised, when my companion pointed out to me that great philosopher in person, who had actually taken his seat in the theatre, and was sitting between Alcibiades and Antipho the son of Pericles; by the side of Alcibiades sate Euripides, and at Antipho's left hand sate Thucydides; I never beheld two more venerable old men than the poet and the historian, nor such comely persons as Alcibiades and Antipho: Socrates was exceedingly like the busts we have of him, his head was bald, his beard bushy, and his stature low; there was something very deterring in his countenance; his person was mean and his habit squalid; his vest of loose drapery thrown over his left shoulder after the fashion of a Spanish Capa, and seemed to be of coarse cloth, made of black wool undyed; he had a short staff in his hand of knotted wood with a round head, which he was continually rubbing in the palm of his hand, as he talked with Alcibiades, to whom he principally addressed his discourse: Thucydides had lately returned from exile upon a general amnesty, and I observed a melancholy in his countenance mixed with indignation; Euripides seemed employed in examining the countenances of the spectators, whilst Antipho with great modesty paid a most respectful attention to the venerable philosopher on his right hand. Whilst I was engaged in observing this respectable group, my conductor whispered the following words in my ear: — " This is the second attack from the same hands upon Socrates; that of last year was defeated by Alcibiades; but if this night's comedy succeeds, I predict that our philosopher is undone: and in truth his

school is much out of credit; for some of the worst
characters of the age have come out of his hands
of late."

'When the players came first on the stage there
was so great a murmur in the theatre, that I could
scarce hear them; after a short time however the
silence became pretty general, and the plot of the
play, such as it was, began to open. I perceived
that the poet had devised the character of an old
clownish father, who being plunged in debt by the
extravagances of a flaunting wife and a spendthrift
son, who wasted his fortune upon horse-races, was
for ever puzzling his brains to strike upon some expedient for cheating his creditors. With this view
he goes to the house of Socrates to take counsel of
that philosopher, who gives him a great many ridiculous instructions, seemingly not at all to the purpose, and amongst other extravagances assures him
that Jupiter has no concern in the government of the
world, but that all the functions of Providence are
performed by The Clouds, which upon his invocation
appear and perform the part of a chorus throughout
the play : the philosopher is continually foiled by the
rustic wit of the old father, who, after being put in
Socrates's truckle-bed, and miserably stung with vermin, has a meeting with his creditors, and endeavours
to parry their demands with a parcel of pedantic
quibbles, which he has learnt of the philosopher, and
which give occasion to scenes of admirable comic
humour : my conductor informed me this incident
was pointed at Eschines, a favourite disciple of Socrates ; a man, says he, plunged in debts and a most
notorious defrauder of his creditors. In the end the
father brings his son to be instructed by Socrates ;
the son, after a short lecture, comes forth a perfect
atheist, and gives his father a severe cudgelling on
the stage, which irreverend act he undertakes to de-

fend upon the principles of the new philosophy he had been learning. This was the substance of the play, in the course of which there were many gross allusions to the unnatural vice of which Socrates was accused, and many personal strokes against Clisthenes, Pericles, Euripides, and others, which told strongly, and were much applauded by the theatre.

'It is not to be supposed, that all this passed without some occasional disgust on the part of the spectators, but it was evident there was a party in the theatre, which carried it through, notwithstanding the presence of Socrates and the respectable junto that attended him: for my part I scarce ever took my eyes from him during the representation, and I observed two or three little actions, which seemed to give me some insight into the temper of his mind, during the severest libel that was ever exhibited against any man's person and principles.

'Before Socrates appears on the stage, the old man raps violently at his door, and is reproved by one of his disciples, who comes out and complains of the disturbance; upon his being questioned what the philosopher may be then employed upon, he answers that he is engaged in measuring the leap of a flea, to decide how many of its own lengths it springs at one hop; the disciple also informs him with great solemnity, that Socrates has discovered that the hum of a gnat is not made by the mouth of the animal, but from behind: this raised a laugh at the expense of the naturalists and minute philosophers, and I observed that Socrates himself smiled at the conceit.

'When the school was opened to the stage, and all the scholars were discovered with their heads upon the floor, and their posteriors mounted in the air, and turned towards the audience, though the poet pretends to account for it, as if they were searching for natural curiosities on the surface of the ground, the action was evidently intended to convey the grossest illusion, and was so received by the audience: when this scene was produced, I remarked that Socrates shook his head, and turned his eyes off the stage; whilst Euripides, with some indignation, threw the sleeve of his mantle over his face; this was observed by the spectators, and produced a considerable tumult, in which the theatre seemed pretty fairly divided, so that the actors stood upright, and quitted the posture they were discovered in.

'When Socrates was first produced standing on a basket mounted into the clouds, the person of the actor and the mask he wore, as well as the garment he was dressed in, was the most direct counterpart of the philosopher himself that could be devised. But when the actor, speaking in his character, in direct terms proceeded to deny the divinity of Jupiter, Socrates laid his hand upon his heart and cast his eyes up with astonishment: in the same moment Alcibiades started from his seat, and in a loud voice cried out—" Athenians! is this fitting?" Upon this a great tumult arose, and very many of the spectators called upon Socrates to speak for himself, and answer to the charge; when the play could not proceed for the noise and clamour of the people, all demanding Socrates to speak for himself, the philosopher unwillingly stept forward and said—" You require of me, O Athenians, to answer to the charge; there is no charge, neither is this a place to discourse in about the gods: let the actor proceed!"—Silence immediately took place, and Socrates's invocation to The Clouds soon ensued; the passage was so beautiful, the machinery of the clouds so finely introduced, and the chorus of voices in the air so exquisitely conceived, that the whole theatre was in raptures, and the poet from that moment had entire possession of

their minds, so that the piece was carried trium-
phantly to its period. In the heat of the applause
my Athenian friend whispered me in the ear and said
—"Depend upon it, Socrates will hear of this in
another place; he is a lost man; and remember I
tell you, that if all our philosophers and sophists
were driven out of Attica, it would be happy for
Athens."—At these words I started and awaked
from my dream.'

## NUMBER CII.

### Natio comœda est.

IF the present taste for private plays spreads as fast
as most fashions do in this country, we may expect
the rising generation will be, like the Greeks in my
motto, one entire nation of actors and actresses. A
father of a family may shortly reckon it amongst the
blessings of a numerous progeny, that he is provided
with a sufficient company for his domestic stage, and
may cast a play to his own liking, without going
abroad for his theatrical amusements. Such a steady
troop cannot fail of being under better regulation
than a set of strollers, or than any set whatever,
who make acting a vocation: where a manager has
to deal with none but players of his own begetting,
every play bids fair to have a strong cast, and in the
phrase of the stage, to be well got up. Happy author, who shall see his characters thus grouped into
a family-piece, firm as the Theban band of friends,
where all is zeal and concord; no bickerings nor
jealousies about stage precedency; no ladies to fall
sick of the spleen, and toss up their parts in a huff;

no heart-burnings about flounced petticoats and silver trimmings, where the mother of the whole company stands wardrobe-keeper and property-woman, whilst the father takes post at the side-scene in the capacity of prompter, with plenipotentiary control over PS's and OP's.

I will no longer speak of the difficulty of writing a comedy or tragedy, because that is now done by so many people without any difficulty at all, that if there ever was any mystery in it, that mystery is thoroughly bottomed and laid open; but the art of acting was till very lately thought so rare and wonderful an excellence, that people began to look upon a perfect actor as a phenomenon in the world, which they were not to expect above once in a century; but now that the trade is laid open, this prodigy is to be met at the turn of every street; the nobility and gentry, to their immortal honour, have broken up the monopoly, and new-made players are now as plentiful as new-made peers.

> Nec tamen Antiochus, nec erit mirabilis illic
> Aut Stratocles, aut cum molli Demetrius Hæmo.

> Garrick and Powell would be now no wonder,
> Nor Barry's silver note, nor Quin's heroic thunder.

Though the public professors of the art are so completely put down by the private practitioners of it, it is but justice to observe in mitigation of their defeat, that they meet the comparison under some disadvantages which their rivals have not to contend with.

One of these is diffidence, which volunteers cannot be supposed to feel in the degree they do who are pressed into the service: I never yet saw a public actor come upon the stage on the first night of a new play, who did not seem to be nearly, if not quite, in as great a shaking fit as the author; but, as there can be no luxury in a great fright, I cannot believe that people of fashion, who act for their amusement only, would subject themselves to it; they must certainly have a proper confidence in their own abilities, or they would never step out of a drawing-room, where they are sure to figure, upon a stage where they run the risk of exposing themselves; some gentlemen perhaps, who have been *mutæ personæ* in the senate, may start at the first sound of their own voices in a theatre, but graceful action, just elocution, perfect knowledge of their author, elegant deportment, and every advantage that refined manners and courtly address can bestow, is exclusively their own. In all scenes of high life they are at home; noble sentiments are natural to them; love-parts they can play by instinct, and as for all the casts of rakes, gamesters, and fine-gentlemen, they can fill them to the life. Think only what a violence it must be to the nerves of an humble unpretending actor to be obliged to play the gallant gay seducer, and be the cockold-maker of the comedy, when he has no other object at heart but to go quietly home, when the play is over, to his wife and children, and participate with them in the honest earnings of his vocation; can such a man compete with the Lothario of high life?

And now I mention the cares of a family, I strike upon another disadvantage, which the public performer is subject to and the private exempt from: the Andromache of the stage may have an infant Hector at home, whom she more tenderly feels for than the Hector of the scene; he may be sick, he may be supperless; there may be none to nurse him, when his mother is out of sight, and the maternal interest in the divided heart of the actress may preponderate over the heroine's: this is a case not within the chances to happen to any lady-actress, who of course consigns the task of education to other hands, and keeps her own at leisure for more pressing duties.

Public performers have their memories loaded and distracted with a variety of parts, and oftentimes are compelled to such a repetition of the same part, as cannot fail to quench the spirit of the representation; they must obey the call of duty, be the cast of the character what it may—

> ——Cùm Thaida sustinet, aut cùm
> Uxorem comœdas agit.

> Subject to all the various casts of life,
> Now the loose harlot, now the virtuous wife.

But, what is worse than all, the veterans of the public stage will sometimes be appointed to play the old and ugly, as I can instance in the person of a most admirable actress, whom I have often seen, and never without the tribute of applause in the casts of Juliet's nurse, Aunt Deborah, and other venerable damsels in the vale of years, when I am confident there is not a lady of independent rank in England of Mrs. Pitt's age, who would not rather struggle for Miss Jenny or Miss Hoyden, than stoop to be the representative of such old hags.

These, and the subjection public performers are under to the caprice of the spectators, and to the attacks of conceited and misjudging critics, are amongst the many disagreeable circumstances which the most eminent must expect, and the most fortunate cannot escape.

It would be hard indeed if performers of distinction, who use the stage only as an elegant and moral resource, should be subject to any of these unpleasant conditions; and yet as a friend to the rising fame of the domestic drama I must observe, that there are some precautions necessary, which its patrons have not yet attended to. There are so many consequences to be guarded against, as well as provisions to be made for an establishment of this sort, that it behoves its conductors to take their first ground with great judgment; and above all things to be very careful that an exhibition so ennobled by its actors, may be cast into such a style and character, as may keep it clear from any possible comparison with spectacles, which it should not condescend to imitate, and cannot hope to equal. This I believe has not been attempted, perhaps not even reflected upon, and yet, if I may speak from information of specimens which I have not been present at, there are many reforms needful both in its external as well as internal arrangement.

By external I mean spectacle, comprehending theatre, stage, scenery, orchestra, and all things else which fall within the province of the *arbiter deliciarum*; these should be planned upon a model new, original, and peculiar to themselves; so industriously distinguished from our public playhouses, that they should not strike the eye, as now they do, like a copy in miniature, but as the independent sketch of a master who disdains to copy. I can call to mind many noble halls and stately apartments in the great houses and castles of our nobility, which would give an artist ample field for fancy, and which with proper help would be disposed into new and striking shapes for such a scene of action, as should become the dignity of the performers. Halls and saloons, flanked with interior columns, and surrounded by galleries, would, with the aid of proper draperies or scenery in the intercolumnations, take a rich and elegant appearance, and at the same time the music might be so disposed in the gallery, as to produce a most animating effect. A very small elevation of stage should be allowed of, and no contraction by side scenes to huddle the speakers together and embarrass their deportment: no shift of scene whatever, and no curtain to draw up and drop, as if puppets were to play behind it; the area, appropriated to the performers, should be so dressed and furnished with all suitable accommodations as to afford every possible opportunity to the performers of varying their actions and postures, whether of sitting, walking, or standing, as their situations in the scene, or their interest in the dialogue may dictate; so as to familiarize and assimilate their whole conduct and conversation through the progress of the drama, to the manners and habits of well-bred persons in real life.

Prologues and epilogues in the modern style of writing and speaking them I regard as very unbecoming, and I should blush to see any lady of fashion in that silly and unseemly situation: they are the last remaining corruptions of the ancient drama; relics of servility, and only are retained in our London theatres as vehicles of humiliation at the introduction of a new play, and traps for false wit, extravagant conceits, and female flippancy at the conclusion of it; where authors are petitioners, and players servants to the public, these condescensions must be made, but where poets are not suitors, and performers are benefactors, why should the free Muse wear shackles? for such they are, though the fingers of the brave are employed to put them on the limbs of the fair.

As I am satisfied nothing ought to be admitted, from beginning to end, which can provoke comparisons, I revolt with indignation from the idea of a lady of fashion being trammelled in the trickery of the stage, and taught her airs and graces, till she is made the mere *fac-simile* of a mannerist, where the most she can aspire to is to be the copy of a copyist: let none such be consulted in dressing or drilling an honorary novitiate in the forms and fashions of the public stage; it is a course of discipline, which neither person will profit by; a kind of barter, in which both parties will give and receive false airs and false conceits; the fine lady will be disqualified by copying the actress, and the actress will become ridiculous by aping the fine lady.

As for the choice of the drama, which is so nice and difficult a part of the business, I scarce believe there is one play upon the list, which in all its parts and passages is thoroughly adapted to such a cast as I am speaking of: where it has been in public use I am sure it is not, for there comparisons are unavoidable. Plays professedly wrote for the stage must deal in strong character, and striking contrast: how can a lady stand forward in a part, contrived to produce ridicule or disgust, or which is founded upon broad humour and vulgar buffoonery?

> Nempe ipsa videtur,
> Non persona loqui.
>
> 'Tis she herself, and not her mask which speaks.

I doubt if it be altogether seemly for a gentleman to undertake, unless he can reconcile himself to cry out with Laberius—

> Eques Romanus, lare egressus meo,
> Domum revertar mimus.
>
> Esquire I sign'd myself at noon,
> At night I countersign'd buffoon.

The drama, therefore, must be purposely written for the occasion; and the writer must not only have local knowledge of every arrangement preparatory for the exhibition, but personal knowledge also of the performers who are to exhibit it. The play itself, in my conception of it, should be part only of the projected entertainment, woven into the device of a grand and splendid *fête*, given in some noble country-house or palace; neither should the specta-

tors be totally excused from their subscription to the
general *gala,* nor left to doze upon their benches
through the progress of five tedious acts, but called
upon at intervals by music, dance, or refreshment,
elegantly contrived, to change the sameness of the
scene and relieve the efforts of the more active corps,
employed upon the drama.

And now let me say one word to qualify the
irony I set out with, and acquit myself as a moralist.

There are many and great authorities against this
species of entertainment, and certainly the danger is
great, where theatrical propensities are too much indulged in young and inexperienced minds. Tertul-
lian says (but he is speaking of a very licentious
theatre) *Theatrum sacrarium est Veneris*—' A playhouse is the very sacristy of Venus.' And Juvenal,
who wrote in times of the grossest impurity, maintains that no prudent man will take any young lady
to wife, who has ever been within the walls of a
theatre—

> Cuneis an habent spectacula totis
> Quod securus ames, quodque indè excerpere possis?

> Look round, and say if any man of sense
> Will dare to single out a wife from hence?

Young women of humble rank and small pretensions should be particularly cautious how a vain ambition of being noticed by their superiors betrays
them into an attempt at displaying their unprotected
persons on a stage, however dignified and respectable. If they have talents, and of course applause,
are their understandings and manners proof against
applause? If they mistake their talents, and merit
no applause, are they sure they will get no contempt
for their self-conceit? If they have both acting
talents and attractive charms, I tremble for their
danger; let the foolish parent, whose itching ears
tingled with the plaudits that resounded through

the theatre, where virgin modesty deposited its blushes, beware how his aching heart shall throb with sorrow, when the daughter *quæ pudica ad theatrum accesserat, indè revertetur impudica. (Cyprian ad Donatum.)*

So much by way of caution to the guardians and protectors of innocence; let the offence light where it may, I care not, so it serves the cause for which my heart is pledged.

As for my opinion of private plays in general, though it is a fashion, which hath kings and princes for its nursing fathers, and queens and princesses for its nursing mothers, I think it is a fashion that should be cautiously indulged and narrowly confined to certain ranks, ages, and conditions, in the community at large. Grace forbid! that what the author of my motto said scoffingly of the Greeks should be said prophetically of this nation; emulate them in their love of freedom, in their love of science; rival them in the greatest of their actions, but not in the versatility of their mimic talents, till it shall be said of us by some future satirist—

Natio comœda est.   Rides? majore cachinno
Concutitur: flet, si lachrymas aspexit amici,
Nec dolet.   Igniculum brumæ si tempore poscas,
Accipit endromidem: si dixeris, æstuo, sudat.
Non sumus ergo pares; melior, qui semper et omni
Nocte dieque potest alienum sumere vultum.

Laugh, and your merry echo bursts his sides;
Weep, and his courteous tears gush out in tides;
Light a few sticks you cry, 'tis wintry—Lo!
He's a furr'd Laplander from top to toe;
Put out the fire, for now 'tis warm—He's more,
Hot, sultry hot, and sweats at every pore:
Oh! he's beyond us; we can make no race
With one, who night and day maintains his pace,
And fast as you shift humours still can shift his face.

Before I close this paper I wish to go back to what I said respecting the propriety of new and oc-

casional dramas for private exhibition : too many
men are in the habit of decrying their contemporaries, and this discouraging practice seems more generally levelled at the dramatic province than any
other ; but whilst the authors of such tragic dramas
as *Douglas, Elfrida,* and *Caractacus,* of such comic
ones as *The School for Scandal, The Jealous Wife,
The Clandestine Marriage,* and *The Way to Keep Him,*
with others in both lines, are yet amongst us, why
should we suppose the state of genius so declined
as not to furnish poets able to support and to supply their honorary representatives? Numbers there
are, no doubt, unnamed and unknown, whom the
fiery trial of a public stage deters from breaking
their obscurity : let disinterested fame be their prize,
and there will be no want of competitors.

Latet anguis in herba.

'There is a serpent in the grass,' and that serpent
is the emblem of wisdom ; the very symbol of wit
upon the watch, couching for awhile under the
cover of obscurity, till the bright rays of the sun
shall strike upon it, give it life and motion to erect
itself on end, and display the dazzling colours of its
burnished scales.

> Though thou, vile cynic, art the age's shame,
>     Hope not to damn all living fame ;
>     True wit is arm'd in scales so bright,
>     It dazzles thy dull owlish sight ;
>     Thy wolfish fangs no entrance gain,
>     They gnaw, they tug, they gnash in vain,
> Their hungry malice does but edge their pain.

> Avaunt, profane! 'tis consecrated ground :
>     Let no unholy foot be found
> Where the Arts mingle, where the Muses haunt,
> And the Nine Sisters hymn their sacred chant,
>     Where Freedom's nymph-like form appears,
>     And high 'midst the harmonious spheres
> Science her laurel-crowned head uprears.

Ye moral masters of the human heart!
  And you advance, ye sons of Art!
Let Fame's far-echoing trumpet sound
To summon all her candidates around :
  Then bid old Time his roll explore,
  And say what age presents a store
In merit greater or in numbers more.

  Come forth and boldly strike the lyre,
  Break into song, poetic choir!
Let Tragedy's loud strains in thunder roll:
With pity's dying cadence melt the soul;
  And now provoke a sprightlier lay;
  Hark! Comedy begins to play,
She smites the string, and Dulness flits away.

  For envious Dulness will essay to fling
  Her mud into the Muse's spring,
Whilst critic curs with pricking ears
Bark at each bard as he appears!
  Ev'n the fair dramatist, who sips
  Her Helicon with modest lips,
Sometimes, alas! in troubled water dips.

But stop not, fair one, faint not in thy task,
  Slip on the sock and snatch the mask,
Polish thy clear reflecting glass,
And catch the manners as they pass;
  Call home thy playful Sylphs again,
  And cheer them with a livelier strain;
Fame weaves no wreath that is not earn'd with pain.

  And thou, whose happy talent hit
  The richest vein of Congreve's wit,
Ah! fickle rover, false ungrateful loon,
Did the fond easy Muse consent too soon,
  That thou should'st quit Thalia's arms
  For an old Begum's tawny charms,
And shake us, not with laughter, but alarms!

Curst be ambition! Hence with musty laws!
Why pleads the bard but in Apollo's cause?
Why move the Court and humbly apprehend
But as the Muse's advocate and friend?
  She taught his faithful scene to shew
  All that man's varying passions know,
Gay-flashing wit and heart-dissolving woe.

Thou too, thrice happy in a Jealous Wife,
Comic interpreter of nuptial life,
    Know that all candid hearts detest
    Th' unmanly scoffer's cruel jest,
  Who for his jibes no butt could find
  But what cold palsy left behind,
A shaking man with an unshaken mind.

    And ye, who teach man's lordly race,
    That woman's wit will have its place,
  Matrons and maidens who inspire
The scenic flute, or sweep the Sapphic lyre,
    Go warble in the sylvan seat,
    Where the Parnassian sisters meet,
And stamp the rugged soil with female feet.

    'Tis ye, who interweave the myrtle bough
With the proud palm that crowns Britannia's brow,
    Who to the age in which ye live
Its charms, its graces, and its glories give ;
    For me, I seek no higher praise,
    But to crop one small sprig of bays,
And wear it in the sunshine of your days.

# NUMBER CIII.

I do not know a man in England better received in
the circles of the great than Jack Gayless : though
he has no one quality for which he ought to be respected, and some points in his character for which
he should be held in detestation, yet his manners
are externally so agreeable, and his temper generally
so social, that he makes a holiday in every family
where he visits. He lives with the nobility upon the
easiest footing, and in the great houses where he is
in habits of intimacy, he knows all the domestics by
name, and has something to say to every one of them
upon his arrival : he has a joke with the butler at the
side-board during dinner, and sets the footman a

tittering behind his chair, and is so comical and so familiar—he has the best receipt-book in England, and recommends himself to the cook by a new sauce, for he is in the secrets of the king's kitchen at Versailles: he has the finest breed of spaniels in Europe, and is never without a puppy at the command of a friend: he knows the theory of hunting from top to bottom, is always in with the hounds, can develop every hit in a check, and was never known to cheer a wrong dog in a cover, when he gives his tongue: if you want an odd horse to match your set, Jack is your man; and for a neat travelling-carriage, there is not an item that he will not superintend, if you are desirous to employ him; he will be at your door with it, when the builder brings it home, to see that nothing is wanting, he is so ready and obliging: no man canvasses a county or borough like Jack Gayless; he is so pleasant with the freeholders, and has so many songs and such facetious toasts, and such a way with him among their wives and daughters, that flesh and blood cannot hold out against him: in short, he is the best leader of a mob, and of course ' the honestest fellow in England.'

A merchant's daughter of great fortune married him for love; he ran away with her from a boarding-school, but her father after a time was reconciled to his son-in-law, and Jack, during the life of the good man, passed his time in a small country-house on Clapham Common, superintending the concerns of about six acres of ground; being very expert however in the gardens and grape-house, and a very sociable fellow over a bottle with the citizen and his friends on a Saturday and Sunday, he became a mighty favourite: all this while he lived upon the best terms with his wife; kept her a neat little palfrey, and regularly took his airing on the common by her side in the most uxorious manner: she was in fact a most excellent creature, of the sweetest temper and mildest manners, so that there seemed no interruption to their happiness, but what arose from her health, which was of a delicate nature. After a few years the citizen died, and Jack, whose conviviality had given him a helping hand out of the world, found himself in possession of a very handsome sum of money upon casting up his affairs at his decease.

Jack Gayless having no farther purpose to serve, saw no occasion to consult appearances any longer, and began to form connexions, in which he did not think it necessary for his wife to have a share. He now set out upon the pursuit of what the world calls pleasure, and soon found himself in the company of those whom the world calls the Great. He had the address to recommend himself to his new acquaintance, and used great dispatch in getting rid of his old ones: his wife was probably his greatest encumbrance on this occasion; but Jack possessed one art in perfection, which stood him in great stead; he had the civilest way of insulting that could be imagined; and as the feelings of his wife were those of the fondest susceptibility, operating upon a weak and delicate constitution, he succeeded to admiration in tormenting her by neglect, at the same time that he never gave her a harsh expression, and in particular, when any body else was present, behaved himself towards her in so obliging a manner, that all his acquaintance set him down as the best tempered fellow living, and her as a lady, by his report, rather captious and querulental. When he had thus got the world on his side, he detached himself more and more from her society, and became less studious to disguise the insults he put upon her: she declined fast in her health, and certain symptoms began to appear, which convinced Jack that a perseverance in his system would in a short time lay her in the grave, and leave him without any farther molestation. Her habit was consumptive, for where is the human frame that can long resist the agony of the heart? In this extremity she requested the assistance of a certain physician, very eminent in these cases: this little gentleman has a way of hitting off the complaints of his patients, which is not always so convenient to those expectant parties, who have made up their minds and reconciled themselves to the call of nature. As Jack had one object, and the doctor another, they did not entirely agree in their process, and she was sent down by her husband into a distant county for the benefit of the air, in a low situation and a damp house. Jack and the physician had now a scene of altercation, in which it was evident that the least man of the two had the greatest spirit and the largest heart, and Jack certainly put up with some expressions, which could only be passed over by perfect innocence or absolute cowardice: the little doctor, who had no objection to send Jack out of the world, and a very longing desire to keep his lady in it, spoke like a man who had long been in the practice of holding death at defiance; but what Jack lost in argument he made up in address, and after professing his acquiescence in the measures of his antagonist, he silently determined to pursue his own, and the doctor's departure was very soon followed by that of his patient. The dying wife made a feeble stand for awhile, but what can a broken heart do against a hardened one?

After Jack had taken such zealous pains to overrule the doctor's advice, it is not to be supposed but he would have accompanied his wife to the place of her destination, if it had been only for the satisfaction of contemplating the effects of his own greater sagacity in her case; and he protested to her, in the kindest manner, that nothing should have robbed

him of the pleasure of attending her on the journey,
but the most indispensable and unexpected business;
he had just then received letters from two friends,
which would be attended with the greatest breach
of honour, if neglected; and she knew his nicety of
principle in those affairs: he would not read them
to her, and she was in too weak a condition (he observed) to attend to business, but she might rest assured, he would, if possible, overtake her on the
way, or be with her in a few hours after her arrival,
for he should be impatient to be a witness of her recovery, which he persuaded himself would soon take
place, when she had made experiment of the place
he had chosen for her.  When he had finished his
apology, his wife raised her eyes from the ground,
where she had fixed them whilst he was speaking,
and with a look of such mild languor, and such dying softness, as would almost have melted marble
into pity, mournfully replied—*farewell!* and resign-
ing herself to the support of her maid and a nurse,
was lifted into her carriage, and left her husband to
pursue his business without reproach.

Jack Gayless now lost no farther time in fulfilling
the promise he had made to his wife, and immediately began to apply himself to the letters, which
had so indispensably prevented him from paying her
those kind offices, which her situation was in so
much need of.  These letters I shall now insert, as
some of my readers may probably think he wants a
justification on this occasion.  The first was from a
great lady of unblemished reputation, who has a
character for public charity and domestic virtues,
which even malice has not dared to impeach.  Her
ladyship was now at her country-seat, where she pre-
sided at a table of the most splendid hospitality, and
regulated a princely establishment with consummate
judgment and decorum: in this great family Jack

had long been a welcome visitor, and as he had received a thousand kindnesses at her hands, gratitude
would dispose him to consider her requests as commands the most pressing. The important contents
were as follow, viz.

'DEAR JACK,

' I am sorry your wife's so sick; but methinks
you'd do well to change the scene, and come
amongst us, now home's so dull. You'll be griev'd
to hear I have clapp'd Tom Jones in the back sinews:
Ned has put a charge to him, but he is so cruelly let
down, I am afraid he must be scor'd with a fine iron,
and that will be an eye-sore, to say no worse on't.
My lord you know hates writing, so he bids me tell
you to bring Moll Ross with you, as he thinks there
is a young man here will take her off your hands;
and as you have had the best of her, and she is rather under your weight, think you'll be glad to get
well out of her. Would you believe it, I was eight
hours in the saddle yesterday: we dug a fox in Lady
Tabby's park: the old dowager goes on setting
traps; all the country round cries out upon it:
thank the fates, she had a py'd peacock and a whole
brood of Guinea fowls carried off last night: my
lord says 'tis a judgment upon her. Don't forget
to bring your Highland terrier, as I would fain have
a cross with my bitch Cruel.

Dear Jack, yours,  * * *.'

As Jack Gayless was not one of those milksops,
who let family excuses stand in the way of the more
amiable office of obliging his friends, and saw in its
just light the ridicule he would naturally expose
himself to, if he sheltered himself under so silly a
pretence as a wife's sickness, he would infallibly
have obeyed her ladyship's commands, and set out
with the Highland terrier instead of Mrs. Gayless,

if he had not been divided by another very pressing attention, which every man of the world will acknowledge the importance of. There was a certain young lady of easy virtue, who had made a tender impression on his heart as he was innocently taking the air in Hyde-park : he had prevailed so far with her as to gain her consent to an appointment for that day : not foreseeing, as I should suppose, or perhaps not just at that moment recollecting, his wife's journey, and the call there would be upon him on that account. This young lady, who was wanting in no other virtue but chastity, had learned some particulars of Mr. Gayless, which she had not been informed of when she yielded to the assignation, and in consequence had written him the following perplexing billet :

'SIR,

'I am sorry it is not possible for me to receive the honour of your visit, and the more so, as I am afraid my reason for declining it, though insuperable with me, will not appear a sufficient one in your opinion. I have just now been informed that you are a married man; this would have been enough, if I had not heard it with the addition, that your lady is one of the most excellent and most injured women living—if indeed she be yet living, for I learn from the same authority that she is in the last stage of a rapid decline.

'In what light must I regard myself, if I was to supply you with a motive for neglecting that attention, which her situation demands of you? Don't let it surprise you, that a woman who has forfeited her claim to modesty, should yet retain some pretensions to humanity : if you have renounced both the one and the other, I have a double motive for declining your acquaintance. I am, &c.

***'

The style of this letter seemed so extraordinary to Jack, and so unlike what he had been used to receive from correspondents of this lady's description, that it is not to be wondered at, if it threw him into a profound meditation: not that the rebuke made any other impression on him, than as it seemed to involve a mystery which he could not expound; for it never entered into his head to suppose that the writer was in earnest. In this dilemma he imparted it to a friend, and with his usual gaiety desired his help to unriddle it: his friend perused it, and with a serious countenance told him he was acquainted with the lady, and gave her perfect credit for the sincerity of the sentiments it contained: she was a romantic girl, he told him, and not worth a farther thought; but as he perceived he was chagrined with the affair, he advised him to take post for the country, and attend the summons of his noble correspondent, for that he himself had always found the dissipation of a journey the best remedy in all cases of vexation, like the present. This friendly advice was immediately followed by an order for the journey, and Jack Gayless put himself into his post-chaise, with his terrier by his side, ordering his groom to follow with Moll Ross by easy stages.

Whilst Jack was rapidly posting towards the house of jollity and dissipation, his suffering and forsaken wife by slow stages pursued her last melancholy journey: supported in her coach by her two women, and attended by an old man-servant of her father's, she at last reached the allotted house, where her miseries were to find a period. One indiscretion only, a stolen and precipitate marriage, had marked her life with a blemish, and her husband, who in early youth had betrayed her artless affection into that fatal mistake, was now the chosen instrument of chastisement. She bore her complicated afflictions with the most patient resignation; neither sickness nor sorrow forced a complaint from her; and Death, by the gentleness of his advances, seemed to lay aside his terrors, and approach her with respect and pity.

Jack was still upon his visit, when he received the news of her death: this event obliged him to break off from a most agreeable party, and take a journey to London; but as the season had happened to set in for a severe frost, and the fox-hounds were confined to their kennel, he had the consolation to reflect that his amusements were not so much interrupted as they might have been. He gave orders for a handsome funeral, and deported himself with such outward propriety on the occasion, that all the world gave him credit for his behaviour, and he continues to be the same popular character amongst his acquaintance, and universally caressed: in short, Jack Gayless (to use the phrase of fashion) is ‘ the honestest fellow in England,’ and—a disgrace to human nature.

---

## NUMBER CIV.

---

THE conduct of a young lady, who is the only daughter of a very worthy father, and some alarming particulars respecting her situation which had come to my knowledge, gave occasion to me for writing my paper, No. XXVII. in which I endeavour to point out the consequences parents have to apprehend from novels, which though written upon moral plans, may be apt to take too strong a hold upon young and susceptible minds, especially in the

softer sex, and produce an affected character, where
we wish to find a natural one.

As the young person in question is now happily
extricated from all danger, and has seen her error, I
shall relate her story, not only as it contains some
incidents which are amusing, but as it tends to il-
lustrate by example the several instructions, which
in my paper before-mentioned I endeavour to convey.

Sappho is the only child of Clemens, who is a
widower; a passionate fondness for his daughter,
tempered with a very small share of observation or
knowledge of the world, determined Clemens to an
attempt (which has seldom been found to succeed)
of rendering Sappho a miracle of accomplishments,
by putting her under the instructions of masters in
almost every art and science at one and the same
time: his house now became an academy of musicians, dancing-masters, language-masters, drawing-
masters, geographers, historians, and a variety of
inferior artists male and female; all these studies
appeared the more desirable to Clemens, from his
own ignorance of them, having devoted his life to
business of a very different nature. Sappho made
just as much progress in each, as is usual with
young ladies so attended; she could do a little of
most of them, and talk of all: she could play a
concerto by heart, with every grace her master had
taught her, note for note, with the precise repetition
of a barrel-organ: she had stuck the room round
with drawings, which Clemens praised to the skies,
and which Sappho assured him had been only
' touched up a little' by her master: she could tell
the capital of every country, when he questioned her
out of the newspaper, and would point out the very
spot upon the terrestrial globe, where Paris, Madrid,
Naples, and Constantinople, actually were to be
found: she had as much French as puzzled Clemens,

and would have served her to buy blond-lace and
Paris netting at a French milliner's; nay, she had
gone so far as to pen a letter in that language to a
young lady of her acquaintance, which her master,
who stood over whilst she wrote it, declared to be
little inferior in style to Madame Sevigné's: in history, both ancient and modern, her progress was pro-
portionable, for she could run through the twelve
Cæsars in a breath, and reckon up all the kings from
the conquest upon her fingers, without putting one
out of place; this appeared a prodigy to Clemens,
and in the warmth of his heart he fairly told her she
was one of the world's wonders? Sappho aptly set
him right in this mistake, by assuring him that there
were but seven wonders in the world, all of which
she repeated to him, and only left him more convinced that she herself was deservedly the eighth.

There was a gentleman about fifty years old, a
friend of Clemens, who came frequently to his house,
and being a man of talents and leisure, was so kind
as to take great pains in directing and bringing Sappho forward in her studies: this was a very acceptable service to Clemens, and the visits of Musidorus were always joyfully welcomed both by him
and Sappho herself: Musidorus declared himself
overpaid by the delight it gave him to contemplate
the opening talents of so promising a young lady;
and as Sappho was now of years to establish her
pretensions to taste and sentiment, Musidorus made
such a selection of authors for her reading, as were
best calculated to accomplish her in those particulars: in settling this important choice, he was careful to put none but writers of delicacy and sensibility
into her hands; interesting and affecting tales or
novels, were the books he chiefly recommended,
which, by exhibiting the fairest patterns of female
purity (suffering distress, and even death itself from

the attacks of licentious passion in the grosser sex), might inspire her sympathetic heart with pity, and guard it from seduction by displaying profligacy in its most odious colours.

Sappho's propensity to these studies, fully answered the intentions of her kind director, and she became more and more attached to works of sentiment and pathos. Musidorus's next solicitude was to form her style, and with this view he took upon himself the trouble of carrying on a kind of probationary correspondence with her: this happy expedient succeeded beyond expectation, for as two people, who saw each other every day, could have very little matter to write upon, there was so much the more exercise for invention; and such was the copiousness and fluency of expression which she became mistress of by this ingenious practice, that she could fill four sides of letter-paper with what other people express upon the back of a card: Clemens once, in the exultation of his heart, put a bundle of these manuscripts into my hands, which he confessed he did not clearly understand, but nevertheless believed them to be the most elegant things in the language; I shall give the reader a sample of two of them, which I drew out of the number, not by choice, but by chance; they were carefully folded, and labelled at the back in Sappho's own hand, as follows: ' Musidorus to Sappho, of the 10th of June;' underneath she had wrote with a pencil these words:

PICTURESQUE!
ELEGANT!
HAPPY ALLUSION TO THE SUN!
KING DAVID NOT TO BE COMPARED TO
MUSIDORUS.

Here follows the note, and I cannot doubt but

the reader will confess that its contents deserve all
that the label expresses.

' June the 10th, 1785.

' As soon as I arose this morning, I directed my
eyes to the east, and demanded of the sun if he had
given you my good-morrow: this was my parting
injunction last night, when I took leave of him in
the west, and he this moment plays his beams with
so particular a lustre, that I am satisfied he has fulfilled my commission, and saluted the eyelids of
Sappho: if he is described to " come forth as a
bridegroom out of his chamber," how much rather
may it be said of him, when he comes forth out of
*yours!* I shall look for him to perform his journey
this day with a peculiar glee; I expect he will not
suffer a cloud to come near him, and I shall not be
surprised, if, through his eagerness to repeat his next
morning's salutation, he should " whip his fiery-
footed steeds to the west" some hours before their
time; unless, indeed, you should walk forth whilst
he is descending, and he should delay the wheels
of his chariot, to look back upon an object so pleasing.   You see, therefore, most amiable Sappho, that
unless you fulfil your engagement, and consent to
repeat our usual ramble in the cool of the evening,
our part of the world is likely to be in darkness before it is expected, and that Nature herself will be
put out of course, if Sappho forfeits her promise to
Musidorus.'

' SAPPHO IN REPLY TO MUSIDORUS.

' If Nature holds her course till Sappho forfeits
her word to Musidorus, neither the setting nor the
rising sun shall vary from his appointed time.   But
why does Musidorus ascribe to me so flattering an
influence, when, if I have any interest with Apollo,
it must be to his good offices only that I owe it?   If

he bears the messages of Musidorus to me, is it not
a mark of his respect to the person who sends him,
rather than to her he is sent to? and whom should
he so willingly obey, as one whom he so copiously
inspires? I shall walk as usual in the cool hour of
even-tide, listening " with greedy ear" to that discourse, which, by the refined and elevated sentiments it inspires, has taught me to look down with
silent pity and contempt upon those frivolous beings,
who talk the mere language of the senses, not of the
soul, and to whose silly prattle I neither condescend
to lend an ear, or to subscribe a word. Know, then,
that Sappho will reserve her attention for Musidorus,
and if Apollo " shall delay the wheels of his chariot"
to wait upon us in our evening ramble, believe me
he will not stop for the unworthy purpose of looking
back upon Sappho, but for the nobler gratification
of listening to Musidorus.'

The evening walk took place as usual, but it was
a walk in the dusty purlieus of London, and Sappho
sighed for a cottage and the country: Musidorus
seconded the sigh, and he had abundance of fine
things to say on the occasion: retirement is a
charming subject for a sentimental enthusiast; there
is not a poet in the language, but will help him out
with a description; Musidorus had them all at his
fingers' ends, from ' Hesperus that led the starry
host,' down to a glow-worm.

The passion took so strong a hold of Sappho's
mind, that she actually assailed her father on the
subject, and with great energy of persuasion moved
him to adopt her ideas; it did not exactly suit Clemens to break up a very lucrative profession, and
set out in search of some solitary cottage, whose
romantic situation might suit the spiritualized desires
of his daughter, and I am afraid he was for once in
his life not quite so respectful to her wishes, as he

might have been. Sappho was so unused to contradiction, that she explained herself to Musidorus
with some asperity, and it became the subject of
much debate between them: not that he held a contrary opinion from hers; but the difficulty which
embarrassed both parties was, where to find the
happy scene she sighed for, and how to obtain it
when it was found. The first part of this difficulty
was at last surmounted, and the chosen spot was
pointed out by Musidorus, which according to his
description was the very bower of felicity: it was
in a northern county, at a distance from the capital,
and its situation was most delectable: the next
measure was a strong one; for the question to be
decided was, if Sappho should abandon her project
or her father; she called upon Musidorus for his
opinion, and he delivered it as follows:—' If I was
not convinced, most amiable Sappho, that a second
application to Clemens would be as unsuccessful as
the first, I would advise you to the experiment; but
as there is no doubt of this, it must be the height of
imprudence to put that to a trial, of which there is
no hope: it comes, therefore, next to be considered,
if you shall give up your plan, or execute it without
his privity; in other words, if you shall or shall not
do that, which is to make you happy: if it were not
consistent with the strictest purity of character, I
should answer no; but when I reflect upon the innocence, the simplicity, the moral beauty of the
choice you make, I then regard the duty you owe
to yourself as superior to all others, which are falsely
called natural; whereas, if you follow this in preference, you obey nature herself: if you were of an
age too childish to be allowed to know what suits
you best, or, if being old enough to be entitled to a
choice, you wanted wit to make one, there would be
no doubt in the case: nay, I will go so far as to say,

that if Clemens was a man of judgment superior to your own, I should be staggered with his opposition; but, if truth may ever be spoken, it may on this occasion, and who is there that does not see the weakness of the father's understanding; who but must acknowledge the pre-eminence of the daughter's? I will speak yet plainer, most incomparable Sappho, it is not fitting that folly should prescribe to wisdom: the question, therefore, is come to an upshot, shall Sappho live a life she despises and detests, to humour a father, whose weakness she pities, but whose judgment she cannot respect?'

'No,' replied Sappho, 'that point is decided; pass on to the next, and speak to me upon the practicability of executing what I am resolved to attempt.'—'The authority of a parent,' resumed Musidorus, 'is such over an unprotected child, that reason will be no defence to you against obstinacy and coercion. In the case of a son, profession gives that defence: new duties are imposed by a man's vocation, which supersede what are called natural ones; but in the instance of a daughter, where shall she fly for protection against the imperious control of a parent, but to the arms—? I tremble to pronounce the word; your own imagination must complete the sentence.'—'Oh! horrible!' cried Sappho, interrupting him, 'I will never marry: I will never so contaminate the spotless lustre of my incorporeal purity: no, Musidorus, no,—*I'll bear my blushing honours still about me.*'—'And fit you should,' cried Musidorus, 'what demon dare defile them? Perish the man that could intrude a sensual thought within the sphere of such repelling virtue!—But marriage is a form; and forms are pure; at least they may be such; there's no pollution in a name; and if a name will shelter you, why should you fear to take it?'—'I perceive,' answered Sappho, 'that I am in

a very dangerous dilemma; since the very expedient
which is to protect me from violence of one sort, exposes me to it, under another shape too odious to
mention.'—' And is there, then,' said Musidorus,
sighing, ' is there no human being in your thoughts
in whom you can confide? Alas for me! if you believe you have no friend who is not tainted with the
impurities of his sex: and what is friendship! what,
but the union of souls? and are not souls thus united
already married? For my part, I have long regarded our pure and spiritualized connexion in this light,
and I cannot foresee how any outward ceremony is
to alter that inherent delicacy of sentiment, which is
inseparable from my soul's attachment to the soul
of Sappho: if we are determined to despise the
world, we should also despise the constructions of
the world: if retirement is our choice, and the life
and habits of Clemens are not to be the life and habits of Sappho, why should Musidorus, who is ready
to sacrifice every thing in her defence, not be thought
incapable of abusing her confidence, when he offers
the protection of his name? If a few words muttered over us by a Scotch blacksmith will put all our
troubles to rest, why should we resort to dangers
and difficulties, when so easy a remedy is before us?
But why should I seek for arguments to allay your
apprehensions, when you have in me so natural a
security for my performance of the strictest stipula-
tions?'—' And what is that security?' she eagerly
demanded. Musidorus now drew back a few paces,
and with the most solemn air and action laying his
hand upon his heart, replied, ' My age, Madam!'—
' That's true,' cried Sappho; and now the conversation
took a new turn, in the course of which they agreed
upon their plan of proceeding, settled their rendezvous
for the next day, and Musidorus departed to prepare
all things necessary for the security of their expedition.

# NUMBER CV.

Tange Chloen semel arrogantem.—HORAT.

O Cupid, touch this rebel heart!

UPON the day appointed, Sappho, with her father's consent, set out in a hired post-chaise upon a pretended visit to a relation, who lived about twenty miles from town on the northern road: at the inn where she was to change horses, she dismissed her London postilion with a short note to her father, in which she told him she should write to him in two or three days' time: here she took post for the next stage upon the great road, where she was met by Musidorus, and from thence they pressed forward with all possible expedition towards Gretna Green.

The mind of Sappho was visited with some compunctions by the way; but the eloquence of her companion, and the respectful delicacy of his behaviour, soon reconciled her conscience to the step she had taken: the reflections which passed in Musidorus's breast, were not so easily quieted: the anxiety of his thoughts, and the fatigues of the journey, brought so violent an attack upon him, that when he was within a stage or two of his journey's end, he found himself unable to proceed; the gout had seized upon his stomach, and immediate relief became necessary: the romantic visions with which Sappho hitherto had indulged her imagination, now began to vanish, and a gloomy prospect opened upon her; in place of a comforter and companion by the way to soothe her cares, and fill her mind with soft healing sentiments, she had a wretched ob-

ject before her eyes, tormented with pain, and at the
point of death.

The house in which she had taken shelter was of
the meanest sort, but the good people were humane
and assiduous, and the village afforded a medical
assistant of no contemptible skill in his profession:
there was another consolation attended her situation, for in the same inn was quartered a dragoon
officer with a small recruiting party; this young
cornet was of a good family, of an engaging person,
and very elegant address; his humanity was exerted
not only in consoling Sappho, but in nursing and
cheering Musidorus. These charitable offices were
performed with such a natural benignity, that Sappho must have been most insensible if she could
have overlooked them; her gentle heart on the contrary overflowed with gratitude, and in the extremity of her distress she freely confessed to him, that
but for his support she must have sunk outright.
Though the extremity of Musidorus's danger was
now over, yet he was incapable of exertion; and
Sappho, who was at leisure to reflect upon her situation, began to waver in her resolution, and to put
some questions to herself, which reason could not
readily answer. Her thoughts were so distracted
and perplexed, that she saw no resource but to un-
burden them, and throw herself upon the honour
and discretion of Lionel, for so this young officer
was called. This she had frequently in mind to do,
and many opportunities offered themselves for it,
but still her sensibility of shame prevented it. The
constant apprehension of pursuit hung over her, and
sometimes she meditated to go back to her father;
in one of these moments she had begun to write a
letter to Clemens to prepare him for her return,
when Lionel entered the room, and informed her
that he perceived so visible an amendment in Musido-

rus, that he expected to congratulate her on his recovery in a very few days—' and then, Madam,'
added he, ' my sorrows will begin where yours end;
be it so! if you are happy I must not complain: I
presume this gentleman is your father or near relation?'—' Father!' exclaimed Sappho:—She cast her
eyes upon the letter she was inditing and burst into
tears. Lionel approached, and took her hand in
his; she raised her handkerchief to her eyes with
the other, and he proceeded—' If my anxious solicitude for an unknown lady, in whose happiness my
heart is warmly interested, exposes me to any hazard
of your displeasure, stop me before I speak another
word; if not, confide in me, and you shall find me
ready to devote my life to serve you. The mystery
about you, and the road you are upon (were it not
for the companion you are with), would tempt me to
believe you was upon a generous errand, to reward
some worthy man, whom fortune and your parents
do not favour; but this poor object above stairs
makes that impossible. If, however, there is any
favoured lover, waiting in secret agony for that expected moment, when your release from hence may
crown him with the best of human blessings, the
hand, which now has hold of yours, shall be devoted
to his service: command me where you will; I never
yet have forfeited my honour, and cannot wrong
your confidence.'—' You are truly generous,' replied
Sappho: ' there is no such man; the hand you hold
is yet untainted, and till now has been untouched;
release it, therefore, and I will proceed. My innocence has been my error; I have been the dupe of
sentiment: I am the only child of a fond father, and
never knew the blessing of a mother; when I look
back upon my education, I perceive that art has
been exhausted, and nature overlooked in it. The
unhappy object above stairs has been my sole ad-

viser and director; for my father is immersed in business: from him, and from the duty which I owe him, I confess I have seceded, and my design was to devote myself to retirement. My scheme I now perceive was visionary in the extreme; left to my own reflections, reason shews me both the danger and the folly of it. I have therefore determined upon returning to my father, and am writing to him a letter, which I shall send by express, to relieve him from the agonies my silly conduct has occasioned.'
—'What you have now disclosed to me,' said Lionel, 'with a sincerity that does equal honour to yourself and me, demands a like sincerity on my part, and I must therefore confess to you, that Musidorus, believing himself at the point of death, imparted to me not only every thing that has passed, but all the future purposes of this treacherous plot, from which you have so providentially escaped; these I shall not explain to you at present, but you may depend upon it, that this attack upon his life has saved his conscience. I cannot as a man of honour oppose myself to your resolution of returning home immediately; and yet, when I consider the ridicule you will have to encounter from the world at large, the reflections that will arise in your mind, when there is perhaps no friend at hand to assuage them, but above all when I thus contemplate your charms, and recollect that affectation is expelled, and nature reinstated in your heart, I cannot resist the impulse nor the opportunity of appealing to that nature against a separation so fatal to my peace; yes, loveliest of women, I must appeal to nature; I must hope this heart of yours, where such refined sensations have resided, will not be shut from others of a more generous kind. What could the name of Musidorus do, which Lionel's cannot? Why should you not replace an unworthy friend with one of

fairer principles: with one of honourable birth, of equal age, and owner of a heart that beats with ardent passion towards you? Had you been made the sacrifice of this chimera, this illusion, what had your father suffered? If I am honoured with your hand in marriage, what can he complain of? My conduct, my connexions, and my hopes in life, will bear the scrutiny: suffer me to say you will have a protector, whose character can face the world, and whose spirit cannot fear it. As for worldly motives, I renounce them; give me yourself and your affections; give me possession of this hand, these eyes, and the soul which looks through them; let your father withhold the rest. Now, loveliest and most beloved, have you the heart to share a soldier's fortune? Have you the noble confidence to take his word? Will you follow where his honour bids him go, and whether a joyful victory or a glorious death attends him, will you receive him living, or entomb him dying in your arms?"

Whilst Lionel was uttering these words, his action, his emotion, and that honest glow of passion, which nature only can assume, and artifice cannot counterfeit, had so subdued the yielding heart of Sappho, that he must have been dull indeed, if he could have wanted any stronger confirmation of his success, than what her looks bestowed: never was silence more eloquent; the labour of language and the forms of law had no share in this contract: a sigh of speechless ecstasy drew up the nuptial bond; the operations of love are momentary: tears of affection interchangeably witnessed the deed, and the contracting parties sealed it with an inviolable embrace.

Every moment now had wings to waft them to that happy spot, where the unholy hand of law has not yet plucked up the root of love: freedom met them on the very extremity of her precincts; nature held out her hand to welcome them, and the Loves and Graces, though exiled to a desert, danced in her train.

Thus was Sappho, when brought to the very brink of destruction, rescued by the happy intervention of Providence. The next day produced an interview with Clemens, at the house to which they returned after the ceremony in Scotland : the meeting, as might well be expected, was poignant and reproachful : but when, Sappho in place of a superannuated sentimentalist, presented to him a son-in-law, in whose martial form and countenance he beheld youth, honour, manly beauty, and every attractive grace that could justify her choice, his transports became excessive ; and their union, being now sanctified by the blessing of a father, and warranted by love and nature, has snatched a deluded victim from misery and error, and added one conjugal instance to the scanty records of unfashionable felicity.

Let not my young female readers believe that the extravagance of Sappho's conduct is altogether out of nature, or that they have nothing to apprehend from men of Musidorus's age and character ; my observation convinces me to the contrary. *Gravity,* says Lord Shaftesbury, *is the very essence of imposture ;* and sentimental gravity, varnished over with the experienced artifice of age and wisdom, is the worst of its species.

---

## NUMBER CVI.

I THINK the ladies will not accuse me of busying myself in impertinent remarks upon their dress and attire, for indeed it is not to their persons my services are devoted, but to their minds: if I can add to them any thing ornamental, or take from them any thing unbecoming, I shall gain my wish; the rest I shall leave to their milliners and mantua-makers.

Now if I have any merit with them for not intruding upon their toilets, let them shew me so much complaisance, as not to read this paper, whilst they are engaged in those occupations, which I have never before interrupted; for as I intend to talk with them a little metaphysically, I would not wish to divide their attention, nor shall I be contented with less than the whole.

In the first place I must tell them, gentle though they be, that human nature is subject to a variety of passions, some of these are virtuous passions, some, on the contrary, I am afraid are evil; there are however a number of intermediate propensities, most of which might also be termed passions, which by the proper influence of reason, may become very useful allies to any one single virtue, when in danger of being overpowered by a host of foes: at the same time they are as capable of being kidnapped by the enemies of reason, and, when enlisted in the ranks of the insurgents, seldom fail to turn the fate of the battle, and commit dreadful havoc in the peaceful quarters of the invaded virtue. It is apparent then, that all these intermediate propensities are a kind of balancing powers, which seem indeed to hold a neutrality in moral affairs, but, holding it with arms in their hands, cannot be supposed to remain impartial spectators of the fray, and therefore must be either with us or against us.

I shall make myself better understood when I proceed to instance them, and I will begin with that which has been called the universal passion, *The love of Fame.*

I presume no lady will disavow this propensity: I would not wish her to attempt it; let her examine it however; let her first inquire to what point it is likely to carry her, before she commits herself to its conduct: if it is to be her guide to that fame only, which excels in fashionable dissipation, figures in the first circles of the gay world, and is the loadstone to attract every libertine of high life into the sphere of its activity, it is a traitorous guide, and is seducing her to a precipice, that will sooner or later be the grave of her happiness: on the contrary, if it proposes to avoid these dangerous pursuits, and recommends a progress through paths less tempting to the eye, perhaps, but terminated by substantial comforts, she may securely follow a propensity, which cannot mislead her, and indulge a passion, which will be the moving spring of all her actions, and but for which her nature would not want energy, and her character be no otherwise distinguished than by avoidance of vice without the grace and merit of any positive virtue. I can hardly suppose, if it was put to a lady's choice at her outset into life, which kind of fame she would be distinguished for, good or evil, but that she would at once prefer the good; I must believe she would acknowledge more gratification in being signalized as the best wife, the best mother, the most exemplary woman of her time, than in being pointed out in all circles she frequents as the most fashionable rake, the best dressed voluptuary in the nation: if this be rightly conjectured, why will not every woman, who has her choice to make, direct her ambition to those objects, which will give her most satisfaction when attained? There can be no reason but because it imposes on her some self-denials by the way which she has not fortitude to surmount; and it is plain she does not love fame well enough to be at much pains in acquiring it; her ambition does not reach at noble objects, her passion for celebrity is no better than that of a buffoon's, who for the vanity of being conspicuous submits to be contemptible.

*Friendship* is a word which has a very captivating sound, but is by no means of a decided quality; it may be friend or foe, as reason and true judgment shall determine for it. If I were to decry all female friendships in the lump, it might seem a harsh sentence, and yet it will seriously behove every parent to keep strict watch over this propensity in the early movements of the female mind. I am not disposed to expatiate upon its dangers very particularly; they are sufficiently known to people of experience and discretion; but attachments must be stemmed in their beginnings; keep off correspondents from your daughters as you would keep off the pestilence: romantic misses, sentimental novelists and scribbling pedants, overturn each other's heads with such eternal rhapsodies about friendship, and refine upon nonsense with such an affectation of enthusiasm, that if it has not been the parent's study to take early precautions against all such growing propensities, it will be in vain to oppose the torrent, when it carries all before it, and overwhelms the passions with its force.

*Sensibility* is a mighty favourite with the fair sex; it is an amiable friend or a very dangerous foe to virtue: let the female, who professes it, be careful how she makes too full a display of her weakness; for this is so very soft and insinuating a propensity, that it will be found in most female glossaries as a synonimous term for love itself; in fact, it is little else than the *nomme-de-guerre*, which that insidious adventurer takes upon him in all first approaches; the pass-word in all those skirmishing experiments, which young people make upon each other's affections, before they proceed to plainer declarations; it is the whetstone upon which love sharpens and prepares his arrows: if any lady makes a certain show of sensibility in company with her admirer, he must be a very dull fellow, if he does not know how to turn the weapon from himself to her. Now sensibility assumes a different character when it is taken into the service of benevolence, or made the sentinel of modesty; in one case it gives the spring to pity, in the other the alarm to discretion; but whenever it assails the heart by soft seduction to bestow that pity and relief, which discretion does not warrant, and purity ought not to grant, it should be treated as a renegado and a spy, which, under the mask of charity, would impose upon credulity for the vilest purposes, and betray the heart by flattering it to its ruin.

*Vanity* is a passion to which I think I am very complaisant, when I admit it to a place amongst these convertible propensities, for it is as much as I can do to find any occupation for it in the family concerns of virtue; perhaps, if I had not known Vanessa I should not pay it even this small compliment: it can however do some under offices in the household of generosity, of cheerfulness, hospitality, and certain other respectable qualities; it is little else than an officious, civil, silly thing, that runs on errands for its betters, and is content to be paid with a smile for its good-will, by those who have too much good-sense to shew it any real respect: when it is harmless, it would be hard to wound it out of wantonness; when it is mischievous, there is merit in chastising it with the whip of ridicule; a lap-dog may be endured, if he is inoffensive and does not annoy the company, but a snappish, barking pett, though in a lady's arms, deserves to have his ears pulled for his impertinence.

*Delicacy* is a soft name, and fine ladies, who have a proper contempt for the vulgar, are very willing to be thought endowed with senses more refined and exquisite than nature ever meant to give them; their nerves are susceptible in the extreme, and they are of constitutions so irritable, that 'the very winds of heaven' must not be allowed to 'visit their face too roughly.' I have studied this female favourite with some attention, and I am not yet able to discover any one of its good qualities: I do not perceive the merit of such exquisite fibres, nor have I observed that the slenderest strings are apt to produce the sweetest sounds, when applied to instruments of harmony; I presume the female heart should be such an harmonious instrument, when touched by the parent, the friend, the husband; but how can these expect a concert of sweet sounds to be excited, from a thing which is liable to be jarred and put out of tune by every breath of air? It may be kept in its case, like an old-fashioned virginal, which nobody knows, or even wishes to know, how to touch: it can never be brought to bear its part in a family concert, but must hang by the wall, or at best be a solo instrument for the remainder of its days.

*Bashfulness*, when it is attached to modesty, will be regarded with the eye of candour, and cheered with the smile of encouragement; but bashfulness is a hireling, and is sometimes discovered in the livery of pride, oftentimes in the cast-off trappings of affectation; pedantry is very apt to bring it into company, and sly, secret consciousness will frequently 'blush because it understands.' I do not say I have much to lay to its charge, for it is not apt to be troublesome in polite societies, nor do I commonly meet it even in the youngest of the female sex. There is a great deal of blushing I confess in all the circles of fine ladies, but then it is so universal a blush and withal so permanent, that I am far from imputing it always to bashfulness, when the cheeks of the fair are tinged with roses. However, though it is sometimes an impostor, and for that reason may deserve to be dismissed, I cannot help having a consideration for one, that has in past times been the handmaid of beauty, and therefore as merit has taken modesty into her service, I would recommend to ignorance to put bashfulness into full pay and employment.

*Politeness* is a charming propensity, and I would wish the fine ladies to indulge it, if it were only by way of contrast between themselves and the fine gentlemen they consort with. I do not think it is altogether becoming for a lady to plant herself in the centre of a circle with her back to the fire, and expect every body to be warmed by the contemplation of her figure or the reflection of her countenance; at the same time I am free to confess it an attitude, by which the man of high breeding is conspicuously distinguished, and is charming to behold, when set off with the proper accompaniments of leather breeches, tight boots, and jockey waistcoat. I will not deny however but I have seen this practised by ladies, who have acquitted themselves with great spirit on the occasion; but then it cannot be done without certain male accoutrements, and presupposes a slouched hat, half-boots, short waistcoat and riding dress, not to omit broad metal buttons with great letters engraved upon them, or the signature of some hunt, with the indispensable appendage of two long dangling watch-chains, which serve to mark the double value people of fashion put upon their time, and also shew the encouragement they bestow upon the arts; with these implements the work may be done even by a female artist, but it is an art I wish no young lady to study, and I hope the present pro-

fessors will take no more pupils, whilst the acade-
mies of Humphries and Mendoza are kept open for
accomplishments, which I think upon the whole are
altogether as becoming.   Politeness, as I conceive,
consists in putting people at their ease in your company, and being at your ease in theirs: modern
practice I am afraid is apt to misplace this process,
for I observe every body in fashionable life polite
enough to study their own ease, but I do not see
much attention paid to that part of the rule, which
ought to be first observed: it is well calculated for
those who are adepts in it, but if ever such an out-
of-the-way thing as a modest person comes within
its reach, the awkward novice is sure to be distress-
ed, and whilst every body about him seems reposing
on a bed of down, he alone is picketted upon a seat
of thorns: 'till this shall be reformed by the ladies
who profess to understand politeness, I shall turn
back to my red-book of forty years ago, to see what
relicts of the old court are yet amongst us, and take
the mothers for my models in preference to their
daughters.

---

## NUMBER CVII.

Alter in obsequium plùs æquo pronus, et imi
    Derisor lecti, sic nutum divitis horret,
Sic iterat voces, et verba cadentia tollit.—HORAT.

I AM bewildered by the definitions, which metaphysical writers give us of the human passions: I can
understand the characters of Theophrastus, and am
entertained by his sketches; but when your profound
thinkers take the subject in hand, they appear to me
to dive to the bottom of the deep in search of that

which floats upon its surface; if a man in the heat of anger would describe the movements of his mind, he might paint the tempest to the life; but as such descriptions are not to be expected, moral essayists have substituted personification in their place, and by the pleasing introduction of a few natural incidents, form a kind of little drama in which they make their fictitious hero describe those follies, foibles, and passions, which they who really feel them are not so forward to confess.

When Mr. Locke in his Essay on the Human Understanding describes all pity as partaking of contempt, I cannot acknowledge that he is speaking of pity, as I feel it: when I pity a fellow-creature in pain (a woman, for instance, in the throes of childbirth), I cannot submit to own there is any ingredient of so bad a quality as contempt in my pity: but if the metaphysicians tell me that I do not know how to call my feelings by their right name, and that my pity is not pity properly so defined, I will not pretend to dispute with any gentleman whose language I do not understand, and only beg permission to enjoy a sensation, which I call pity, without indulging a propensity which he calls contempt.

The flatterer is a character, which the moralists and wits of all times and all nations have ridiculed more severely and more successfully than almost any other: yet it still exists, and a few pages perhaps would not be misapplied, if I was to make room for a civil kind of gentleman of this description (by name Billy Simper), who, having seen his failings in their proper light of ridicule, is willing to expose them to public view for the amusement, it is hoped, if not for the use and benefit of the reader.

I beg leave therefore to introduce Mr. Billy Simper to my candid friends and protectors, and shall leave him to tell his story in his own words :—

'I am the younger son of a younger brother: my father qualified himself for orders in the university of Aberdeen, and by the help of an insinuating address, a soft counter-tenor voice, a civil smile, and a happy flexibility in the vertebræ of his back-bone, recommended himself to the good graces of a right reverend patron, who, after a due course of attendance and dependance, presented him to a comfortable benefice, which enabled him to support a pretty numerous family of children. The good bishop it seems was passionately fond of the game of chess, and my father, though the better player of the two, knew how to make a timely move so as to throw the victory into his lordship's hand after a hard battle, which was a triumph very grateful to his vanity, and not a little serviceable to my father's purposes.

'Under this expert professor I was instructed in all the shifts and movements in the great game of life, and then sent to make my way in the world as well as I was able. My first object was, to pay my court to my father's elder brother, the head of our family: an enterprise not less arduous than important. My uncle Antony was a widower, parsimonious, peevish, and recluse, he was rich, however, egregiously self-conceited, and in his own opinion a deep philosopher and metaphysician: by which I would be understood to say that he doubted every thing, disputed every thing, and believed nothing. He had one son, his only child, and him he had lately driven out of doors and disinherited for non-suiting him in an argument upon the immortality of the soul: here then was an opening no prudent man could miss, who scorned to say his soul was his own, when it stood in the way of his interest: and as I was well tutored beforehand, I no sooner gained admission to the old philosopher, than I so far worked my way into his good graces, as to be allowed to take possession of a truckle-bed in a spare garret of the family mansion : envy must have owned (if envy could have looked asquint upon so humble a situation as mine was), that considering what a game I had to play, I managed my cards well; for uncle Antony was an old dog at a dispute, and as that cannot well take place, whilst both parties are on the same side, I was forced at times to make battle for the good of the argument, and seldom failed to find Antony as completely puzzled with the zig-zaggeries of his metaphysics, as uncle Toby of more worthy memory was with the horn-works and counterscraps of his fortifications.

' Amongst the various topics, from which Antony's ingenuity drew matter of dispute, some were so truly ridiculous, that if I were sure my reader was as much at leisure to hear, as I am just now to relate them, I should not scruple the recital. One morning having been rather long-winded in describing the circumstances of a dream, that had disturbed his imagination in the night, I thought it not amiss to throw in a remark in the way of consolation upon the fallacy of dreams in general. This was enough for him to turn over to the other side, and support the credit of dreams *totis viribus:* I now thought it advisable to trim, and took a middle course between both extremes, by humbly conceiving dreams might be sometimes true and sometimes false; this he contended to be nonsense upon the face of it, and if I would undertake to shew they were both true and false, he would engage to prove by sound logic they could be neither one nor the other :—" But why do we begin to talk," added he, " before we settle what we are to talk about ? What kind of dreams are you speaking of, and how do you distinguish dreams?"—" I see no distinction between them," I replied : " Dreams visit our fancies in sleep, and are

all, according to Mr. Locke's idea, made up of the
waking man's thoughts."—" Does Mr. Locke say
that?" exclaimed my uncle. " Then Mr. Locke's
an impostor for telling you so, and you are a fool for
believing him: wiser men than Mr. Locke have
settled that matter many centuries before its was
born or even *dreamt* of: but perhaps Mr. Locke forgot to tell you how many precise sorts of dreams
there are, and how to denominate and define them?
perhaps he forgot that I say." I confessed that I
neither knew any thing of the matter myself, nor did
I believe the author alluded to had left any clue towards the discovery.

" " I thought as much," retorted my uncle Antony,
in a tone of triumph," and yet this is the man who
sets up for an investigator of the human understanding; but I will tell you, Sir, though he could not,
that there are neither more nor less than five several
sorts of dreams particularly distinguished, and I defy
even the seven sleepers themselves to name a sixth.
The first of these was by the Greeks denominated
*Oneiros*, by the Latins *Somnium* (simply a *dream*),
and you must be asleep, to dream it."—" Granted,"
quoth I. " What is granted?" rejoined the philosopher, " Not that sleep is in all cases indispensable to
the man who dreams."—" Humph!" quoth I.—My
uncle proceeded.

" " The second sort of dreams you shall understand
was by the aforesaid Greeks called *Orama*, by the
Latins *Visio*, or as we may say a *vision;* in this case
take notice, you may be asleep, or you may be
awake, or neither, or as it were between both: your
eyes may be shut, or they may be open, looking in-
wards or outwards or upwards, either with sight or
without sight, as it pleases God, but the *vision* you
must see, or how else can it rightly be called a vision?"—" True," replied I, " there is a sect who are

particularly favoured with this kind of visions."—
"Prythee, don't interrupt me," said my uncle, and
again went on.

'"The third sort of dreams, to speak according to
the Greeks, we shall call *Chrematismos*, according to
the Latins we must denominate it *Oraculum* (an
*oracle);* now this differs from a *vision*, in as much as
it may happen to a man born blind as well as to
Argus himself, for he has nothing for it but to listen,
understand, and believe, and whatever it tells him,
shall come true, though it never entered into his
head to preconceive one tittle of what is told him:
and where is Mr. Locke and his waking thoughts
here?"—"He is done for," I answered, "there is
no disputing against an oracle."

'"The fourth sort," resumed he, "is the *Enuption*
of the aforesaid Greeks, and answers to the Latin
*Insomnium*, which is in fact a dream and no dream!
a kind of *reverie*, when a man dozes between sleeping and waking, and builds castles (as we say) in the
air upon the ramblings of his own fancy.

'"The fifth and last sort of dreams is, by Greeks
and Latins, mutually styled *Phantasma*, a word
adopted into our own language by the greatest poet
who ever wrote in it: now this *phantasma* is a visitation peculiar to the first mental absence or slumber,
when the man fancies himself yet waking, and in
fact can scarce be called asleep; at which time
strange images and appearances seem to float before
him and terrify his imagination. Here then you
have all the several denominations of dreams perfectly distinguished and defined," quoth the old sophist, and throwing himself back in his chair with
an air of triumph, waited for the applause, which I
was not backward in bestowing upon this pedantic
farrago of dogmatizing dulness.

'It will readily be believed that my uncle Antony

did not fail to revive his favourite controversy, which
had produced such fatal consequences to his discarded son : in fact he held fast with those ancient
philosophers, who maintained the eternity of this
material world, and as he saw no period when men
would not be in existence, no moment in time to
come when mortality shall cease, he by consequence
argued that there could be no moment in time,
when mortality shall commence. There were other
points respecting this grand stumbling-block of his
philosophy, the human soul, upon which he was
equally puzzled, for he sided with Aristotle against
Plato in the unintelligible controversy concerning its
power of motion : but whilst my uncle Antony was
thus unluckily wedded to the wrong side in all cases,
where reason ought to have been his guide, in points
of mere quibble and sophistry, which reason has
nothing to say to, and where a wise man would take
neither side, he regularly took both, or hung suspended between them like Socrates in the basket.

   ' Of this sort was the celebrated question—*Ovumne
prius fuerit, an gallina*—viz. "Whether the egg was
anterior to the hen, or the hen to the egg?"—This
inquiry never failed to interest his passions in a peculiar degree, and he found so much to say on both
sides, that he could never well determine which side
to be of : at length, however, hoping to bring it to
some point, he took up the cause of Egg versus Hen,
and having composed a learned essay, published it
in one of the monthly magazines, as a lure to future
controversialists. This essay he had so often avowed
in my hearing, and piqued himself so highly upon it,
that I must have been dull indeed not to have understood how to flatter him upon it : but when he
had found month after month slip away, and nobody
mounting the stage upon his challenge, he felt angry
at the contempt with which his labours were passed

over, and without imparting to me his purpose, furnished the same magazine with a counter-essay, in
which his former argument was handled with an
asperity truly controversial, and the hen was tri-
umphantly made to cackle over the new-laid egg,
decidedly posterior to herself.

'I am inclined to think, that if Antony had any
partiality, it was not to this side; but as the second
essay was clearly posterior to the first (whatever
the egg may have been to the hen), it had the advantage of being couched in all the spirit of a reply,
with an agreeable tinge of the malice of one, so that
when at length it came down printed in a fair type,
and respectfully posted in the front of the long-
wished-for magazine, his heart beat with joy, and
calling out to me in a lofty tone of counterfeited
anger, as he ran his eye over it—" By the horns of
Jupiter Ammon," quoth he, "here is a fellow has
the confidence to enter the lists against me in the
notable question of the egg."—" Then I hope you
will break that egg about his ears," replied I. "Hold
your tongue, puppy, and listen," quoth the sophist,
and immediately began to read.

'At every pause I was ready with a pooh! or
pish! which I hooked in with every mark of contempt I could give it, both by accent and action.
At the conclusion of this essay, my uncle Antony
shut the book, and demanded what I thought of the
author?—" Hang him," I exclaimed, " poor Grub-
street Garretteer; the fellow is too contemptible for
your notice; he can neither write nor reason; he is
a mere ignoramus, and does not know the com-
monest rules of logic; he has no feature of a critic
about him, but the malice of one."—" Hold your
tongue," cried Antony, no longer able to contain
himself, " you are a booby; I will maintain it to be
as fine an essay as ever was written."   With these

words he snatched up the magazine and departed: I saw no more of him that night, and early next morning was presented by a servant with the following billet:—" The Grub-street Garretteer finds himself no longer fit company for the sagacious Mr. William Simper; therefore desires him without loss of time to seek out better society than that of a ' mere ignoramus, who does not know the common rules of logic:' one rule, however, he makes bold to lay down, which is, never again to see the face of an impertinent upstart, called William Simper, whilst he remains on this earth. A. S."

## NUMBER CVIII.

Sunt verba et voces, quibus hunc lenire dolorem
Possis, et magnam morbi deponere partem.—HORAT.

' DRIVEN from my uncle Antony's door by my unlucky mistake between the hen and her egg, my case would have been desperate, but that I had yet one string left to my bow, and this was my aunt Mrs. Susanna Simper, who lived within a few miles of my uncle, but in such declared hostility, that I promised myself a favourable reception, if I could but flatter her animosity with a sufficient portion of invective; and for this I deemed myself very tolerably qualified, having so much good-will towards the business, and no slight inducements to spur me to it.

' My aunt, who was an aged maiden, and a valetudinarian, was, at my arrival, closeted with her apothecary: upon his departure I was admitted to my audience, in which I acquitted myself with all the address I was master of. My aunt heard my story through without interrupting me by a single word. At last, fixing her eyes upon me, she said—" 'Tis very well, child; you have said enough: your uncle's character I perfectly understand; look well to your own, for upon that will depend the terms you and I shall be upon."—She now took up a vial from the table, and surveying it for some time, said to me—" Here is a nostrum recommended by my apothecary, that promises great things, but perhaps contains none of the wondrous properties it professes to have. The label says it is a carminative, sedative mixture; in other words, it will expel vapours and spasms, and quiet the mind and spirits: do you think it will make good what it promises?"—So whimsical a question, put to me at such a moment, confounded me not a little, and I only murmured out in reply, that I hoped it would.—" Take it then," said my aunt, " as you have faith in it; swallow it yourself, and when I see how it operates with you, I may have more confidence in it on my own account."—I was now in a more awkward dilemma than ever, for she had emptied the dose into a cup, and tendered it to me in so peremptory a manner, that, not knowing how to excuse myself, and being naturally submissive, I silently took the cup with a trembling hand, and swallowed its abominable contents.

' " Much good may it do you, child," cried she; " you have done more for me than I would for any doctor in the kingdom. Don't you find it nauseous to the palate?"—I confessed that it was very nauseous.—" And did you think yourself in need of such a medicine?"—" I did not perceive that I was."—" Then you did not swallow it by your own choice, but my desire?"—I had no hesitation in acknowledging that. " Upon my word, child," she replied, " you have a very accommodating way with you." I was now fighting with the cursed drug, and had all the difficulty in life to keep it where it was. My aunt saw my distress, and smiling at it, demanded if I was not sick? I confessed I was rather discomposed in my stomach with the draught.—" I don't doubt it," she replied; " but as you have so civilly made yourself sick for my sake, cannot you flatter me so far as to be well when I request it?" I was just then struggling to keep the nausea down, and though I could not answer, put the best face upon the matter in my power.

' A maid-servant came in upon my aunt's ringing her bell.—" Betty," said she, " take away these things; this doctor will poison us with his doses."—" Foh!" cried the wench, " how it smells!"—" Nay, but only put your lips to the cup," said the mistress, " there is enough left for you to taste it."—" I taste it! I'll not touch it, I want none of his nasty physic!"—" Well, but though you don't want it," rejoined the mistress, " taste it nevertheless, if it be only to flatter my humour."—" Excuse me, Madam," replied Betty, " I'll not make myself sick to flatter any body."—" Humph!" cried my aunt, " how this wench's want of manners must have shocked you, nephew William! you swallowed the whole dose at a word; she, though my servant, at my repeated command, would not touch it with her lips; but these low-bred creatures have a will of their own!"—There was something in my aunt's manner I did not understand; she puzzled me, and I thought it best to keep myself on the reserve, and wait the farther developement of her humour in silence.

' We went down to supper, it was elegantly served, and my aunt particularly recommended two or three dishes to me; her hospitality embarrassed me not a little, for my stomach was by no means reconciled; yet I felt myself bound in good manners to eat of her dishes, and commend their cookery;

this I did, though sorely against the grain, and, whilst my stomach rose against its food, I flattered what I nauseated.

'A grave, well-looking personage stood at the side-board, with whom my aunt entered into conversation.—" Johnson," said she, " I think I must lodge my nephew in your room, which is warm and well-aired, and dispose of you in the tapestry-chamber, which has not lately been slept in."—" Madam," replied Johnson, " I am ready to give up my bed to Mr. William, at your command ; but as to sleeping in the tapestry-chamber, you must excuse me."— " Why?" replied my aunt, " what is your objection ?" —" I am almost ashamed to tell you," answered Johnson, " but every body has his humour ; perhaps my objection may be none to the young gentleman, but I confess I don't choose to pass the night in a chamber that is under an ill name."—" An ill name, for what ?" demanded the lady. " For being haunted," answered the butler, " for being visited by noises, and rattling of chains, and apparitions ; the gentleman, no doubt, is a scholar, and can account for these things ; I am a plain man, and don't like to have my imagination disturbed, nor my rest broken, though it were only by my own fancies."— " What then is to be done ?" said my aunt, directing her question to me ; " Johnson don't choose to trust himself in a haunted chamber ; I shall have my house brought into discredit by these reports : now, nephew, if you will encounter this ghost, and exorcise the chamber by sleeping in it a few nights, I dare say we shall hear no more of it. Are you willing to undertake it ?"

I was ashamed to confess my fears, and yet had no stomach to the undertaking ; I was also afraid of giving umbrage to my aunt, and impressing her with an unfavourable opinion of me ; I therefore assent-

ed, upon the condition of Johnson's taking part of
the bed with me: upon which the old lady, turning
to her butler, said, "Well, Johnson, you have no objection to this proposal."—"Pardon me, Madam,"
said he, "I have such objections to that chamber,
that I will not sleep in it for any body living."—
"You see he is obstinate," said my aunt, "you
must even undertake it alone, or my house will lie
under an ill name for ever."—"Sooner than this
shall be the case," I replied, "I will sleep in the
chamber by myself."—"You are very polite," cried
my aunt, "and I admire your spirit: Johnson, light
my nephew to his room." Johnson took up the
candle, but absolutely refused to march before me
with the light, when we came into the gallery, where,
pointing to a door, he told me that was my chamber,
and hastily made his retreat down the stairs.

'I opened the door with no small degree of terror,
and found a chamber comfortably and elegantly furnished, and by no means of that melancholy cast,
which I had pictured to myself from Johnson's report of it. My first precaution was, to search the
closet; I then peeped under the bed, examined the
hangings; all was as it should be; nothing seemed
to augur a ghost, or (which I take to be worse) the
counterfeit of a ghost. I plucked up as good a spirit as I could, said my prayers and turned into bed:
with the darkness my terrors returned, I passed a
sleepless night, though neither ghost nor noise of
any sort molested me.

'"Why," said I, within myself, "could not I be
as sincere and peremptory as Johnson? He takes his
rest and is at peace, I am sleepless and in terrors:
though a servant by condition, in his will he is independent; I, who have not the like call of duty,
have not the same liberty of mind: he refuses what
he does not choose to obey, I obey all things whe-

ther I choose them or not: And wherefore do I this?
Because I am a flatterer: And why did I swallow
a whole nauseous dose to humour my aunt's caprice,
which her own chambermaid, who receives her wages,
would not touch with her lips? Because I am a
flatterer: And what has this flattery done for me,
who am a slave to it? what did I gain by it at my
uncle's? I was the echo of his opinions, shifted as
they shifted, sided with him against truth, demonstration, reason, and even the evidence of my own senses:
abject wretch, I sunk myself in my own esteem first,
then lost all shadow of respect with him, and was
finally expelled from his doors, whilst I was in the
very act of prostituting my own judgment to his gross
absurdities: and now again, here I am at my aunt's,
devoted to the same mean flattery, that has already
so shamefully betrayed me. What has flattery gained
for me here? A bitter harvest truly I have had of it:
poisoned by an infernal dose, which I had no plea
for swallowing; surfeited by dainties I had no appetite to taste, and now condemned to sleepless hours
within a haunted chamber, which her own domestic
would not consent even to enter: fool that I am to
be the dupe of such a vapour as flattery! despicable
wretch, not to assert a freedom of will, which is the
natural right of every man, and which even servants
and hirelings exercise with a spirit I envy, but have
not the heart to imitate: I am ashamed of my own
meanness: I blush for myself in the comparison, and
am determined, if I survive till to-morrow, to assert
the dignity of a man, and abide by the consequences."

'In meditations like these night passed away, and
the dawn of morning called me from my bed: I rose
and refreshed my spirits with a walk through a most
charming plantation: I met a countryman at his work
—"Friend," said I, "you are early at your labour."
—"Yes," answered he, "'tis by my labour I live,

and whilst I have health and strength to follow it, I have nothing to fear, but God alone." So! thought I, here is a lesson for me: this man is no flatterer; then why do I worship what a clown despises?

' I found my aunt ready for breakfast: she questioned me about my night's rest: I answered her with truth that I had enjoyed no rest, but had neither seen nor heard any thing to alarm me, and was persuaded there were no grounds for the report of her chamber being haunted. "I am as well persuaded as yourself of that," she replied; "I know 'tis only one of Johnson's whims; but people you know will have their whims, and it was great courtesy in you to sacrifice a night's rest to his humour: my servants have been spoiled by indulgence, but it is to be hoped they will learn better submission by your example." There was a sarcastic tone in my aunt's manner of uttering this, which gave it more the air of ridicule than compliment, and I blushed to the eyes with the consciousness of deserving it.

' After breakfast she took me into her closet, and desiring me to sit down to a writing-table: "Nephew," says she, "I know my brother Antony full well; he is a tyrant in his nature, a bigot to his opinions, and a man of a most perverted understanding, but he is rich, and you have your fortune to make; he can insult, but you can flatter; he has his weaknesses, and you can avail yourself of them; suppose you write him a penitential letter."—I now saw the opportunity present for exerting my new-made resolution, and felt a spirit rising within me, that prompted me to deliver myself as follows: "No, Madam, I will neither gratify my uncle's pride, nor lower my own self-esteem, by making him any submission: I despise him for the insults he has put upon me, and myself for having in some sort deserved them; but I will never flatter him or any living creature more; and if I am to forfeit your favour by resisting your commands, I must meet the consequences, and will rather trust to my own labour for support, than depend upon the caprice of any person living; least of all on him."—" Heyday," cried my aunt, " you refuse to write!—you will not do as I advise you?"—" In this particular," I replied, " permit me to say I neither can nor will obey you." —" And you are resolved to think and act for yourself?"—" In the present case I am, and in all cases, let me add, where my honour and my conscience tell me I am right."—" Then," exclaimed my aunt, " I acknowledge you for my nephew: I adopt you from this hour;" and with that she took me by the hand most cordially; " I saw," said she, " or thought I saw, the symptoms of an abject spirit in you, and was resolved to put my suspicions to the test; all that has passed here since your coming has been done in concert and by way of trial; your haunted chamber, the pretended fears of my butler, his blunt refusal, all have been experiments to sound your character, and I should totally have despaired of you, had not this last instance of a manly spirit restored you to my esteem: you have now only to persist in the same line of conduct to confirm my good opinion of you, and ensure your own prosperity and happiness."

' Thus I have given my history, and if the example of my reformation shall warn others from the contemptible character, which I have fortunately escaped from, I shall be most happy, being truly anxious to approve myself the friend of mankind, and the Observer's very sincere well-wisher,

WILL. SIMPER.'

END OF VOL. XXXIX.

Printed by J. F. DOVE, St. John's Square.